JOHN PAUL II
1920–2005
ILLUSTRATED BIOGRAPHY

July 27, 2016

To Hamsie, Andrew, Rosie
and ...

with the best wishes
and hopes for
future meetings
in the Pope's town

JOHN PAUL II

1920–2005

ILLUSTRATED BIOGRAPHY

Andrzej Nowak

KLUSZCZYŃSKI

Copyright © by Wydawnictwo Ryszard Kluszczyński
Kraków 2005
30-110 Kraków, ul. Kraszewskiego 36
tel./fax +48 (12) 421 22 28, e-mail: kluszcz@kki.krakow.pl

Text copyright © Andrzej Nowak

Edited by: Justyna Chłap-Nowakowa

Translated by: Marta Kapera (pp. 7-34), Barbara Śpiewak (pp. 34-62),
Władysław Chłopicki (pp. 63-102), Agnieszka Trzaska (103-126) and Anna Wyrwa (pp. 127-144)

Cover design by: Leon Kowalski

Illustrations selected by: Andrzej Nowak

Sources of illustrations:
Agencja BE&W, Archives of the Cracow Metropolitan Curia, Cracow Regional Archives,
Polish Photographic Agency "Forum", Polish Press Agency "PAP",
Janusz Kozina, Krystyna Litewkowa, Stanisław Markowski, L'Osservatore Romano – Servizio fotografico/Arturo Mari,
Jacek Walczewski, Jan Walczewski, Tadeusz Warczak, Archiwum Wydawnictwa

DTP
look STUDIO, Kraków, ul. Wielopole 17,
tel./fax +48 (12) 429 18 31, e-mail: lookstudio@kki.pl, www.lookstudio.pl

The Editor and the author wish to thank the following individuals for making available the stories
and documents concerning the Holy Father:
**Jan Adamski, Father Andrzej Bardecki, Halina Kwiatkowska,
Krystyna Litewkowa, Archbishop Józef Michalik,
Professor Stanisław Nagy, Bishop Kazimierz Nycz,
Marek Skwarnicki, Archbishop Ignacy Tokarczuk,
Jacek Walczewski**

ISBN 83-7447-028-3

TABLE OF CONTENTS

CHAPTER I
Family and neighborhood (1920–1938)

On 18 May 1920, St Alexander's Church in Warsaw resounded with the solemn hymn of *Te Deum*. The Head of the State, Józef Piłsudski, had just returned from the front and the fight with the Soviet Russia: the fight for the political future of entire Eastern Europe. The day was his moment of triumph; the troops of the Polish Army, re-built after years of foreign occupation, entered Kiev. The threat of imposing the alien, communist system on Poland and its neighbors seemed no longer imminent. Independent Poland was to stand side by side with independent Ukraine. This victory, the first one after 250 years, was yet another proof of the strength of Polish, Christian bulwarks on the eastern frontier. After Mass was celebrated in thanksgiving for the day and in hopeful prayer for the future, Piłsudski went to meet the Parliament. He was greeted by Marshal Wojciech Trąmpczyński's lofty words: "Since [the victorious battle of] Chocim, the Polish nation has never experienced such a military triumph. The victorious march to Kiev empowered the nation and reinforced its faith in its independent future."

The same day was marked by a different kind of joy in the family of a modest army clerk in Wadowice. Lieutenant Karol Wojtyła, extremely busy in those times of war and working for the Regional Draft Board, had to forget his duties at least for a while when he learned that his wife Emilia née Kaczorowska had just given birth to their second son. The new-born inhabitant of Wadowice had two Christian names Karol Józef; the former after his father and the latter after the last rulers of the Austro-Hungarian Empire, to whom Lieutenant Wojtyła had proved a loyal subject before Poland regained independence.

On 20 June, when little Lolek (as he was nicknamed in the family) was baptized in the parish church in the main square of Wadowice, there was no trace left of the feeling of triumph that had previously filled the country. The huge offensive of the Red Army rushed across Belarus towards Warsaw while the Polish troops were pushed back from Ukraine and more Soviet soldiers marched on towards Lwów. Eight weeks later the Soviets were already at the gates of Warsaw. Their commander, Mikhail Tukhachevsky, gave orders in which he clearly stated the aims of the offensive: over the dead body of "white" Poland to Berlin, to the West, to the global communist revolution. The political education commissar of the second Soviet front (which was to ring Lwów), yet unknown to the world Joseph Stalin, assigned his soldiers equally ambitious tasks: right after the conquest of Poland, the countries to be "revolutionized" were Hungary, the Czech Lands and Italy; Romania was to be partitioned.

If the success of the Soviet offensive had lasted for another week or two, would Poland exist at all? Could Europe defend itself? Would little Karol and the subsequent generations of Poles have got a chance to learn to pray? The Soviet bayonets, according to the ideology preached by the Soviet political leaders, were to "liberate the masses" from the "ignorance of superstition," that is from Christianity, which Lenin described in Bolshevist terms as "vodka for the masses."

But 15 August 1920, the Assumption of the BVM, saw the collapse of the Soviet offensive. The counterattack prepared by Piłsudski averted the danger which, as the then Pope Benedict XV

Father Skorupka – Poland holding the Cross against the Bolsheviks
(painting by Jan Rosen in the Papal Chapel at Castel Gandolfo, commissioned by Pope Pius XI)

Parish church in Wadowice: baptismal font

John Paul II pays homage to the defenders of Europe during the pilgrimage to Poland in 1999

In his UNESCO address, the Pope emphasizes the dignity of his nation

put it, hung over Poland, Europe, Christianity and its culture. Seventy-nine years later, the Polish Pope John Paul II could in person pay homage to the Polish soldiers whose heroism and sacrifice contributed to the victory in the battle of Warsaw. On 13 June 1999, in the fields near Radzymin, John Paul II called that victory a "battle for our freedom and for yours, for our freedom and Europe's." This freedom was saved in August 1920, but not for everybody and not for long. Poland lacked the military power to complete the task of saving entire Eastern Europe and to completely eliminate the totalitarian spell of communism. Nineteen years later the Soviet system hit Poland back in revenge, joining forces with the Nazi invasion of September 1939. The nineteen years of freedom and independence of the Polish state were, however, of enormous value. They made it possible to raise a whole generation: the generation of Karol Wojtyła.

That generation lost very many of its valuable members who sacrificed their lives in the Second World War and in their fight against communism, and Karol Wojtyła, a representative of that generation, gave testimony to the significance of patriotic upbringing and cultural education he received during the nineteen years of freedom. The testimony was especially manifest in his UNESCO address on 2 June 1980 in Paris. He said: "I am a son of the nation that has survived the most horrible historical experiences and that on many occasions was sentenced to death by its neighbors, but it has survived and retained its true character. It has preserved its identity and, despite the partitions and occupation, its autonomy as a nation, not on the basis of any other power, but solely on the basis of its culture, which proved much more powerful than any [political] powers."

It fell to John Paul II, who was born on the day of premature triumph over the totalitarian invasion from the east, to make the triumph complete seventy years later. Yet his was not a triumph of a strong

bulwark of Christianity, but of a bridge of Christian freedom, spanning between the east and the west. Also, the triumph was made complete by different means than those used by Piłsudski in 1920. The winning power was that of spirit, not the sword. But such spirit would not have been born in Soviet-dominated Poland; it was born in free Poland, which could cultivate its religious and patriotic traditions, in this Poland that was saved in the year when Karol Wojtyła was born.

* * *

For Karol Wojtyła, the immediate neighborhood was the south-west of pre-war Poland. The scenic range of the Beskid Mały, with the incised valleys of the Skawa and Soła, had marked the horizon for many generations of the Wojtyła family. However, their first seat was not Wadowice but the village of Czaniec near Kęty, lying close by. The genealogy of Karol Wojtyła, as documented in the parish books in Czaniec, can be traced back to the early nineteenth century. His great-great-grandfather Bartłomiej married Anna née Hudecka and had four children, among them a son named Franciszek, who in turn married Franciszka née Gałuszka and also had four sons. One of them, Maciej, born in 1852, had one son by his first wife Anna née Przeczek. He was born in 1879 and named Karol, and he was the Pope's father. All of them were small farmers. Additionally, Maciej worked as a tailor and so did his son before he was drafted to the Austrian army in 1900.

Karol Wojtyła Sr, having done his service in Lwów, was in 1904 transferred to Wadowice to the local 56th Infantry Regiment, and later on was sent to do quartermaster work in Cracow. At that time (the exact date is unknown) he married Emilia.

Emilia and Karol Wojtyłas with their elder son, Edmund

Parish church at the Wadowice town square

The Kaczorowskis, that is the Pope's mother's family, came from Biała, a town that nowadays forms a part of Bielsko-Biała. The genealogy of John Paul II on his mother's side can also be traced back to the first half of the nineteenth century. In the parish of Biała in 1849 Feliks Kaczorowski was born, a son of Mikołaj and Urszula née Malinowska. (In the recent years, in connection with John Paul II's pilgrimage to Lviv and Kiev, some Ukrainian roots were discovered: the newly found death certificate of Feliks Kaczorowski confirms that he was born and initially lived in Michałów near Szczebrzeszyn, that is in the region inhabited by both Poles and Ukrainians, and only later moved to Biała.) Feliks, a saddler by trade, married Maria née Scholz and they had nine children. One of them was Emilia (b. 1884), the future wife of Karol Wojtyła Sr. When she was one year old, the Kaczorowskis moved to Cracow. It was probably here that Emilia, who had attended the eight-form primary school of the Daughters of Divine Charity in Pędzichów Street, met her future husband. They may have been married in the Church of SS Peter and Paul, which at that time was the garrison church in Cracow. They also lived in Cracow, possibly until 1918. And it was in Cracow that in 1906 their first son Edmund was born.

From 1918 onwards Edmund was registered among the pupils of the state high school for boys in Wadowice. The Wojtyła family may have moved to this town on the River Skawa due to the father's reassignment. They rented an apartment on the second floor of the house owned by an affluent Jewish merchant, Chaim Balamuth, in the town square, just a stone's throw from the parish church of Our Lady. Such was the family home of little Karol Wojtyła. Wadowice became his hometown.

A guidebook on the region of Galicia, published before the First World War, does not say much about this town. It had eight thousand inhabitants, including 1,300 Jews, boasted two hotels, three restaurants, a cake shop and a cafe, a parish church and the new churches of the Carmelites, the Sisters of the Holy Family of Nazareth and the Pallottini Fathers. "No historical buildings." After 1918 it did not change much. The landscape – the panorama of the Beskid Mały range – was delineated by

Emilia née Kaczorowska with young Karol

Karol wearing the school uniform

Karol's elder brother, Edmund, with their mother

the hills of Gancarz, Magórka and Leskowiec and remained as beautiful as ever, which was remarked upon by all the authors of guidebooks.

Wadowice, nevertheless, was not a cultural desert. A symbol of the town's traditions and aspirations was the figure of Marcin Wadowita (1567–1641). He was a peasant's son, then became the parish priest at St Florian's in Cracow and a doctor of philosophy. He received a post-doctoral degree in Rome, for over fifty

The house at the Wadowice town square (now at Kościelna 7), residence of the Wojtyłas

years worked as a professor of theology at the Jagiellonian University and finally became its Rector. In many respects his pioneering venture resembled that of Karol Wojtyła 350 years later. Marcin Wadowita was several times summoned to Rome to participate in theological disputes and he became renowned there for his "angelic knowledge and diabolic voice." His ministry and scholarly work in Cracow were remarkable for tolerance (e.g. he saved Faustus Socinus, the leader of a radical Reformation sect, from being lynched) and even more for his rapport with young people, whom he often supported not only with his expertise, but with his savings as well.

At the time of Karol Wojtyła Jr's childhood and youth in Wadowice, the town also boasted several eminent personages. At one extreme was Emil Zegadłowicz, whose novels (such as *Zmory* [Nightmares]) scandalized all Poland. At the other extreme was Jędrzej Wowro, the local sculptor and self-educated philosopher. His solemn images of the Man of Sorrow, carved in wood, were expressions of folk piety and taught viewers – including Karol Wojtyła, who often remembered Wowro in his early poems – to respect that piety.

For the future Pope, the first model of faith was most of all his family, and the first source of knowledge and culture

was his school in Wadowice. He went to the four-year elementary school in 1926. Later on, until 1930 he attended, just like his elder brother, the local high school, a memorial school of Marcin Wadowita. But these years were not altogether happy for young Karol, they were marred by the family tragedy. In 1929 died his mother Emilia. Three years later, in December 1932, the family had to attend another funeral after the death of Karol's beloved brother Edmund. He had just graduated

Rakowice Military Cemetery in Cracow: tomb of the Wojtyłas and the Kaczorowskis

from his medical studies in Cracow and worked as an intern in a hospital in Bielsko, where he contracted scarlet fever. Trying to save the life of a patient, he lost his own life. The only survivors in the Wojtyła family were two Karols: the father and the son. The father retired so as to devote more time to his younger, surviving son. He was a very religious man and demanded a great deal both from himself and from his son. Karol Wojtyła Sr was always remembered by John Paul II as a man of "continuous prayer." With his son, he read the Bible, said the Rosary and went on pilgrimages to Kalwaria Zebrzydowska and Częstochowa. The father and son learned together how to accept the decrees of Providence that had affected their family so harshly.

Before classes, Karol Wojtyła Jr often served at Mass. After classes, he went with his father to have lunch to the dairy-cum-cafeteria run by Maria Banaś. Sometimes, homework finished, they played football – even at home! Karol Wojtyła Sr, who had served in the Austrian army for eighteen years, taught his son German. During strolls and evening talks, he also introduced him to the problems of Polish history and of patriotic, especially Romantic, literature. To the future Pope, his father was both the mentor and a friend.

The façade of the high school in Wadowice, which was built in the late nineteenth century, bears a Latin inscription: *Casta placent superis – pura cum veste venite / Et manibus puris sumite fontis aquam*. Those who graduated from the school in the same year as Karol Wojtyła Jr remember the motto till this day: "Superior beings prefer pure things, therefore draw from this pure well in vestal attire and with clean hands." For them, this was not the parody of a school described by Emil Zegadłowicz in his novel *Zmory*. In the school named after Marcin Wadowita one could really draw from the pure fountain of knowledge. And there Karol was really able to build upon the upbringing he received at home, in the spirit that was typical of pre-war Poland, full of respect for the patriotic tradition and for great Polish literature. The latter was Karol's absolute fascination. He studied hard all school subjects and received the best grades at the end of the school year. The highest grades in religion and Polish were accompanied by the teachers' notes: "studied with much passion."

Karol could prove his passion on the stage of the school theater and on a second stage arranged in the Catholic House by the religious supervisor, Father Edward Zacher. In Class 6 Karol played Gustave in *Śluby panieńskie* [The Virgins' Vows] by Aleksander Fredro and Haemon in Sophocles' *Antigone*. In Class 7 he was cast as Kirkor and Kostryn in Słowacki's *Balladyna* and with Father Zacher he directed Krasiński's *Nie-Boska komedia* [The Un-Divine Comedy], in which he also played the main hero Count Henry. In Class 8, the last one, he co-directed Wyspiański's drama *Zygmunt August*, again playing the protagonist. In the majority of the performances, the accompanying major female roles were played by Halina Królikiewiczówna (whose later married name was Kwiatkowska), daughter of the school's director. Young Karol competed with her for theatrical talent on the amateur stage in Wadowice. Halina held a very high opinion of her rival: "He was well-built and handsome; endowed with a beautiful voice, a good memory, and a perfect articulation; he was very reflective and sensitive; and therefore predisposed to the acting profession." However, it was Halina who won in the recitation contest that was organized in their final year at school. Karol, who chose and extremely difficult text, Norwid's *Promethidion*, came second best. And in the years to come, on every occasion the Pope met his

Karol Wojtyła (back row, first from the left) among his classmates

Among the group of altar boys (first row, second from the left) bidding farewell to their priest, Fr Kazimierz Figlewicz

On a school trip to Wieliczka salt mine: Karol Wojtyła Jr (second row, second from the right) and Karol Wojtyła Sr (fourth from the right)

former classmates, he used to wag his finger at his victorious rival, saying: "You beat me then…"

On 16 June 1999 in Wadowice, when he spoke about his childhood surroundings, John Paul II, obviously moved, recollected his first steps on stage. He enumerated the names of other actors and actresses, quoted passages from the part of Haemon he had played fifty-four years earlier, and lastly he regretted there was no amateur theater in his hometown any longer.

Mount Leskowiec: backdrop of Karol's hiking trips

Karol in service of the paramilitary Academic League (first from the right)

Metropolitan of Cracow visiting the Wadowice parish

The Pope thanks God for his baptism during the first trip to Poland (1979)

His interest in theater and in the spoken word grew even more when he met and in 1938 made friends with Mieczysław Kotlarczyk. Kotlarczyk also came from Wadowice, was fourteen years Karol's senior, and worked as a teacher of Polish in a Carmelite high school. He lived for the idea of his own theater which was founded on the presupposition about the quasi-mystical significance of the spoken word, especially of the recited works of Polish Romanticism. He passed on this idea to Karol Wojtyła and a group of his friends. Together, in Wadowice, they analyzed Słowacki's *Król-Duch* [King Spirit] and subsequently went on with the analysis in Cracow, even under the Nazi occupation.

Karol Wojtyła shared with his friends not only artistic interests. He was also fond of sports. In his soccer team he was usually the goalkeeper. In winter he frequently skied. He never went away on vacation, but went on pilgrimages with his father, on trips to Wieliczka and Cracow and on tours to Andrychów and Kalwaria with his school theater. He hiked in the mountains, in the Beskid Mały and Beskid Żywiecki. And they were his "little homeland," his neighborhood.

Which way to go? How and where to broaden spiritual horizons? Karol Wojtyła had to find the answers to such questions on the threshold of his adult life, in his last year at school. He passed his final examinations on 14 May 1938. He was the best student at school and it was he who on behalf of his schoolmates thanked the teachers for the received education. A week earlier, as the graduates were to be confirmed, the school was visited by Metropolitan Adam Stefan Sapieha, a man of great spirit, who was greeted by the representative of the students, Karol Wojtyła. This tall young man, an active member of the Marian Sodality and of the Association of Catholic Youth, drew the attention of the Metropolitan, who asked Father Zacher whether that promising student did not by any chance intend to join the clergy.

Karol clearly had to choose between literature and theater or priesthood, to which he seemed predisposed by his deep religiousness. In 1938 he was absolutely decided to choose literature. When in Zubrzyca Górna he completed the obligatory, four-week vocational practice, during which his jobs were peeling potatoes and building the road between Zubrzyca and Krowiarki, he began his Polish studies at the Jagiellonian University. In the summer of 1938 he and his father moved to Cracow. They lived in the house of the Kaczorowski family at 10 Tyniecka Street in the district of Dębniki, close to the meandering Vistula, on the other bank of which stood the majestic towers and walls of Wawel Castle. The parish and school in Wadowice were left behind by Karol, then an eighteen-year-old. They had given him so much. And Cracow, the University, physical work, the experience of the Nazi occupation, and lastly the seminary, complemented his education.

CHAPTER II
The word and blood: first years in Cracow (1938–1944)

Because it has a great number of beautiful churches in the Old Town, Cracow is sometimes called a Polish Rome. For

Image of Merciful Christ, as envisioned by Sister Faustyna Kowalska

centuries, it has also been a town of Polish saints, patrons of all Poland and of Cracow: the bishop and martyr St Stanislaus of Szczepanów, Blessed Wincenty Kadłubek, the Dominican St Jacek Odrowąż, St Jadwiga the Queen, and St John of Kęty (near Wadowice), who is buried in the collegiate church of St Anne and is the patron saint of Catholic schools and youth. Cracow was also a town of saints when Karol Wojtyła arrived there. In the year when he began to live in the district of Dębniki, Sister Faustyna (Maria Helena Kowalska), a mystic and apostle of the Divine Mercy, was dying in the nearby Congregation of the Sisters of Our Lady of Mercy in Łagiewniki. The pre-war Cracow vividly remembered and was full of the traces of the activity of Adam Chmielowski, Brother Albert, who died

itual aura of his Cracow. When living there, Karol Wojtyła never gave up his personal development in the religious dimension. He still regularly served at Mass in Wawel Cathedral, where he met his old religious instructor from Wadowice, Father Kazimierz Fuglewicz. He organized the meetings of youth in his parish in Dębniki and was active in the Marian Sodality at the Jagiellonian University. In Karol's hometown Wadowice, the window of the room where he had his writing table looked straight upon a wall of the church that bore a Latin inscription: *Tempus fugit, aeternitas manet* ("The time flies, the eternity waits"). This motto accompanied the young graduate and student. The direction had been set for him and he followed it even in Cracow. He did not want to waste time in any aspect.

Entrance to the new apartment of the Wojtyłas in the Cracow district of Dębniki

St Anne's Church in Cracow: John Paul II praying at the tomb of St John of Kęty

Royal Castle of Wawel

in 1916. He was an eminent painter who dedicated his life to the poorest and organized shelters for the homeless. Earlier, he fought for Poland's independence in the 1863 Uprising. Aniela Salawa (d. 1922) used to work in Cracow as a servant in bourgeois households. Strong ties joined the town of Cracow and Bishop Józef Sebastian Pelczar (d. 1924), Rector of the Jagiellonian University and founder of the Congregation of Sister Servants of the Most Sacred Heart of Jesus, who were so close, literally and figuratively, to Karol Wojtyła. And the Cracow seat of the Franciscans was frequently visited by Father Maksymilian Maria Kolbe, who in the 1930s carried out incessant missionary work on a worldwide scale.

St Maksymilian, St Albert, Blessed Aniela, Blessed Józef Sebastian, St Faustyna – with time, thanks to his prerogatives, John Paul II could officially show all of them as examples of sainthood to the faithful of the Catholic Church. They created the spir-

First and foremost, Cracow was for him a fountain of knowledge and a center of culture. It had the university and theater. He wanted to fill his time primarily with studies. In the first year he took thirty-six hours of classes per week, while the minimum specified by the regulations was ten hours. He was taught the history of theater and drama by Stanisław Pigoń, theory of drama by Stefan Kołaczkowski, Polish etymology by Kazimierz Nitsch, and his classes in the history of Polish literature were conducted by Kazimierz Wyka. These lecturers are the legend of the Polish studies of the nineteenth century, and they undoubtedly encouraged one to use the most opportunities that were offered by the University. In Professor Pigoń's seminar, Karol Wojtyła prepared his first extensive dissertation on the theory of European Romanticism. He also joined the Polish philologists' club,

Courtyard of Collegium Maius, heart of the Jagiellonian University

Ecce Homo, *the most renowned painting by Adam Chmielowski (now St Albert)*

led by Professor Kołaczkowski, and worked there as a librarian. However, in the very difficult examinations after his first year, he did not manage to obtain as high grades as he used to get in high school: in descriptive grammar, he received a good grade from Professor Nitsch and a fair grade in Old Church Slavonic grammar from Mieczysław Małecki. Studies had to be reconciled with two other time-consuming passions: poetry and theater.

In that respect, Karol Wojtyła's interests were nothing special among his fellow students, and he found many kindred souls. Other students at that time were Wojciech Żukrowski, Tadeusz Hołuj, and Tadeusz Kwiatkowski, who later became writers; Mieczysław Kieta, Jerzy Bober and Krystyna Zbijewska, who became journalists; Halina Królikiewiczówna (married name Kwiatkowska), the award-winning reciter, moved from Wadowice to Cracow to study Polish too. Karol made friends also with Juliusz Kydryński, who studied law. The merry company embraced Wojtyła as its regular member. They made up couplets to describe students, and in one of them Karol Wojtyła is expected to "move the whole world in the future" (and in a limerick from that time, he is remembered not so much for his personality, but for his characteristic, long and unruly hair). The same circles formed in October 1938 the Club of Young Artists, whose star was Tadeusz

Hołuj, the only one among them who could boast of his first published volume of poetry.

Karol had been writing poetry since his high school. Already in Class 5 it was noticed by one of the inquisitive pupils, who "blabbed" about it at school. As a first-year student, Karol began to write his earliest mature poems. It was a series of sonnets in which memories of the Beskidy and his neighborhood were intertwined with admiration for the "Renaissance splendor" of Cracow and with elements of Slavonic and Christian messian-

Karol Wojtyła as a student of the Polish Department in Cracow

ism. Culture and religion conjoined in desire for freedom: that was the unique message of his poetry. Its dynamics were described by the author: "from Wawel to Acropolis, I join spirits in unity," "from polonaise to hymn." Besides the sonnets, in the spring of 1939 Karol Wojtyła wrote another important poem styled as the hymn *Magnificat*: the praise of God, the Father of All Poetry. The coda contains an incredibly strong note of trust in the special, both cultural and religious, mission of the Slavonic world.

*May the Slav Book of Yearnings at last
        resound
with the spring music of resurrection
        chants,
with the holy, chaste songs of praise
        profound
and the hymn of mankind,
        Magnificat.*

His poetry was self-sufficient, independent from any other poetic trend that was present in the literary life of pre-war Poland. Wojtyła did not follow that life too closely. He was acquainted with and appreciated, as we learn from the accounts of his fellow students, the new, outstanding poetry by Czesław Miłosz (*Trzy zimy* [Three Winters]), but he was a more avid reader of philosophical and mystical works than of the then popular books by Gombrowicz, Uniłowski, Andrzejewski, or of poems by Czechowicz. His poetic models, and especially the models of his spiritual program, were the heritage of Mickiewicz, Słowacki (the author of *Król-Duch*), Norwid and Wyspiański. Karol Wojtyła was the follower of the Polish Romantic tradition, not only in poetry.

An opportunity to introduce himself to the public as a poet occurred during a common performance of poetry-writing students. The debut took place exactly forty years before Wojtyła's debut in the most important role of his life. On 15 October 1938, in the Blue Room of the Catholic House (which nowadays is the rehearsal room of the Cracow Philharmonic Orchestra), rented for that evening thanks to the recommendation of the officer of the Polish Army, father of the student Jerzy Bober, a literary meeting was organized under the somewhat odd title *Drogą topolowy most* [The Way of the Poplar Bridge]. Four students, among them young Karol Wojtyła, presented their poetry. Poems were also recited by other students of the first year. Karol recited his poems by himself. Halina Królikiewiczówna-Kwiatkowska, who took part in the meeting, remembered that Wojtyła's recitation was modern, balanced, focused on the sense of the uttered words and much different from the exaggerated gestures and "inspired" facial expression that were the confirmed habit of pre-war film acting. The actor and poet's first night was actually a success. All the tickets (priced 30 groszy for the youth and 49 groszy for the adults) were sold out and the room was "bursting at the seams." Part of the earnings was donated to the organization that aided Poles in the region of Cieszyn and the rest was divided between the young artists (2 zloty per person). The majority of the poets decided to spend the money to celebrate their success in a wine-vault in Mały Rynek (Small Market Square). Karol, however, did not join the party. All his friends from the University unanimously claim that he usually had no time for such entertainment. The only exception to the rule was the party to celebrate the passed examinations at the end of the first year, a dancing and drinking party hosted by one of female students. One of the women participants recollects that "Karol danced like anybody else, but he was more interested in conversation than in dancing."

And he was absolutely fascinated with theater. He joined the Theatrical Confraternity formed by Tadeusz Kudliński within the Association of Polish Writers. In January 1939 it was turned into Studio 39

Jagiellonian University Polish Department building in Gołębia Street

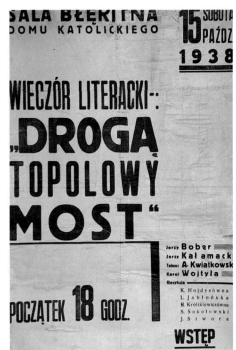

Poster announcing the poetic debut of Karol Wojtyła

Venue of the debut performance: Catholic Hall in Cracow (currently Philharmonic Hall)

for amateurs who wanted to become better acquainted with the acting profession. It offered classes with professionals from the Julisz Słowacki Theater, with playwrights and other experts on theater (e.g. Ludwik Hieronim Morstin, Adam Polewka, Roman Dyboski). Soon there emerged an idea that the students from Studio 39 should prepare a performance for the Days of Cracow, municipal festivities held in the summer. It was to be the first practical examination of the first-year students in Cracow's only school of acting at that time. Especially for this occasion a play was written about legendary Master Twardowski, a Polish Doctor Faustus. One more play was commissioned about Brother Albert Chmielowski, but the ap-

proaching war thwarted its completion. Eventually, it was written by Karol Wojtyła when he became a priest. The examination session of June 1939 was supplemented with the staging of the play about Master Twardowski, in which Wojtyła played a Zodiac sign, Taurus. The performance, shown in the beautiful yard of Collegium Nowodworskiego, was an entertaining and atmospheric one, and became widely popular. For each spectacle, the actors received a fee of 10 zloty, which was not little for students and meant a lot in the modest household of the Wojtyłas. The play was staged espe-

*September 1939, makeshift grave of
a defender of Warsaw*

*Queen Jadwiga's Cross in Wawel Cathedral:
Karol Wojtyła prayed here on 1 September 1939*

cially on 14 and 15 August during the Cracow meeting of the soldiers of the Polish Legions, and those were the last performances of the young actors before the war.

In July 1939 Karol Wojtyła took part in a training of the paramilitary Academic League near Sądowa Wisznia (between Przemyśl and Lwów), and the students' additional task there was to improve the relations between the local people of Polish and Ukrainian origin. On 30 August, after the training, Karol returned to the University his military uniform. Two days later came the first Friday in the month and Karol wanted to go to confession and receive the Eucharist. So, early in the morning he set out from Dębniki towards Wawel Cathedral. As usual, he assisted Father Figlewicz at Mass. All around the sirens were wailing and the bombs were falling down. It was 1 September 1939. The Nazi invasion of Poland began the Second World War.

For the whole 1920 generation, that is for the generation of Karol Wojtyła, the war was the most dramatic experience. Ten friends of Karol from his high school were either killed in action or murdered by the Germans. The majority of his Jewish friends and their families, both from Wadowice and Cracow, met a tragic fate. Karol's response to such a challenge was a remarkable one and proved pivotal for the whole course of his life.

In September, just like hundreds of thousands of other Poles, Karol and his

father went on foot towards the eastern regions to escape the Nazi offensive. They reached as far as the River San but, exhausted, decided to return when the effort proved futile: Poland was invaded from the east by the Soviet Union. There was no possibility of escape. The Wojtyłas came back to Cracow, which was appointed the capital of the General-Gouvernement (GG). Wadowice was incorporated to Germany and subjected to total germanization. Karol managed to enroll in the second year, but on 6 November the Germans dispelled all such illusions: the Gestapo carried out a brutal action, arresting 183 professors of the Cracow university and other schools of higher edu-

cation and transporting them to the concentration camp in Sachsenhausen. Among the professors who died there was Stefan Kołaczkowski, one of Karol's mentors; also Stefan Bednarski, a lecturer in Russian, died there. Three days after the Sonderaktion Krakau, the Nazis arrested a great number of high school teachers. Polish institutions of higher education and of secondary comprehensive education were officially liquidated. The majority of other cultural institutions, such as theaters, museums, libraries and the press, were banned. The Nazis systematically destroyed the monuments of Polish history and historical objects. In the spring of 1940 they began a campaign to destroy the elites and the leaders of the nation: from May to July, in mass executions they shot to death almost four thousand teachers, priests, artists, writers, and political activists. The meaning of such actions was made all too lucid by Hitler at the meeting during which he summed up the first year of the functioning of the GG: he presented the province as a reservoir of cheap labor force for unskilled work. "The Poles may have only one master, that is the Germans. There can be no two masters, and so the representatives of Polish intelligentsia have to be eliminated. It sounds cruel but such is the law of life."

Karol Wojtyła and a small group of his friends acted against that "law." Since the Nazis aimed at the destruction of the Polish language, Polish culture and Polish tradition, it was they, and not the military equipment, that had to serve as

*Collegium Novum: university professors were
escorted out from here by the Germans
on 6 November 1939*

weapons in the fight for the survival of Poland. And then, of what kind of Poland? This perpetual question was posed by Karol Wojtyła in the face of the 1939 defeat. And the answer was given in his literary works, which he wrote with more zeal than ever. At that time he composed his dramas *Hiob* [Job] and *Jeremiasz* [Jeremiah]. The latter dealt with the defeat in the 1620 battle of Cecora during the war with the Turks and therefore concentrated on the response towards the ultimate threat to the existence of the nation. In this drama the answer resulted from the dialogue between the ghosts of Hetman Stanisław Żółkiewski and Father Piotr Skarga and it was an appeal to start a spiritual crusade. Thanks to it, Poland was expected to resist the terrible power of two totalitarian systems which threatened Europe and Christianity. The slavery was supposed to force the Poles to engage in massive action: not necessarily in any military enterprise, but rather in morality and culture. The same spiritual program was recorded by the nineteen-year-old Karol in his correspondence with Mieczysław Kotlarczyk; the letters were smuggled right across the border to the Reich, to Wadowice, by Halina Królikiewiczówna. In the letter dated 2 November 1939, Karol wrote directly: "our liberation should be the gate of Christ. I think about «Athenian» Poland, but more perfect than Athens thanks to the enormous significance of Christianity. And such Poland was conceived by our great Romantic poets, our prophets in Babylonian Captivity."

In order to sustain the "Athenian" Poland underground, they needed theater: the place of the spoken word and of the poetry of Karol's favorites: Mickiewicz, mystic Słowacki, Norwid and Wyspiański. Even in October 1939 Karol began regular meetings with a few friends, the survivors of Studio 39: Tadeusz Kwiatkowski, Juliusz Kydryński, Danuta Michałowska. They recited the greatest works of Romantic literature. The return of Tadeusz Kudliński, the founder of the group, and a meeting with Juliusz Osterwa, the master of the theatrical art from before the war, provided an even stronger stimulus to rehearse again, of course illegally. The first spectacle (based on excerpts from *Przepióreczka* [The Quail] by Żeromski), in which Karol played Smugoń, was given in the apartment of the Kydryńskis, at 10 Felicjanek Street. It was the group's immediate response to yet another assault of the Nazis on Polish

culture and tradition. In August 1940, on the same day when Osterwa watched the clandestine performance of *Przepióreczka*, the Germans pulled down the monument of Adam Mickiewicz, which had stood in Cracow's Market Square. Karol Wojtyła and Juliusz Kydryński were at that time frequent guests at Osterwa's, who suggested to the young adherents of theater that they should work on the classics. Karol was commissioned to modernize the translation of *King Oedipus* by Sophocles (Wojtyła could prove his knowledge of Greek, which he learned in high school in Wadowice). The next rehearsals (e.g. of *Wesele* [The Wedding] and *Wyzwolenie* [Liberation] by Wyspiański) in the second half of 1940 took place in the apartment of Tadeusz Kudliński at 15 Słoneczna Street (now Prusa Street).

Kudliński introduced Karol Wojtyła to the resistance organization called Unia [the Union]. Established by the poet and philosopher Jerzy Braun, Unia was not

Wyspiański's stained-glass window: one of the "Athenian" visions which inspired Karol Wojtyła

Apartment of Tadeusz Kudliński (15 Prusa Street), who ran the clandestine theater

only a military organization, but also an ideological and educational movement that aimed at preparing Poland for restructuring and implementing Christian ideas in practice. Karol's friends, among others Wojciech Żukrowski and Tadeusz Kwiatkowski, joined the organization, too. Karol Wojtyła was sworn in the section called Unia Kultury, where the second-in-command was Tadeusz Kudliński. This section was to offer as many as possible forms of resistance against the Nazi occupation in the field of culture. So it established a network of underground theaters, held series of lectures and discussions and published an underground newspaper *Kultura Jutra* [The Culture of Tomorrow]. Such a formula of underground activity was undoubtedly very close to the spiritual program of Karol Wojtyła, who was twenty at the time.

The intensity of the cultural life in which he was immersed during the first months of the Nazi occupation is quite astonishing. And one should not forget that it was only part of his life. He had to work, just like all adult men in the General-Gouvernement, and at the beginning of 1940 he accepted a permanent job as an errand boy for a restaurant. But ultimately one was able to avoid forced labor in Germany only by taking a physical job in a plant that was of strategic importance to the industry of the Reich. Karol found such a job in September 1940 in a caustic soda plant called Solvay, which was re-named by the Germans as the Ost Deutsche Chemische

Former Solvay stone quarry area, today Lake Zakrzówek

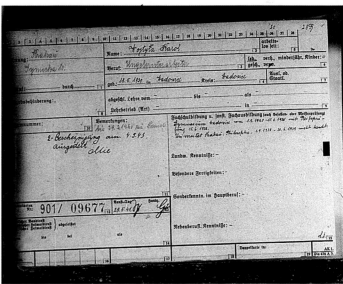

Karol Wojtyła's work record from Ost Deutsche Chemische Werke

Werke. He managed to secure this job thanks to the recommendation of Jadwiga Lewaj, his French teacher. She approached the Polish director of the plant who, tolerated by the Germans, had kept his pre-war position. But the price for being saved from slave labor in Germany was not small.

At first Karol was sent to work in the plant's stone quarry in Pychowice; limestone was exploited there as it was needed in the production process of soda. There were two shifts: 6 am to 2 pm and 2 pm to 10 pm. The former students (besides Wojtyła, Żukrowski and Kydryński were employed) had to crush limestone blocks with pickaxes and to load them on the cars of the narrow-gauge train that took limestone to the plant. Soon Karol was promoted to the position of a "blasting assistant": he had to prepare tamping, that is a mixture of sand and clay and to carry it in metal containers to the holes in the face of the quarry where the explosives were to be inserted. Then, supervised by the blaster, he took the explosives from the storage room and again carried them to the proper place. For safety reasons, it was prohibited for one worker to carry more than 20 kilos of explosives at a time. When they were put in the holes and tamped with the sand and clay, they were blasted with the help of an electric detonator. These things could be done by a trained assistant, but during the explosions, regrettably, sometimes workers lost their lives.

In the summer of 1941 Karol Wojtyła was transferred to the so-called "refinery" in the Solvay plant in the district of Borek Fałęcki and he had to work also nights shifts there. A worker's wages amounted to 80-90 groszy per hour. For a small fee he could get a meal: half a liter of soup and ten dekagrams of bread. The actor of an underground theater, using a wooden yoke, carried buckets full of milk of lime, which was used to soften water, and sacks of phosphate and soda. After forty years, in a conversation with the French journalist André Frossard, John Paul II recollected: "Four years of physical work, a period of belonging to the numerous working community, were to me a special gift of Providence. I learned to hold that period and that experience in high esteem. Sometimes I said that they were perhaps more valuable than my doctorate (although I greatly respect scholarship and university degrees)." No modern-time Pope ever had a comparable experience, and obviously its worth should not be underestimated for John Paul's

perception of social and moral problems that were connected with human labor in the twentieth century.

Under the Nazi occupation, Karol Wojtyła, a poet and a worker, made progress along yet another path of personal and spiritual development. He became involved in the life of his parish in the district of Dębniki, with the Church of St Stanislaus Kostka, which was managed by the Salesians. From February 1940, Karol participated in spiritual guidance meetings for young men. The Salesians, like other religious orders dedicated to pastoral tasks, were under the increasing pressure of the Nazis, who did not want any rivals in the area of education in the country occupied by them. Therefore the priests decided to educate a group of lay spiritual guides who could carry on, underground, with their work with the youth. One of the first guides was a very special tailor, Jan Tyranowski, who lived in the Wojtyłas' neighborhood, at 11 Różana Street. He was almost twenty years older than Karol and his friends, and initially seemed somewhat comical or perhaps stuffy to the young men. But when in 1949, in one of his first articles in *Tygodnik Powszechny*, Father Wojtyła remembered a "man called Jan," he showed how the feeling of distance towards Tyranowski had gradually changed into the youngsters' recognition that they were dealing "with a real saint." Tyranowski assigned himself the task of becoming a saint. And he wanted to set the same task to the group of young people whom he met in order to say the Rosary. Jan's apostleship mostly consisted in intimate conversation, in the example of his own spiritual life, and in the encouragement to read books that could open up the boys' minds to new, hitherto undiscovered dimensions of mystic spirituality.

This strange tailor introduced Karol to the world of the Spanish mystics and their books, which he studied on his own. First of all, Tyranowski presented to him the record of reflection and thought of St John of the Cross, the sixteenth-century reformer of the Carmelite Order. Following Jan from Różana Street and St John of the Cross, whose mysticism he later discussed in his doctoral dissertation, Karol, as a young worker from Solvay, climbed the narrow path in the footsteps of Christ. "A spiritual alpinist," the term that describes Tyranowski and captures the experience of any mystic, could well be applied to Karol Wojtyła, then about twenty years of age. However, he did not climb his steep path alone but, just like his spiritual guide, wanted others to join him. When the misgivings of the Salesians proved well-founded and almost all of them were arrested by the Gestapo in May 1941 (eleven of the clergy from the parish of St Stanislaus Kostka, including the parish priest, died in concentration camps), Jan Tyranowski divided his wards into four groups of fifteen and Karol became a spiritual guide to one of these groups. Discussions of moral problems, praying together and mutual assistance (e.g. Karol helped Mieczysław Maliński, a future priest, to learn Latin) were the simplest forms of activity that gave young people support during the dangerous and demoralizing time of the Nazi occupation.

Meeting Jan Tyranowski and reading the Spanish mystics coincided with the most painful experience of young Karol. On 18 February 1941 his father, his closest friend, died. When Karol worked in the quarry, took part in clandestine rehearsals, or met the youth of the parish, his father ran the house: he prepared meals using the rationed products that Karol had managed to buy (peas, groats, jam) and mended their shoes and clothes. On Sundays they went to Mass together, usually to the Franciscan Church. In the winter of 1940-1941, Karol Wojtyła Sr, then sixty-one years old, fell ill. The son received the kind assistance of the Kydryńskis, the family of his friend Juliusz. The latter's mother prepared meals for them, which Karol took back home for his ill father. On 18 February Karol came home with Juliusz's younger sister Maria, who was to heat the food up. Karol's father was dead. The son found it hard to accept the blow. He voiced his regret: "I was absent when my mother died, I was absent when my brother died, and I was absent when my father died." He had no living relative any more. The trauma of his father's death brought back to his mind the idea of priesthood, which he had previously put aside.

Although the idea was revived, the final choice was not made yet. Immediately following the death of his father, Karol temporarily moved to the apartment of the Kydryńskis in Felicjanek Street, whence he and Juliusz every morning went to work in the Solvay plant. They continued to rehearse in Tadeusz Kudliński's clandestine theater. Karol did not want to return to the apartment in Tyniecka Street, which was filled up with bitter memories. But soon another tenant appeared who brought new life to the basement lodging in Dębniki. In the summer of 1941 Mieczysław Kotlarczyk, the man who had both shared and inspired Karol's theatrical fascinations, managed to steal across the border from Wadowice to Cracow. Kotlarczyk wanted to flee the Gestapo, which persecuted and killed representatives of Polish intelligentsia in the territories that were incorporated in the Third Reich (his brother, who also had worked as a teacher in Wadowice, did not manage to escape his doom: he was murdered in a concentration camp). Kotlarczyk found in Cracow a place to live and a relatively safe job: he was a tram driver. He and his wife moved to one room in the Tyniecka Street basement and Karol returned to the other room.

The two friends were then able to form their common vision of theater in face-to-face conversation after work, no longer through correspondence that had been illegally carried across the border between Cracow in the General-Gouvernement and Wadowice in the Reich. Later on, Father Wojtyła returned to the essence of their idea of theater in several articles. He stressed the primacy of the word over gesture, which was to reflect the primacy of man's thought over his impulse and movement. "Theater, whose primary element is the word, entails the need to think." A meeting that began the process of putting the idea

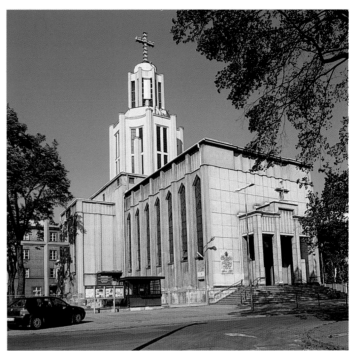

Parish church of St Stanislaus Kostka in Dębniki district

Kydryński family apartment in Felicjanek Street

John Paul II prayed at his parents' tomb on each visit to Cracow

*Mieczysław Kotlarczyk during a Rhapsodic Theater performance
(post-war picture)*

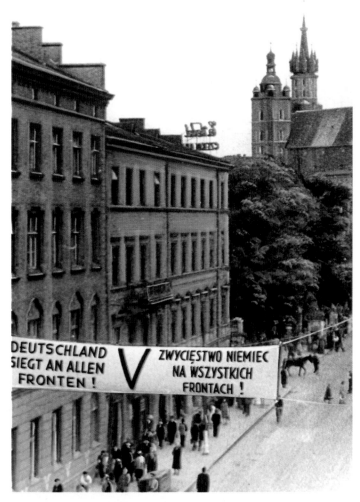

DEUTSCHLAND SIEGT AN ALLEN FRONTEN !

V ZWYCIĘSTWO NIEMIEC NA WSZYSTKICH FRONTACH !

*Streets of German-occupied Cracow were dominated
by Nazi propaganda*

They formed the core of the clandestine Rhapsodic Theater. The name alluded to their first performance, the rhapsodies of *Król-Duch* by Juliusz Słowacki. Additionally, in ancient Greece rhapsodes were itinerant singers who traversed the perpetually war-stricken country and brought comfort to its people by reciting the poetry by Homer and earlier epic poets. The same factor was present in the artistic program of Kotlarczyk and Wojtyła: they wanted to reassure the sorrowful listeners and to show them things that were more powerful than the occupying powers, to evoke a vision of strong Poland and its cultural and spiritual mission using the word of the great Romantic poets and their followers.

So they started with excerpts from *Król-Duch*, and the first "staging," after many evening rehearsals, took place on 1 November 1941, at 7 Komorowskiego Street. The set consisted of a carpet that marked the area of the stage, a grand piano with a white rose in a vase on top, and an open book of Słowacki's poetry. The clandestine first night, during which Karol played the tragic King Bolesław the Bold, was attended by professional actors who sympathized with the "rhapsodic" group, Zdzisław Mrożewski and Władysław Woźnik. The subsequent performances (*Beniowski* by Słowacki, *Hymny* [Hymns] by Kasprowicz, excerpts from Wyspiański's works and Norwid's works, excerpts from *Pan Tadeusz* by Mickiewicz) were attended by eminent representatives of Polish underground culture: Zofia Kossak-Szczucka, who co-founded the Council for the Assistance to the Jews; professors Stanisław Pigoń and Kazimierz Wyka, Karol's university lecturers; Jerzy Braun, the leader of the Union; the excellent conductor Witold Rowicki; and Juliusz Osterwa, who constantly assessed the achievements of his younger colleagues. It was in the presence of Osterwa that a particularly dramatic performance of *Pan Tadeusz* was held. In the vicinity of the apartment at 5 Rynek Kleparski, where the performers and the viewers had to come one by one so as not to raise suspicion, stood one of the hateful street loudspeakers which boomed official announcements about the consecutive victories of the German army on all fronts. At the moment when Karol began to recite the confession speech of Jacek Soplica, the loudspeaker roared out the next military report of the Wehrmacht. But the actor neither stopped speaking nor raised his voice so as to outshout Goebbels's words with those of Mickiewicz. "When the loudspeaker was almost finished with the praise of the German atrocities, Mickiewicz praised the reconciliation between Soplica and Klucznik." Those who watched the performance could never forget the feeling.

To the great astonishment of people who had already seen Karol's acting abilities and his passion for the theater of the spoken word, he finally decided to follow a different career. Even before *Pan Tadeusz* was staged, in October 1942, he had an important talk with Mieczysław Kotlarczyk. Karol did not want to be cast in the next plays because, as one of his biographers said, he "wished to dedicate his life to the Living God and the only drama that he wanted to perform in was the sacrifice of Christ." The thought had matured in him for over a year since the death of his father. The prospect of using his talents in priesthood seemed feasible thanks to the experience of working with fifteen young boys in the parish of Dębniki. Amid these experiences, his work at Solvay, clandestine rehearsals and hours spent on writing his own poetry, his awareness of the priest's calling, John Paul II recollected, "grew as an internal fact, absolutely transparent and unambiguous in

of such theater in practice occurred on 22 August 1941, in the apartment of Krystyna Dębowska at 7 Komorowskiego Street. Kotlarczyk presented his artistic program and engaged, besides his housemate from Tyniecka Street, one more former inhabitant of Wadowice, Halina Królikiewiczówna, as well as Danuta Michałowska and Krystyna Dębowska (whose fiancé, Tadeusz Ostaszewski, became the troupe's stage set designer).

my view. I realized what I was leaving behind and what I was to strive for, never looking back." He became completely sure that it was not he who had chosen – it was he who had been chosen. With this certainty, he could not be dissuaded by the troupe, who argued that he should not hide his light under a bushel and that he should not squander the gift of God, his immense acting talent.

Tadeusz Kudliński, Karol's first mentor in theatrical matters, claimed credit for a slight modification in the plans of the future priest. Having talked to Karol all night long, he apparently convinced him at least not to join the strict, closed Order of Discalced Carmelites. That was indeed the original intention of Karol, who was fascinated by the great Carmelite mystics from Spain. In the fall of 1942 he enquired if it was possible to become a novice at the monastery in Czerna (where Father Rafał Kalinowski, canonized later by John Paul II, had for many years served as a confessor). However, this turned out to be impossible, and there was no chance for a young man to join a religious order and abandon his job in an industrial plant that was "of strategic importance for the Third Reich." No matter whether the decision was affected by Kudliński's power of persuasion or whether it simply resulted from the circumstances of the Nazi occupation, Karol's resignation from living in a closed order should be perceived as providential. In a religious community he would have been able to reach the summit of spiritual development, but he would not have become the shepherd of the Cracow Church and of the entire Catholic Church. Karol Wojtyła began to serve God's Fold in October 1942, when he became a student of the clandestine Seminary of the Cracow Archdiocese.

Under the Nazi occupation it was strictly forbidden to accept new students to seminaries. The Cracow Metropolitan, Prince Adam Sapieha, decided nevertheless to violate that law. In the fall of 1942 he allowed the Seminary Rector, Father Jan Piwowarczyk, to accept ten new students, of course in the greatest secrecy. One of those ten young men was Karol Wojtyła. In this way, four years after the visit of Archbishop Sapieha to the parish of Wadowice and after his enquiry about the promising graduate, Karol appeared before the Cracow Metropolitan, now sure about his decision. Archbishop Sapieha became his fourth master of spiritual growth, following his father, Mieczysław

Kotlarczyk and Jan Tyranowski. In the times of war, the Cracow Archbishop of aristocratic origin became the moral leader of all the Polish Church. Primate August Hlond, just like the Polish government, remained in exile. The Cracow Metropolitan not only represented the local Catholic community, but also the whole nation threatened by the German invaders. He retained his dignity and refused to collaborate with the Nazis in any way. At the same time, by all means possible, he

attempted to safeguard the Poles and to protect the hiding Jews against the rising waves of persecution. His decision that the Seminary should secretly admit new students stemmed from the conviction that the occupation sooner or later had to end and that it would be necessary to replace those members of the pastoral network of the Church who were murdered by the Nazis (in the Second World War, over 3,000 of Polish priests and members of religious orders were killed).

Prince Adam Stefan Sapieha, Archbishop Metropolitan of Cracow

Karol Wojtyła as a seminary graduate just after his ordination

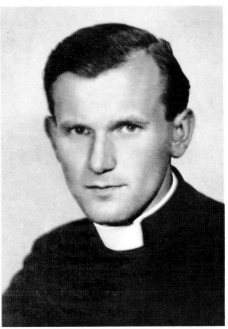

Archbishops' Palace in Cracow, wartime headquarters of the clandestine seminary

The studies at the underground Seminary did not release the student from the obligatory work for the Nazi state. The classes were held secretly in private homes, churches and monasteries. As a seminarian, Karol Wojtyła did not lead a much different life than that from before October 1942. He kept carrying buckets at Solvay, but in the breaks he read not so much poetry as tough seminary handbooks of ontology or general metaphysics, rather remote from the highly emotional Spanish mysticism. He still lived in Tyniecka Street, sharing the apartment with the Kotlarczyks. He made no departure from the Rhapsodic Theater either and continued to perform both in *Pan Tadeusz*, a new spectacle, and in *Król-Duch*, a revived one. Wojtyła also agreed to play his last main part of Samuel Zborowski in Słowacki's drama. The first night took place in March 1943 and the spectacle had the highest number of shows, i.e. as many as six (one of them was watched by the representatives of the underground Polish government). From the middle of 1943 Karol Wojtyła was no longer an actor. He was preparing for a new role of a priest, and he was more and more preoccupied by that. He even decided to give up writing poetry before graduating and being ordained (the only exception to this rule was *Pieśń o Bogu ukrytym* [Hymn about Hidden God] from 1944).

But the country was still under the occupation and the danger was on the increase. Before the war was over, Karol Wojtyła escaped death at least on two occasions. On 29 February 1944, when, as usual, he returned from his double (day and night) shift at Solvay in his rubber-lined coat, drill trousers and clogs, he was hit by a German military truck. A Wehrmacht officer who passed by a few minutes later ordered that the unconscious worker be lifted from the pavement and taken to hospital. After a fortnight in the surgical ward in Kopernika Street and a short recuperation at his friends the Szkockis', Karol returned to work. When an uprising broke out in Warsaw, the Germans feared it might spread all over the General-Gouvernement. On 6 August 1944 they arranged roundups in Cracow to arrest young men. They also searched the house at 10 Tyniecka Street but, in a hurry, overlooked the entrance to the basement where the Kotlarczyks and Karol Wojtyła stayed. On that day in Cracow 8,000 men were arrested and the majority of them were soon afterwards transported to concentration camps.

The Metropolitan decided – as the liberation seemed to be near – that there was no point in risking the lives of the young seminarians. Therefore he summoned them to come to the Archbishops' Palace and to stay there until the end of the occupation. They managed to gather in the palace, in Franciszkańska Street, in front of the Archbishop. He declared that from then on he was going to be the Rector of their Seminary, and that the seat of the Seminary would be the Palace. When Karol was taken under the wing of Sapieha, he abandoned his work in a plant of "strategic importance." Therefore an arrest warrant was issued on him, as demanded by the Arbeitsamt, but eventually Father Kazimierz Figlewicz persuaded the Polish manager of Solvay to strike Wojtyła's name off the register of employees.

It was the end of Wojtyła's lay life, abundant in experiences that gave the young priest a great deal of knowledge about the world outside the walls of the Seminary: much more knowledge than many of his colleagues could have since they usually decided to become priests right after they finished high school. On 9 November 1944, the ex-student of the Polish Department, actor, worker, poet and sworn member of an underground resistance organization, bereaved of all his family, was ordained as a deacon by the Cracow Metropolitan.

CHAPTER III
Priesthood
and scholarship
(1945–1958)

Clandestine seminary studies were a unique experience. The seminarians lived in the halls of their bishop's palace, next to his modest rooms, and were close enough to observe the concentration and spirituality of Prince Sapieha, who taught them and prayed with them on a daily basis. The lectures were held in one of the palace halls as well. One of the lecturers was Juliusz Osterwa, whose task was to teach the seminarians the art of the spoken word, which is so much needed in pastoral work. But Karol Wojtyła had already mastered that art and he could use it on 8 December 1944, when the Seminary organized a Marian celebration during which he recited Norwid's *Litania do Matki Boskiej* [Litany to Our Lady].

On 18 January 1945 the German occupation was over. Cracow saw the tanks of the First Ukrainian Front of the Soviet Army. That moment was remembered by Cardinal Wojtyła during the retreat with Paul VI in Vatican: "I can never forget the impact of the conversation I had with a Soviet soldier in 1945. (…) He knocked at the gate of the Seminary in Cracow, and the building was still partly in ruin. I asked what he wanted, and when he asked if he could be admitted to the Seminary,

Seminary building in Cracow, rebuilt following wartime damage

I started a conversation that lasted for several hours. Although he did not join the Seminary, I learned a great deal in the course of this lengthy talk about how God can find His way to the human mind in the circumstances of systematic negation, presenting Himself as the Truth that cannot be obliterated. My interlocutor had never been to church and he constantly heard at school and at work that there was no God. <And anyway I always knew,> he reiterated, <that God exists. And now I would like to learn about Him even more>."

The end of the Nazi occupation was not tantamount to absolute liberation. The Soviet tanks brought to Poland another system of enslavement, and one of its basic assumptions was the "systematic negation" of the existence of God. This meant that Poland was to be torn away from its spirituality and Catholic tradition and that the influence of the Church was to be limited in every aspect of social life and in the national education. The first harbingers of such a policy were the decrees of the communist-dominated Provisional Government, dated September 1945, including the decree that declared the concordat between Poland and the Holy See null and void. The leader of the Communist Party and the Deputy Prime Minister, Władysław Gomułka, directly threatened the Church: "We broke the concordat, and if the Church plays up, we'll put them in their place." The new reality, created by the ideologues and implementers of the Soviet system, was in due time opposed by the priests who had received their education at the hands of the Cracow Archbishop.

In the first stage of the introduction of the new system in Poland, no full-scale attack on the Church was launched yet. The communists wanted first to eliminate their political opponents and the anti-communist military resistance. This is why seminaries re-opened. Also, other Catholic institutions of higher education began to function, such as the Theological Faculty of the Jagiellonian University or the Catholic University of Lublin (KUL). The Cracow Archbishop permitted that a new periodical, *Tygodnik Powszechny*, should be issued under his patronage. It was to propagate and develop Catholic culture under the altered political circumstances. The first issue, edited by the hitherto supervisor of clandestine seminarians, Jan Piwowarczyk, was published on 24 March 1945.

At that time Karol and his friends were busy renovating the Seminary building (situated near Wawel Castle), which the SS used as a prison until the end of the occupation. He did an intensive course of Spanish and worked in Professor Ignacy Różycki's seminar on his master's thesis concerning faith in the writings of St John of the Cross. On 1 April 1945, almost two weeks after the University re-opened, he received a position of a junior assistant at the Theological Faculty. In this way, as a third-year student, he began his academic career that was crowned with the honorary doctorate he received from the University in 1983. Moreover, while sitting virtually dozens of regular exams, he was involved in yet another type of activity, the student government. With the support of the Archbishop, he was elected the deputy chairman of the University Association for Mutual Assistance. The supervisor of the Association was his former lecturer in the history of drama, Stanisław Pigoń, and the chairman of the law committee was Father Andrzej Deskur, later a close friend of Bishop Wojtyła in the Roman Curia. The Association distributed American food parcels among those in need, provided accommodation and protected the students who were persecuted by the new regime. The political problems emerged

Karol Wojtyła (second from the right) at a meeting of Class 1946

Corpus Christi procession among the ruins of Warsaw (troops were still allowed to take part)

Primate August Hlond celebrates Mass at Jasna Góra ramparts

*St Leonard's Crypt at Wawel, venue of
Fr Wojtyła's first Mass*

in Cracow on a large scale when on 3
May 1946 the students spontaneously
celebrated the anniversary of the voting
of the 1791 Constitution of the Third of
May: the police and secret police dis-
persed the celebrators with extreme violence.

Karol Wojtyła, however, was not directly involved in political activity. He had to
study hard in Professor Różycki's seminar
devoted to dogmatic theology, while being employed as an assistant and working
towards his master's thesis. The time of

*St Angelo's bridge and castle in Rome,
the regular walking route of Wojtyła,
the Angelicum student*

his final examinations and the ordination
was approaching. Following a six-week
retreat conducted by Father Stanisław
Smoleński, Karol Wojtyła swore to live in
celibacy and to say his daily breviary
prayers. On 1 November 1946, Archbishop Sapieha, who had been appointed Cardinal a few months earlier, ordained
Wojtyła in his private chapel in the Archbishops' Palace. "May the blessing of the
almighty God, the Father, the Son, and
the Holy Ghost, descend upon you, that
you may be blessed in the priestly order,
and offer up the sacrifice of propitiation
for the sins and offenses of the people to
almighty God, to whom be honor and glo-
ry forever and ever." Wojtyła became
a priest. The sense of the mystery for which
he had been preparing was pondered in
his poetry, in *Pieśń o Bogu ukrytym*, which

at that time was anonymously published
in *Głos Karmelu*:

*I hold a land – transparent –
and a boat, and a fishermen's quay
lit up by Lake Genezareth,
where the waves lap peacefully.
And I hold great multitudes of hearts
of which One Single Heart got hold,
the simplest Heart in the world,
the gentlest of all.*

This vision, which had been written
down in 1944, presented the new role of
the ex-actor. Now he was to work as a fish-
erman and capture people's hearts, the
multitudes of hearts that were waiting for
the Gospel. On the day following his ordination by the Cardinal, Father Wojtyła
celebrated his first Mass in the same special place where he had found himself
seven years earlier, at the outbreak of the
war: in St Leonard's Crypt at Wawel.
There, on All Souls' Day (2 November
1946), with Father Kazimierz Figlewicz,
whom he assisted at Mass on 1 September 1939, Wojtyła celebrated Mass thrice
for the souls of his parents and his brother. The Crypt, which holds the tombs of
Polish national heroes, such as King Jan III
Sobieski, General Tadeusz Kościuszko
and Prince Józef Poniatowski, is one of
the major memorial places. On Wawel
Hill some Polish monarch are also buried, and in a special crypt at Wawel Cathedral the ashes of the great Romantic
poets, Adam Mickiewicz and Juliusz
Słowacki (who inspired Wojtyła's poetry
and thinking) are interred. The newly
ordained priest chose the most sacred
Polish crypt for his first Masses in order
to, as he said, accentuate the living spiritual bond between himself and the history of his nation and to pay homage to
its great poets and heroes whose tombs
he could see around and who were so
important for his Christian and patriotic
education (*Dar i tajemnica* [Gift and
Mystery]). St Leonard's Crypt was the silent witness of the first fruits of Karol
Wojtyła's calling, thanks to which he
joined the ranks of the national heroes as
the spiritual leader of the Poles at the turn
of the second and third millennium. Subsequent masses were offered by Father
Wojtyła in his parish in Dębniki, where
his new role was a source of joy to his
former spiritual guide Jan Tyranowski; in
Wawel Cathedral, where he was met by
many of his fellow students from the Polish Department, his friends from the Sem-

inary and the troupe of the Rhapsodic Theater; and, lastly and most solemnly, in his hometown Wadowice. Father Wojtyła embraced new responsibilities such as administering the sacraments. As early as ten days after his ordination, he baptized a little daughter of his friends, Halina née Królikiewiczówna and Tadeusz Kwiatkowski.

Cardinal Sapieha decided to send the best graduate of the Seminary to study in Rome, as soon as possible. He had been observing the unique scholarly skills and the profundity of Wojtyła's spirituality since 1942 and he wanted to use them to the greatest benefit of the Cracow Catholic community and of the Church in general. Father Wojtyła was advised to continue his studies at the Angelicum, the Dominican Pontifical University. On 15 November 1946 he went by train via Paris to Rome. As instructed by Cardinal Sapieha, he lived in the Belgian College on the Quirinal, next to St Andrew's Church, where St Stanislaus Kostka, a patron saint of Poland, is buried. Soon after he had arrived in the Italian capital with the credentials of the Cracow Cardinal, he was kindly received by the Polish Primate August Hlond, who stayed in Rome at the time. Later, at a special audience, Pope Pius XII received all the priests and students (about twenty of them) of the Belgian College. The stay in the College allowed Father Wojtyła to master his French, which he had diligently studied under the occupation besides Italian, Spanish and, *nolens volens*, German.

The crowning achievement of the first stage of studies at the best of Catholic universities was Wojtyła's final examination in July 1947, during which he obtained the highest score possible, that is forty points. In October he began his second year at the Angelicum, working towards his doctoral degree. The supervisor of the dissertation was one of the then greatest theological authorities of the Church and the reviver of the traditional teaching of St Thomas Aquinas, Father Reginald Garrigue-Lagrange, and the subject of the dissertation was the doctrine of the faith in the writings of St John of the Cross, who constantly fascinated Father Wojtyła. In June 1948 the dissertation was brilliantly defended. However, the author could not afford to publish it, which was a formal requirement at the Angelicum for granting doctoral degrees. (The dissertation was published only after Karol Wojtyła became Pope, in several languages at the same time.) So the degree was eventually granted in Poland, the thesis having been officially presented at the Jagiellonian University, by its Theological Faculty in December 1948.

Young priests from Cracow (Karol Wojtyła and Stanisław Starowiejski, who also lived in the Belgian College) spent their holidays on trips and pilgrimages across Italy. They visited Father Pio, the famous confessor and stigmatic, in San Giovanni Rotondo; the places connected with St Francis; Monte Cassino; Naples and Capri. In the summer of 1947, as permitted by Cardinal Sapieha, Father Wojtyła was able to visit France (and, for the first time, its Marian sanctuary at Lourdes), Belgium and Holland. His task was to observe pastoral work in great modern towns, especially among the working class. How is it possible to prevent the increasing secularization and religious indifference of modern societies? How to bridge the gap between the outstanding Catholic intellectuals of various convictions and the masses who abandoned the Gospel in their lives and modes of thinking? The questions that Father Wojtyła formulated in France were to prove universal problems of his service as a priest, bishop and pope, and were not limited to the experience of a few weeks' stay in Paris or Marseilles. In France, in 1947, Father

Pope Pius XII receives the Monte Cassino Prior's staff from General Władysław Anders

Wojtyła found about the local answer to the question: the movement of worker-priests, *mission de France.*

He described that movement in the first article that he published in *Tygodnik Powszechny* in 1949, stressing that those priests who had found employment as common workers so as to preach the Gospel directly to a completely de-Christianized community had intuitively sensed that was the right thing to do. In a situation when any religious tradition is defunct, the testimony of the priest's life becomes the most important. This testimony has to be reliable and comprehensible at the same time. It is also crucial that the apostleship should neither involve negating nor opposing; instead, it should make allowances for the circumstances of the present day, for modern psyche, for today's social and mental preconditions, and "try to draw all these changes into the orbit of the Gospel, thus striving to create a new model of Christian culture." Lastly, it is important that the priest should not succumb to secularization himself by totally replacing spiritual exercise with physical work and involvement in social issues. The fruit of the stay in France, Belgium and Holland in 1947 was reflection on the opportunities and threats connected with the efforts of the Church to make its presence felt in the quickly changing world of the twentieth century. Moreover, this experience considerably broadened the horizons of the young minister. He got acquainted and established contacts with outstanding theologians, includ-

View of the Notre-Dame Cathedral in Paris; Karol Wojtyła saw it for the first time in 1947

Fr Karol Wojtyła, curate from Niegowić, leads the funeral cortege of the mother of Jan Adamski, a friend from the Rhapsodic Theater

Fr Karol Wojtyła (now a bishop) among the First Communion children

ing many high officials of the Church (then and in the future), gathered in the Roman Curia. This undoubtedly proved useful in preparing Father Karol Wojtyła for important positions in the Church.

The Cracow Metropolitan, who had been watching from a distance over the achievements of his ward, sent him immediately after his return from Rome to work in a small parish. Straight from the grand world of theology, intellectual dispute and the Church officialdom, Karol Wojtyła entered the reality of the Polish countryside. He became a curate at Niegowić, a small village between Wieliczka and Bochnia, near Cracow. The Cardinal trusted that the local parish priest, Kazimierz Buzała, who had much experience in pastoral work in the country, would be able to introduce the graduate of the Angelicum to his new responsibilities. Or he wanted, as one of the biographers of John Paul II supposed, the extremely emaciated new curate to "put on a little flesh" in a typical provincial parish after his voyages all over Europe. When Father Wojtyła arrived at the borders of the parish on foot, he knelt down and kissed the ground. He always did that when beginning a new stage in his priestly career. Wojtyła had acquired that habit (recorded in photos from his numerous pilgrimages), as he

admitted fifty years later, from Jean-Marie Vianney, a saint and confessor from Ars, a town Wojtyła visited in 1947 when traveling in France. Working in Niegowić, he had to go in farmers' carts to teach religion in nearby villages; he organized Rosary prayer meetings like he used to do in Dębniki; he established a theatrical group and engaged in the construction of a new church in the parish. Apart from that he served at baptisms, weddings, funerals, confessions, and the First Holy Communions, that is administered the sacraments, which is a vital part of any priest's vocation. He fulfilled similar responsibilities in a new parish, at St Florian's in Cracow, where he was transferred in March 1949 based on the Cardinal's decision. In the new place he was also supervised by a parish priest in whom the Cardinal had absolute confidence: his former chaplain, Tadeusz Kurowski. Another curate at St Florian's was Marian Jaworski, the future Archbishop of Lviv and Cardinal, and Wojtyła's close friend. St Florian's parish in Cracow is at least 800 years old and there, perhaps more profitably than in Niegowić, Wojtyła – a priest, actor and poet of good education and considerable experience in the life and problems of lay people and his contemporaries – could develop his pastoral talents. St Florian's parish, besides St Anne's parish, became a centre of pastoral work with students. Two schools of higher education, the Institute of Technology and the Academy of Fine Arts, are located close to St Florian's Church, and the parish priest Tadeusz Kurowski had previously worked in St Anne's parish, so he attracted some students of the Jagiellonian University.

This kind of work: meeting young people, especially students, who are about to make their mature choices but are still open and perceptive of the deepest questions of existence, was of particular interest to Wojtyła. He did not wait for young people to approach him or to come to the church, but himself visited students' halls of residence. He looked for new forms of prayer and meditation, not only during retreats or prayer meetings, but in studying the theology of St Thomas Aquinas or involving in activities that required a special talent (e.g. singing Gregorian chant). Pastoral work was not confined solely to the church: the energetic priest took young people on trips (hiking, cycling or skiing) in the neighborhood of Cracow, in the Beskidy and in the Tatras. Karol Wojtyła, endearingly nicknamed "Uncle" by the students, gained in this way a hiker's medal, awarded to him by the Polish Tourist Society (PTTK) in 1954. At the same time he maintained contact with the Rhapsodic Theater and Mieczysław Kotlarczyk and introduced the students to the world of Christian culture: went with them to the theater and discussed the spectacles, and in the parish directed plays presenting Christ's Passion, based on medieval mystery plays. New friendships were formed between Karol Wojtyła and the students at St Florian's, which survived until the end of his life. He and his friends were called a "little family" or a "gang."

In this environment, for the first time in the Cracow diocese, Karol Wojtyła organized the first course that prepared engaged couples for marriage. Whenever it was possible, he tried to prepare for this sacrament each of the 160 couples that he joined in marriage when he worked at St Florian's (until 1958). Remaining in close contact with them, he tried to build their and his own understanding of married love, responsible parenthood and honest life in a family. In the conversations with his young interlocutors, he was open enough to tackle the most delicate aspects of love, including sensual love. He was far from discrediting it; to the contrary, he stressed its positive meaning both in the act of procreation and in the evolution of love between the married man and woman. He wanted to convince them that in order to foster that love it is necessary to show patience, mutual understanding and constant acceptance. "The surface of love has its current, which is swift, glittering and changing. The current is sometimes so swift that it carries away people, women and men. Love is not an adventure. Love tastes of the whole person. (...) It cannot be momentary." The knowledge that he presented at St Florian's and that he had acquired on the basis of young people's experience became fundamental in his reflection on love. Soon it was given the form of a scholarly treatise *Miłość i opowiedzialność* [Love and Responsibility] as well as a theater play which described young people's dilemmas (*Przed sklepem jubilera* [In Front of a Jeweler's]). Eventually this knowledge shaped his reflection on the significance of family and married life, about the calling of women and men to love, which reflection was vital throughout the pontificate of John Paul II.

Cardinal Sapieha, who made sure Father Wojtyła progresses in his vocation, did not intent to limit his interests to parish pastoral work any longer, even if it involved working with young people, which Karol Wojtyła cherished so much. In the spring of 1955 the Cardinal allowed St Florian's curate to proceed with his scholarly work and to prepare his post-doctoral dissertation. Karol Wojtyła's sabbatical was to start after the summer vacation. However, before it was over, on 23 July 1951, the Metropolitan died at the age of eighty-four. Karol Wojtyła lost a spiritual father for the first time in March 1947: Jan Tyranowski died when he studied theology far away in Rome. The death of Cardinal Sapieha meant a loss of another spiritual father. When as a thirty-one-year-old curate he stood at the open coffin of the Metropolitan, he did not foresee that in time he would succeed him as the Cracow Archbishop. But it may have occurred to Cardinal Sapieha in the last years of his ministry that Karol Wojtyła, whom he had noticed at the Wadowice high school, should be prepared for the responsibilities and honors of religious communities larger than a parish. In 1951 the obvious candidate to replace the dead Metropolitan was the Archbishop of Lwów, Eugeniusz Baziak, whom the Red Army banished from his seat. Therefore Pope Pius XII nominated him to become the Cracow Archbishop. The decision was vetoed by the communist regime in Poland. Archbishop Baziak in practice fulfilled his responsibilities although formally he was not allowed to do that and this strange pseudo-vacancy lasted until 1964, when Bishop Karol Wojtyła took the position after the investiture.

In 1951 the conflict between the Church authorities and the communist state as to the successor of Cardinal Sapieha was only one symptom of the radically altered, anti-Church policy of the

Niegowić parishioners bring altar gifts to their former curate during Mass in 1966

St Florian's Church in Cracow, venue of the pastoral work of Fr Wojtyła until 1958

St Florian's curate greets his former parishioners as Bishop of Rome

Monument to Prince Cardinal Adam Sapieha in front of the Archbishops' Palace in Cracow

Cardinal Karol Wojtyła and his auxiliary bishops (Julian Groblicki and Jan Pietraszko) celebrate Mass on the 25th anniversary of the death of Cardinal Adam Sapieha

regime. In January 1950 the communists illegally took control over the head office of Caritas, an organization that coordinated charity work of the Church on the national scale. Cardinal Sapieha voiced his most vigorous protest and expressed his indignation in a special telegram he sent to President Bierut. In response, there was a wave of arrests among the priests and of the police searches in the Church institutions under the pretext of embezzlement. Stefan Wyszyński, who was nominated Primate after the death of August Hlond, decided to accept a compromise. In this way he wanted to assure that the Church would be able to function within a communist state. On his initiative an agreement was made between the Church and the state in April 1940 (which was very strongly opposed by Cardinal Sapieha, who did not consider the communist authorities a reliable partner). That temporarily averted anti-Church repressions but did not prevent them completely. Towards the end of 1951 almost 900 priests were in prison, accused of anti-state activities.

The year 1952 saw the intensification of the campaign to remove religious instruction from school curricula. Not only priests were arrested, abut also bishops who protested against the atheist model of education. In November 1952 the provocation of the secret police led to a large-scale repressive action against the Cracow Curia. Its primary objective was to tarnish the reputation of the late Cardinal Sapieha as the greatest authority of the Church in Poland at that time. Those who had been closest to him were accused of having "betrayed their nation," spying for the "American imperialism," illegal trading in foreign currencies and possession of firearms. Father Andrzej Bardecki, who was present at the trial, said: "They wanted to present the Cardinal as a traitor to the Polish nation. One of the priests who had to testify before the tribunal mentioned a few years later that an investigation officer had threatened: <We'll arrange for such a trial that Sapieha will turn in his grave.>" Even Archbishop Baziak was arrested. In a show trial that was carried out in January 1953 according to the classic Stalinist models, three priests from the Cracow Curia were sentenced to death. Even *Tygodnik Powszechny* approved of the condemnation of the alleged "agents of the USA" and a letter of protest against "traitors in cassocks" was signed by the Cracow luminaries of culture (among others, by Sławomir Mrożek, Wisława Szymborska, and Jan Błoński). Archbishop Baziak could no longer run the diocese and he was replaced by a temporarily appointed administrator, assisted by two trusted curates selected by the communist authorities from among the so-called "priests patriots." In March 1953, when Stalin died, the editors of *Tygodnik Powszechny* did not want to publish a sufficiently laudatory obituary of the dictator. The authorities then closed the paper which was a living monument to the spiritual efforts of Cardinal Sapieha. Even earlier, *Gość Niedzielny*, a Catholic weekly of mass circulation, had been suspended, while the number of copies of the weekly *Niedziela* had been reduced as many as ten times: the journalists had not agreed to condemn the Germans for the mass murder [of Polish Army officers] at Katyń [which in fact was committed by the Soviets]. Lastly, in September 1953 Primate Stefan Wyszyński was arrested. The independence of the Catholic Church in Poland was in jeopardy.

As decided by Cardinal Sapieha and later on sustained by Archbishop Baziak, Karol Wojtyła was absent from the front-line confrontation with the state. In September 1951 he began his two-year sabbatical leave to complete his post-doctoral dissertation. He had to give up being a curate at St Florian's and the only responsibilities that he was allowed to retain were his work with students in the parish. Archbishop Baziak supplemented that with pastoral work with healthcare personnel in Cracow. As a sub-tenant, Wojtyła moved to the apartment of his former professor, Father Ignacy Różycki, at 19 Kanonicza Street. And it was Father Różycki who suggested to his sometime doctoral student that he should concentrate upon the *oeuvre* of Max Scheler, a German philosopher and phenomenologist from the turn of the twentieth century. The sense of Wojtyła's research in the area is best summed up by

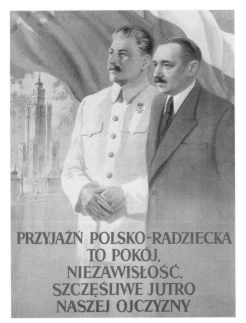

"Fathers of the Nations" look ahead into the glamorous future without God

Propaganda picture from the trial of priests from the Cracow Metropolitan Curia

Kanonicza Street; here Fr Wojtyła lived (first at no 19, then 21) until he was nominated Archbishop

the title of his post-doctoral thesis: *Assessment of Possibilities of Building Christian Ethics on the Assumptions of Max Scheler's System.*

Under the impact of his pastoral experience (and especially his work with young people who sought answers to burning moral issues), Father Wojtyła's scholarly interests shifted towards practical ethics. Phenomenology, whose eminent Cracow representative was Roman Ingarden, was discovered by Wojtyła as a sensitive instrument used for examining human experience. Nonetheless, he negatively assessed the possibility mentioned in the title of his dissertation since in Scheler's phenomenology the stress was on the subjective aspect of human awareness and experience: that could end up in negating the real and objective character of moral standards. And in the moral chaos of the contemporary world, aggravated by the pressures of the totalitarian system in communist countries, it was necessary to defend man's capability of differentiating between good and evil as real moral standards and not only subjective, emotional choices and evaluations.

This problem was expressed by Father Wojtyła not only in his post-doctoral thesis but also, in a simpler form, in retreats for students that he conducted in 1954 during Lent. He addressed his listeners at St Florian's in the following way: "What is truth? This question was posed once by Pilate, this question is posed by man, this question is posed by the system. Truth is agreement with reality, agreement of thoughts and attitude with the whole surrounding world. It requires man to submit to reality, and not the other way round: reality cannot be submitted to man. (…) The method of the Kingdom of God is the method of truth. Man should be ready to accept reality, all of it. And contemporary man lives by part of reality, by the applications of civilization, not by the idea of person." The core of the reflection as well as the kind of critique of the errors of modern philosophy of man remained unchanged in the teachings of Wojtyła even when he became the Archbishop of Cracow and the Pope. They found their fullest expression in two encyclicals: *Veritatis splendor* and *Fides et ratio.*

As the post-doctoral dissertation was prepared in a careful and innovative way, it received three positive academic assessments required in the procedure, and the most enthusiastic of them was that by Stefan Swieżawski, a renowned expert on modern philosophy who later became Wojtyła's friend and was his colleague at the Catholic University of Lublin (KUL). The Board of the Theological Faculty, Jagiellonian University, unanimously approved of the dissertation and the accompanying lecture in December 1953 and applied to the Ministry of Higher Education to grant Wojtyła a post-doctoral degree in ethics and moral theology. Wojtyła's post-doctoral dissertation was the last to be defended at the Theological Faculty, which had functioned for over 550 years. It was hit by the anti-Church repressions and liquidated at the beginning of 1954. Father Wojtyła, who in the fall of the previous year had begun his course in Catholic social doctrine, had to move his lectures to the Seminary. At that time he donated a major portion of his modest salary to the Congregation of the Sister Servants of the Most Sacred Heart of Jesus, from where it was taken by Father Andrzej Bardecki to be distributed among the journalists of *Tygodnik Powszechny*, who remained unemployed. In 1954–55 Karol Wojtyła expanded his teaching activities to seminaries in Silesia and Częstochowa. But he could embark upon the career of a university professor only at the Catholic University of Lublin.

In the early 1950s this private Catholic university, founded in 1918 and revived after the Second World War, was extremely limited in its operations by the communist authorities waging war against the Church. The faculties of law, social sciences and teaching suffered liquidation. Besides the faculty of theology, the faculty of philosophy still functioned, and Stefan Swieżawski's intention was to invite Wojtyła to work for the latter. From the fall of 1954 Wojtyła had a temporary contract to lecture on the history of doctrines of ethics and to conduct a seminar. He became a full-time employee of the university only in December 1956, nominally a deputy head in the Chair of Ethics, but practically its head (since the professor in charge was on leave to lecture at the Angelicum in Rome).

Just like several of his colleagues who could not offer seminars or lectures at the Jagiellonian University, Karol Wojtyła became a regular passenger on the trains between Cracow and Lublin. As the travel lasted all night long, he could meet and make friends with other

Professor Karol Wojtyła, "magnet" of Catholic University students

any notes, and sometimes interrupted the lecture to read excerpts from the discussed text (Plato, St Thomas, or Max Scheler) and contemplate its wisdom with students. He was always eager to use practical examples and to present concrete ethical problems by means of images. He frequently spoke about love and problems concerning the ethics of sex. He wanted to give his students individual treatment so as to meet him or her in person. As it was phrased by his colleague and eminent professor, co-founder of the Lublin school of philosophy Father Mieczysław Albert Krąpiec, "For him, philosophy was focused on a single being as an acme of the formation of reality. He accentuated the need to experience a person in face-to-face meetings and especially in this most intimate of meetings, the confession. The drama of the person, staged in the dialogue of the confession, was for Professor Wojtyła an experience of a moral being, which experience should be explained also from the philosophical point of view." The role of confessor and spiritual guide during so many retreats and trips, which he organized to join recreation with meditation, significantly contributed to the knowledge and expertise of Wojtyła as a professor of ethics.

Wojtyła offered a doctoral seminar for a group of his students to whom he could convey his particular "method" as well

Bishop Karol Wojtyła during one of his skiing trips

passengers, his colleagues. Father Franciszek Tokarz, a lecturer in Indian philosophy remembered that Wojtyła had always prayed much and intensively during the journey. "The difference between him and me," said Tokarz, "consists in that I, immediately after I wake up, have to smoke a cigarette, whereas he kneels down at the window and prays on and on." Another of Wojtyła's "railway friends," Father Stanisław Nagy, a lecturer in theology (nowadays the chairman of the Academic Council of the John Paul II Institute at the KUL), confirms this observation and adds that Wojtyła was immensely interested in the new, important achievements in those fields in which he did not specialize. During the travels to Lublin and after, Professor Nagy became Wojtyła's guide in the world of current theological debate as the latter, a professor of ethics, could not devote enough time to it.

Father Wojtyła prayed and listened. He was always able to listen attentively. He spoke a great deal only in the lecture hall and attracted more and more students due to the manner of speaking and to the subject of the lectures. He did not use

as his passion for research and education in ethics. The seminar comprised, among others, Sister Zofia Zdybicka, an Ursuline, now one of the outstanding researchers in the phenomenon of religion; experts on ethics, Stanisław Grygiel and Tadeusz Styczeń, the most loyal follower of Wojtyła and his successor in the KUL Chair; and the 1978, last doctoral student, Father Andrzej Szostek.

While doing ever more intensive research and teaching, Father Wojtyła did not forget his environment, his "little family" from Cracow, that is young people who met in the parish of St Florian. In spare time, they went cycling in the country or hiking in the mountains. Starting in August 1953, they took up one more form of "spiritual tourism," namely canoeing. A great enthusiast of this sport was the young engineer Jerzy Ciesielski from the Cracow Institute of Technology, and it was he who persuaded Wojtyła and the group of friends to arrange the first trip of this kind along the Brda River. Such trips were repeated year after year, until 1978, and of course joined recreation with meditation. In May 1955, Father Wojtyła took part in an international canoeing rally on the Dunajec River, but he punctured the kayak just before the finish in Szczawnica – the only thing that escaped thorough soaking was his breviary. Canoeing or hiking in the mountains with friends were not treated by him as a means of sports achievement. The group included from ten to thirty people. Every day they celebrated Mass on a kayak that was turned bottom up and served as the altar; the cross was made with tied oars. They prayed and sang together (not only religious hymns), talked by the fire, and discussed their reading: excerpts from the Bible or some other book they had taken to reflect upon (e.g. by C. S. Lewis, Chesterton, Cesbron, or parts of the "Uncle's" dissertation on the ethics of marriage that was to go to print). Moreover, they talked about the films they had just seen or talked individually to each other in kayaks. It was Wojtyła's unique parish.

Additionally, he had a few other "adoptive" parishes: at St Catherine's in the Cracow district of Kazimierz, where his Gregorian choir had moved, or at St Mary's, starting from 1953. He regularly offered Mass (on week-days at 6 am, on Sundays and holidays at 7 am) and, academic responsibilities allowing, confessed, usually in the second chapel, right to the mar-

ble crucifix by Veit Stoss. He spared no time on talks in the confessional, on wise spiritual teaching and giving comfort, so he attracted growing numbers of the faithful. The then parish priest at St Mary's and a perfect clergyman, Father Ferdynand Machay, remembers that every now and then young people burst into the sacristy asking for Father Wojtyła. "For God's sake!" he cried out eventually, "You

ask for Wojtyła again and again as if I wasn't here, your parish priest!" Father Wojtyła, with utmost dedication, spent much time on his pastoral work with the healthcare personnel of Cracow, in the Church of the Felician Sisters, organizing

The Pope among his KUL friends; from the left: Fr Stanisław Nagy, Holy Father, Fr Marian Jaworski, Fr Tadeusz Styczeń

Cardinal Wojtyła and the Rector of the KUL, Professor Mieczysław Albert Krąpiec

Stalls in St Mary's Church in Cracow; here Fr Wojtyła served as confessor

John Paul II visited "his" St Mary's Church already during his first trip to Poland

Protest of the workers of Poznań in June 1956

meetings for doctors and nurses. Moreover, he went on doctors' pilgrimages to Częstochowa.

Such a public form of demonstrating the ties of the intelligentsia with the Catholic faith became for a while more acceptable for the authorities after the political "thaw" of 1956. The communist party leadership changed, following a workers' revolt which had been brutally suppressed four months earlier in Poznań, so one could expect more lenient policies. A token of this liberalization (also in the relations between the Church and the state), which unfortunately proved only momentary, was the decision of the new leader of the Communist Party, Władysław Gomułka, from the end of 1956: Primate Stefan Wyszyński was not to be interned any longer. Also Archbishop Eugeniusz Baziak could again undertake the responsibilities of the Cracow Metropolitan, although his nomination had not been accepted by the state authorities yet. And the majority of the journalists with *Tygodnik Powszechny* could return to work.

Father Wojtyła did not take any active part in the political events of that period. His life was filled with academic and pastoral responsibilities, and he had plenty of both. But of course he was not indifferent to the political conditions of the life of the nation or to everyday problems of the faithful and of his friends. He could see that professional careers were often hindered or ruined in the case of young people who did not hesitate to cling to the Church in the worst years of Stalinism and participated in the purely religious ventures at St Florian's. One of the women parishioners was not allowed to complete her higher education only because the hall of residence of her choice was run by nuns. One of the men was not permitted to get his degree because of his participation in devotional practices, including the retreats offered by Father Wojtyła. This caused great pain to their guide. However, he did not suggest to them any means of political resistance, which anyway would be hopeless in the Stalinist years. Instead, he opened up a perspective of inner freedom and trust in Providence and God's grace.

He was very happy to see the practical results of this freedom right after the political thaw of 1956. He had an opportunity then to find out how important it was to publicly manifest one's religion, attachment to tradition and to the Church. Meetings of thousands of the faithful in Częstochowa and at mass pilgrimages (for everybody or representatives of particular professional or social groups) proved the power and the ability to form a community. This was particularly feared by the communists and was feasible only when their position was weakened. Father Wojtyła mentioned it directly when summing up the national pilgrimage of doctors to Częstochowa in October 1957 (he was one of the organizers and ministers). "It was our common act, and act that means something to us. And certainly it did not stem exclusively from devotion. It was not for their special piety that people of the same profession went together to Częstochowa. It seems like this is going to turn into a habit. (...) Thanks to our prayer together we realized that next to us, to the right and to the left, in front of us and behind us, there stands a person who thinks in the same way, who feels and wants the same." That was the really revolutionary program of the spiritual revival of the nation, initiated by Primate Stefan Wyszyński after his internment. In Father Wojtyła's words from the end of 1957 one can also perceive the simple sense of this program and at the same time the motto of the future Pope's pilgrimages to Poland, starting with the breakthrough pilgrimage of 1979.

Father Wojtyła was in a way forced to look at the problem of faith in the system whose aim was to secularize society and to look at the situation of the Church in Poland under the communist rule so that he could perceive it not only through the prism of individual lives of a bunch of students, friends and the faithful from the KUL, the parish of St Florian, the religious group of doctors or his "little family": On 4 July 1958 Pope Pius XII unexpectedly nominated him, a 38-year-old priest, an auxiliary bishop in the archdiocese of Cracow. It was one of the last appointments of the elderly Pope (who died in

Church in Święta Lipka, where Fr Wojtyła received the news of his nomination for bishop

the diocese. However, I did what I considered crucial. I made efforts to assure that the priest whom I consider the most valuable in the entire diocese should become a bishop."

The most interested party, that is Father Wojtyła, held a retreat in the Benedictine Abbey in Tyniec near Cracow and, as usual at this time of the year, went canoeing on the Łyna River in the Masurian Lake District. He wanted to take a "philosophical vacation" organized by the KUL in August 1958 in Święta Lipka. It was a meeting place for young Catholics from the largest Polish towns and for their professors, with whom they could rest, pray and talk. However, on 5 August, at Lake Pluszcze, Father Wojtyła received an

Cardinal Stefan Wyszyński among the faithful in Warsaw

Fr Karol Wojtyła at the morning toilet during one of his kayak trips

Karol Wojtyła, Bishop of Cracow

October 1958) and it made Karol Wojtyła the youngest member of the Polish Episcopate. He became a helper to the ailing Archbishop Baziak in supervising the Cracow Church and he became one of the shepherds of all Poland. That was a new perspective indeed.

Karol Wojtyła owed his nomination to Archbishop Baziak. On the day when Wojtyła was nominated, Father Andrzej Bardecki, who was the Church assistant of *Tygodnik Powszechny* and regularly visited the Archbishop to share with him the political news from the editorial office, heard the following remark: "I'm an old bishop now. My situation is difficult because at that age I cannot do much for

urgent letter from the office of the Polish Primate: he was expected to arrive in Warsaw to meet Cardinal Wyszyński and to answer the formally posed question whether he accepted his nomination as bishop. Wojtyła accepted the Pope's decision without a moment's hesitation. Then he went to the nearby convent of the Ursulines and prayed in their chapel, lying prostrate on the floor for hours that were left to him before his train departed to Cracow. After a conversation with Archbishop Baziak and a preliminary discussion concerning his new responsibilities, he went back by train to the Lake District, to canoe with his friends and students as a newly nominated bishop.

On 1 September he participated for the first time in the plenary conference of the Polish Episcopate in Częstochowa and was introduced to the other bishops by Primate Wyszyński. He had another retreat at Tyniec on 28 September, the Day of St Wenceslas (the patron saint of Wawel Cathedral), and was consecrated bishop by Archbishop Baziak, the Bishop of Opole Franciszek Jop and the Bishop of Wrocław Bolesław Kominek. Archbishop Baziak, who led the ceremony, handed to him the pastoral staff, the mitre and put the episcopal ring on his finger with the words: "Receive the ring, the symbol of fidelity, in order that, adorned with unspotted faith, you may keep inviolably the Spouse of God, namely, His Holy Church." The new bishop adopted as his motto the words of St Louis de Montfort (whose treaty he had diligently studied many years before): *Totus Tuus* ("All Yours"), which express his absolute trust in St Mary. On the next day he left with his "little family" for Częstochowa. He begged Our Lady to protect him on the new, even steeper path of his ministry.

Chapter IV
Servant of the Cracow Church (1958-1964)

The role of an auxiliary bishop is to assist his superior, the ordinary, in the governance of a diocese. Archbishop Baziak was noticeably tired after all he had had to go through for over more than a decade. The Cracow Church needed very much the young and energetic Bishop Wojtyła. He had to harness himself to the whirl of everyday pastoral activities combined with the co-managing of the archdiocese. The circle of those to whom Bishop Wojtyła was to serve widened tremendously.

Fr Karol Wojtyła as Archbishop Metropolitan of Cracow

A children's performance organized in the Archbishops' Palace by its host

Now it was already hundreds of thousands of the faithful, nearly 2,000 priests, dozens of religious orders, literally millions of problems.

The "headquarters" was the Archbishops' Palace at 3 Franciszkańska Street, the seat of the Metropolitan Curia of Cracow. It was here that Bishop Wojtyła attended daily to the administration of the archdiocese, received various visitors, and resolved controversies, such as, for example, the one provoked by his friend from the secret seminary, Father Mieczysław Maliński, whose short and modern sermons, addressed to the pupils of V Secondary School, shocked another priest...Other problem areas came to light during his regular parish visits not only in Cracow but also, or first of all, in smaller towns and villages. Helping to obtain the local authorities' permission for building new churches or for renovating the old

Monument to John Paul II at the Archbishops'
Palace of Cracow

"Deans' House" at 21 Kanonicza Street, where Fr. Wojtyła moved
as Bishop and Vicar of the Chapter

ones, administering the Sacrament of Confirmation, ordaining priests, inspiring and initiating new forms of retreats (e.g. the retreats for the deaf-mute), were but some of the demands of the tightly packed schedule of the bishop suffragan.

On the surface his life did not change much. He moved from his priest's flat at 19 Kanonicza Street to the next-door number 21, the "Deans' House." He did not give up his annual kayaking trips. He tried to combine his new responsibilities with his academic duties. However, in 1962 he had to definitely resign from his teaching post at the Theological Faculty in Cracow. He still would not relinquish his work at the Catholic University of Lublin (KUL) although his trips to Lublin became less and less frequent. From 1960 he worked there only part-time, lecturing on some aspects of ethics and conducting his seminar. But it became somewhat of a tradition for his undergraduate and doctoral students to come to his consultations or seminars to Cracow to Kanonicza Street. Most of his teaching duties were taken over by his colleagues from Lublin, primarily by Father Styczeń, who received his Ph.D. in January 1963. More often than in the seminar rooms of the KUL, the bishop-professor conferred with

his reader on the concerns of the Chair of Ethics during the mountain trips or skiing expeditions when he took brief holidays from his pastoral duties in the diocese.

Despite numerous claims upon his time, the Cracow bishop was determined to continue with his individual studies. In the late 50s he finished writing his major work on the ethics of marital love which he had been working on for years. Published as *Love and Responsibility* in 1960 by the Learned Society of the KUL, the book caused a sort of sensation. The author, a serious bishop, seen on so many occasions with the solemn symbols of his office: the mitre and the crosier, goes into an in-depth analysis of sexual drive and approves of sexual enjoyment in marriage, affirming the dignity of a person. That was unheard of. The future pope was convinced that if the "priests and bishops cannot honestly and humbly discuss with their flock (also) the problem of sexual drive and its fulfillment they fail to observe their pastoral duties." In fact, the book was the continuation of the talk, which Bishop Wojtyła had been having for years with his young friends from St. Florian's "circle," young couples whose marriages he had blessed. None of those couples got divorced. He continued to

see them. In his bishop's flat in Kanonicza Street he organized the carnival balls for their children, asked them to sing Christmas carols together; he cared deeply about the members of his "family" and helped to solve their problems. It was in this circle that he found encouragement for his faith in a responsible marital love, possible without deceit and contraceptives.

To translate this faith into life, Bishop Wojtyła founded in 1960 the Institute of the Family. Its aim was to train the lay counselors, both men and women, to give the families and engaged couples help and advice, based on life experience and the principles of the Catholic ethics alike. He also wished to establish a framework for testing new forms of family pastoral care, such as group prayers of married couples or family retreats, and consequently to create the platform not just for lectures and exams, but for the exchange of ideas and experiences. The bishop himself provided artistic input for this exchange. He continued to write and publish his poems and dramas under the pseudonym Andrzej Jawień. Among them stands out his play *The Jeweler's Shop*, "a meditation" on the Sacrament of Marriage "which from time to time is transformed

Bishop Karol Wojtyła administers the sacrament of marriage (already with Fr. Stanisław Dziwisz at his side – from 1966 on)

After the mass at Wawel Cathedral the Bishop of Cracow greets the faithful

phy of Brother Albert, an insurrectionist and an artist-painter who finally became a monk and a friend of the poor, juxtaposes three concepts of man's activity in the world. The first one is symbolized by Max, an artist and a friend of the title protagonist. He represents an individualistic attitude – what counts in life is personal success, achieved in free competition that should be permitted both in art and in life. His approach is contradicted by a mysterious Stranger, modeled – as admitted many years later by the author himself – on Lenin. He acts as a self-appointed spokesman for all the losers in this world. He wants to forge poverty into class hatred, into a tool of violent revolution which will give him power. Although he appeals to the poor, harmed and humbled, he actually despises them. The main protagonist, Adam, or Brother Albert, appeals to the same people. He understands their sense of wrong and anger and does not want to betray them but offers help. Not only by giving bread to the poor and finding homes for the homeless, but also by trying to restore their dignity. Not everything can be obtained by "force of anger" – such is an answer of Brother Albert to the trap of blind belief in social revolution. Neither egoistical liberalism personified by Max, nor materialistic socialism represented by the Stranger – is Karol Wojtyła's answer to the ideological challenges of his century.

The text with such a message could not be printed under the Communist censorship – at least not in the period of the

A room at St Albert's shelter for the homeless in Cracow

into drama." First published in 1959 in a December issue of the Cracow monthly *Znak,* it describes the feelings of the three couples: Monica and Christopher and their parents. Although the love bond between Christopher's parents, Teresa and Andrew, remained strong and deep, the war deprived Christopher of his father. This is his drama. Monica grieves over the crisis of her parents' marriage: Anna and Stephen. Its most poignant symbol is the scene when Anna wants to sell her wedding ring. The Jeweler, a mysterious character, weighs a wedding ring only to say

that: "one ring weighs nothing – you have to put two on a scale." (Many years later this drama was made into a feature film starring – in one of his last roles – Burt Lancaster as the Jeweler.) In the end, the mystery the young protagonists of this meditation by "Andrzej Jawień" are confronted with turns out to be the mystery of indissolubility of the marriage tie and of giving oneself to another person.

Other problems Bishop Wojtyła (and later also Pope John Paul II) had to face in his pastoral work were described in his drama *Our God's Brother,* written slightly earlier than *The Jeweler's Shop* but published only after his election to the papacy. This work, based on the biogra-

"special vigil" kept on the Catholic Church in Poland after a brief phase of "Thaw" of 1956. The new First Secretary of the Polish United Workers' Party (PZPR), Władysław Gomułka, was strongly committed to his party's monopoly in regard not only to political power but also in regard to the education of the society understood in its broadest sense. Barely had religion made a come back to schools when it started to be forcefully removed from public education. In December 1960 religion classes were conducted in only 8, 000 out of 28 000 schools (mostly village schools). In 1961 religion was excluded from schools altogether while at the same time the authorities sought to control religious instructions given in the parish churches. The police and Security Service (SB) gave "a word of warning" to several thousand parish priests, trying to bully them into accepting such control. Simultaneously, along with refusing building permits for new sacral objects, the Communist regime started a campaign of depriving the Church institutions of their property. In the new, large districts, built to accommodate the villagers migrating to towns, the lack of churches was fast becoming a burning issue.

The main battleground for the confrontation between the Church and the Communist state and a symbol of the Catholic resistance was Nowa Huta. This industrial suburb of Cracow, designed to create the "ideological" counterbalance to the "reactionary," "clerical" city, obtained the permission to build its first church in January 1957, in a brief spell of political liberalization. It was to be built in Nowa Huta-Bieńczyce, on the corner of Mayakovsky and Marx streets. However, already in September 1959 the building permit was withdrawn. All the same, by now, there was a cross erected at the lot designated for the construction of the church. Under this cross Bishop Wojtyła decided to celebrate the nearest Midnight Mass. On Christmas Eve 1959 he was with his flock – the workers from Nowa Huta and their families. He joined them in their prayers for the first church in the new district, already inhabited by over 100, 000 residents.

In April 1960, preparing for Gomułka's visit in Nowa Huta, the district authorities decided to have the cross removed. On 27 April the police set about the task of destroying the cross. Thousands of angry inhabitants of Nowa Huta rioted in the streets. A crowd of many thousands

stood up for the defense of the cross. In the evening, when power was cut in the whole district, the demonstrators seized the center and demolished the seat of the local authorities. The riots were suppressed only by the massive counterattack of the police in which over 1000 policemen took part and the fire-arm was used. The number of victims on the demonstrators' side has remained unknown. According to some unconfirmed sources, 17 people died in hospitals as a result of the wounds received during the riots. The MO (Police) and the SB detained almost 500 protesters. On 28 April Bishop Wojtyła was summoned before the Presidium of the National Council of Cracow. He denied the Church's responsibility for provoking the riots, but agreed to deliver a conciliatory address provided the cross remained. As he was not given such a promise, he did not issue the address. Instead, in May, he sent a memorial to the authorities calmly stating that: "[...] you cannot leave these peo-

Bishop of Cracow administers baptism rites at the parish in Nowa Huta

Mass at the church construction site in Nowa Huta-Bieńczyce (corner of Marx and Mayakovsky streets)

Bishop of Cracow arrives in a parish with a pastoral visit in his "official" ZIS lorry

Benedictines Abbey at Tyniec – the place which Fr. Wojtyła used to visit to pray and collect his thoughts before assuming new posts

ple, who were promised to have a church built […], with the feeling that both this promise and their effort have been meaningless." In 1960, for the second time, he celebrated the Midnight Mass in Nowa Huta. He continued to come to the construction site every year. It was not until 1967 that he managed to obtain another building permit. Ten years later he consecrated a new church – the amazing Ark of the Lord. Then he expressed his views freely, emphasizing the sense of remaining by the cross in Nowa Huta. "This city"

– he spoke on 15 May 1977 – "is not the city of people who belong to nobody. Of people who can be ordered about, who can be manipulated according to the laws or rules of production and consumption. This city is the city of God's sons." In 1983 he returned to Nowa Huta – this time as Pope – to speak up again for the dignity of the persecuted workers and to express his solidarity with them.

The way the Cracow suffragan bishop acted about the Nowa Huta cross, whose defense gave rise to the largest wave of protests between the Poznań Riots of June 1956 and the Baltic Riots of December 1970, was the first dramatic confirmation of the solidarity which binds

the shepherd with the flock entrusted to him – his archdiocese. In June 1962 Bishop Wojtyła assumed even more responsibility for the Cracow Church. Following the death of Archbishop Eugeniusz Baziak, the Cracow Chapter elected Bishop Wojtyła vicar general. As the vicar general he was responsible for running the archdiocese until the pope nominated new Archbishop of Cracow (who had to be approved by the Polish Communist government).

His duties were now even more numerous than during the first four years of his bishopric. 42-year-old priest-professor did not only, as it had been so far, helped in managing the diocese, but now he also represented one of the largest dioceses in Poland, second in prestige only to Gniezno-Warszawa diocese. He represented it before the faithful, before the Polish Episcopate, and also before the civil authorities.

From the very first moment he joined the episcopate he became an active member of the Pastoral Committee. From January 1962 he was in charge of the country ministry for the creative intelligentsia. At the beginning, Primate Wyszyński saw him primarily as an intellectual man, willing and able to dialogue with the academic circles and to communicate with them in a language that was appropriate for modern culture and science. He hoped to make the best use of the young Cracow bishop's talents for the benefit of the whole Church in Poland. For himself he reserved – in front of all the bishops – the leadership in the great program of strengthening the Polish Catholicism.

This program, devised by the Primate at the time of his detention by the communists, was announced at Jasna Góra, even before he was released, on 26 August 1956. It took the form of the renewal of Jasna Góra Vows of the Nation, which had been made three centuries before, at the time of the Swedish and Moscow "Deluge," by King Jan Kazimierz. Relying on the Polish piety whose very essence was particular attachment to the cult of the Mother of Christ, the Primate wanted to entrust the whole nation to the Virgin Mary, begging Her help in freeing the Poles from the enforced government and ideology. So far it had been only individuals who made such commitment, e.g. St Ludwig Grignon de Montfort (followed closely by Father Wojtyła) or St Maximilian Kolbe. The idea of entrusting the whole nation to the Mother of God had obviously its theo-

Paulites Monastery: Home of Our Lady of Częstochowa

Archbishop of Cracow in his suite at Jasna Góra Shrine

logical backup. It referred also clearly to the historical role of Poland as the bulwark of Christendom and Europe and linked up with a special devotion to the Virgin Mary, reflected in the historical annals and in the artistic visions (from the 17th c.-artists through the great Romantic writers of the 19th c. to the poets of the Underground Poland of the World War II). Such an interpretation of the role of Poland and of its historical foundation – anchored in the Polish messianic tradition in the works of Słowacki, Mickiewicz, Norwid and Wyspiański – must have been close to Wojtyła's heart.

The Primate translated his theology of the nation into the program of preparation for the 1000th anniversary of Christianity in Poland. The program of events of the "Great Novena" was mapped out for nine years preceding the Millennium Year: 1966. The spiritual struggle for the souls of the young, threatened by atheism (the leitmotiv of the 6th year of Novena), or the struggle for social justice (the leitmotiv of the 7th year of Novena) – were but some among the targets of the program which the Cracow vicar general was to actively implement. In his address to the priests, the Primate explained the sense

of his program and the high hopes he had for it: "Nine-year long preparation for the Millennium Year should transform Poland spiritually. The fate of Communism will be determined in Poland. As Poland becomes more Christian, she will become a great moral power and Communism will fall on its own. The fate of Communism will be determined not in Russia but in Poland. Poland will show to the whole world how to overthrow Communism and the whole world will be grateful to her!"

In answer to this great religious mobilization of the nation the government intensified the anti-Church campaign. The Cracow bishop-vicar faced it in his archdiocese. He coped in his own unique way throwing the authorities off their balance. When in September 1962 he learnt about the intended annexation of one of the seminary buildings in Cracow, he interrupted his visitation of the parish in the mountains and went straight to the Provincial Committee of the PZPR, where he asked for a private talk with the party's secretary – the real administrator of the Cracow region. Surprised by the unprecedented request of the bishop, the first secretary of the Provincial Party Commit-

tee Lucjan Motyka, agreed to a compromise solution: the Seminary bequeathed its third floor to the authorities but retained the remaining section of the building for its own use. A year later the Cracow vicar intervened with him again – this time to prevent the annexation of the Silesian Seminary building, located also in Cracow. He argued with Motyka on the phone saying that to expel the Silesian Seminary is a shame not on the Church but on Cracow and Poland in whose vital interest was to emphasize her link with Silesia. He also gave his support to the priests and clerics who were ready to organize the protest in defense of this cause.

The Communist authorities held back from their intended action again. After all, the young Bishop of Cracow seemed to adopt a less "confrontational" attitude in his public addresses than the Primate and a few other older members of the episcopate in theirs: in the 1962 report, prepared by the Ministry for Church Affairs, the Primate was accused of 69 "hostile" speeches, the second bishop in this ranking – of 17; Bishop Wojtyła was not included on the list of top ten "enemies." However, according to the recently disclosed reports of the Ministry for Church Affairs, written at the beginning of the 60s, the co-coordinators of the campaign against the Church were irritated by the involvement of the Cracow vicar general in the work among the young and the intelligentsia. These particular circles were to be the bastion of "progress," represented by the PZPR, as opposed to "backwardness," symbolized by the Church. Thus, the fact that Bishop Wojtyła was personally involved in organizing the conferences for students (e.g. in the academic church of St Ann) was definitely frowned on and these meetings with the students were labeled as "illegal gatherings."

The main adversary for the party and its First Secretary, Gomułka, was obviously the Primate, Cardinal Wyszyński. To weaken his position, the communists tried to find the cracks in the monolith of the Polish Church. They hoped to set against the Primate part of the Catholic intelligentsia, including the Cracow circle, which grouped around the revived weekly *Tygodnik Powszechny,* and the monthly *Znak,* and which looked with some suspicion on the program of the national religious revival based on folk piety. Bishop Wojtyła was appointed by the episcopate to monitor *Tygodnik.* Generally he was able to prevent misunderstandings between this circle and the Primate. Although he himself published in *Tygodnik,* in some of his opinions he differed markedly from the opinions of the editorial staff. It became very obvious on the occasion of the 100th anniversary of the January Insurrection of 1863. The editors of the *Tygodnik* acknowledged the anniversary with an aggressive attack of Stanisław Stomma against the insurrectionary tradition and the romantic vision of Polishness. This angle of attack corresponded with the Communist propaganda of the time, which praised "realism" and the policy of conciliation towards the Russian "older brother." Bishop Wojtyła offered a different perception of the Polish history: the one which he had gained at Wadowice school and from his experiences of the World War II, and which was in concord with the program of historical and national education propounded by the Primate.

Particularly strongly did Cracow vicar appeal for the respect of the ethos of Romantic heroism during the Feast of St Stanislaus on 12 May 1963. On this day he blessed the plaque commemorating the insurrectionists of 1863: Father Rafał Kalinowski and Brother Albert Chmielowski. He said then that this in-surrection was noble – tragic but necessary. "All those who at that time, in 1863, leaped up to fight against horrible violence, against unprecedented violence, knew the threat. And therefore their deeds have an inherent greatness: they are marked with the deepest nobility; they point to some great power of human spirit and, at the same time, they are able to develop and nurture this power in others. [...] Let us ask God to raise to the altars the conspirators and the members of the underground movement – as our history compelled us to bore our way to freedom through the underground stratum. Let us pray that all the conspirators and the heroes of the underground may find in them their saint patrons, who will become the spokesmen for the cause of freedom of man and of the nations." The prayer said by Bishop Karol Wojtyła was answered, after many years, by Pope John Paul II who canonized Brother Albert and Father Rafał. The new conspirators, the heroes of the new underground, who grew out of the seed of his papal word sown in Poland, found their saint patrons.

If only had the Communist authorities predicted all this in 1963…Well, they did not predict it. They continued to perceive Bishop Wojtyła as a "lesser evil" than the hated Primate Wyszyński. They did not lose hope that the young bishop-intellectual could somehow be won over against the "peasantish," "conservative" Primate. In this illusory hope there was a

Bishop of Cracow also ran the ministry for the deaf-mute: his sermon is being translated into the sign language

Preparations in the sacristy for the concelebrated High mass (1966)

key to the truly providential history of electing Karol Wojtyła Archbishop of Cracow.

After the death of Archbishop Eugeniusz Baziak, an ordinary of Archdiocese of Cracow, who was recognized by the Church but not recognized by the regime, for the first time an opportunity presented itself of reaching a consensus over finding a common candidate for the successor of Prince Sapieha at the Wawel Cathedral. In 1956 Cardinal Wyszyński agreed to the following procedure of nominating the bishops-ordinaries: the Primate would disclose the names of his candidates to the government and the government had the right of veto. If – within three months – there was no veto, the primate notified the Holy Father of the agreed candidate and, finally, Rome declared his nomination. As a rule, the auxiliary bishop did not become an ordinary of a diocese in which he had worked. Even for this very reason the Cracow vicar, Bishop Wojtyła could not expect the nomination. And although he was Cardinal Wyszyński's loyal co-worker in a difficult time of the government's anti-Church campaign in the beginning of the 60s, the cardinal showed more trust in the other – also excellent – candidates. The newly opened files of the Ministry for Church Affairs reveal that "higher" on the list, handed to the government by the Primate, were Jerzy Stroba (the then auxiliary bishop in Gorzów and a future Archbishop of Poznań) and Father Tadeusz Fedorowicz (the truly heroic priest of the Catholics in Soviet Ukraine, and a later chaplain of the Institution for the Blind in Laski). The very fact, however, that they were the front-runners of the Primate discredited them in the eyes of Gomułka and Zenon Kliszka, responsible, on Gomułka's' behalf, for the Church. On consulting the "priests-patriots", who collaborated with the regime, the Cracow Department for Church Affairs sent a confidential letter to the headquarters in Warsaw with the conclusions, which are worth quoting:

"After getting acquainted with the characteristics of Bishop Stroba and of Father Tadeusz Fedorowicz, the Cracow Department recommends Bishop Karol Wojtyła as the most suitable of the three candidates for the post of Cracow Archdiocese ordinary. On the negative side, we consider Bishop Wojtyła's attitude to be less reactionary than the attitudes of Bishop Stroba and of Father Fedorowicz." Having said that, the last sentence of the candidate's characteristics, enclosed with the letter, left no doubt that their recommendation for Karol Wojtyła was a vote for a "lesser evil" candidate: "Summarizing his views and activities, Bishop Wojtyła is critical of both the authorities and of the political system of the Polish People's Republic and his way of thinking is definitely that of a Roman priest." The author of the report added with some regret that it would be difficult for the police to collect any discrediting materials on the accepted candidate: "To be taken into consideration! Among the local priests Bishop Wojtyła is judged to be a man of extremely soft heart, who never has anything of his own and is completely indifferent to the material things, giving everything to the poor."

And so, just to spite Cardinal Wyszyński, the Communist regime set Karol Wojtyła on the path to the Archbishopric of Cracow. And this, in turn, carried a potential for Wojtyła's participation in the conclave as within the last one hundred years the shepherds of this archbishopric usually received cardinal hats. By becoming Metropolitan Archbishop of Cracow, Karol Wojtyła was offered, by God's Providence, the opportunity to become "a Roman priest," but in a completely different sense than that used by the Communist regime.

The government did not veto his candidature and on 30 December 1963 Pope Paul VI signed the nomination of Father

St Stanislaus, Bishop and Martyr (painting from Cracow's Franciscans Church, 1490)

Box containing the head of St Stanislaus – reliquary from the early 16th century displayed at the most important religious celebrations in Cracow

"Ark of the Lord": parish church at Nowa Huta-Bieńczyce, consecrated finally in 1977

Inauguration ceremony of Archbishop Wojtyła on 8 March 1964: new host of Wawel Cathedral welcomed by the Catholic Cracovians when crossing its threshold

Karol Wojtyła to the position of Metropolitan Archbishop of Cracow. Five days earlier, the bishop-nominee celebrated, as it had become his custom, the Midnight Mass in the "homeless" parish in Nowa Huta. On the day of the official announcement of his nomination, 18 January 1964, he was in Zakopane, presenting the Episcopal Commission for Pastoral Care with his paper on the program of spiritual fight with atheistic ideologies i.e. Communist system. The task which he traced out for himself and for the Church in Poland was one: rechristening.

The last day before the ceremony of inauguration to the Archbishopric of Cracow, the nominee spent on personal retreats in Tyniec – just as he had done before his ordination as bishop. On 8 March 1964 Karol Wojtyła entered the Wawel Cathedral as a successor of St Stanislaus, the 76th bishop of Cracow, and, formally, only the second archbishop after Cardinal Stefan Sapieha (Archbishopric of Cracow was founded in 1925). Dressed in his ermine cape – put on only during the most important church nominations – he received the keys to the cathedral. He went into the cathedral and kneeled to pray, first before the confession of St Stanislaus, then before the crucifix of Queen Jadwiga – the same before which he had served during the morning Mass on 1 September 1939 – and, finally, in the chapel of the Most Blessed Sacrament. After the papal announcement of his appointment, the auxiliary bishops, priests and clerics paid their tributes, and the new archbishop changed in the sacristy to celebrate the first Mass in his new role. He put on a gold chasuble – the gift of Anna the Jagiellon, the sister of the last Jagiellon on the Cracow throne, the 17th-c. miter of Bishop Andrzej Lipski, the 12th-c. ring of Bishop Maurus, and, finally, the rational embroidered with pearls by Queen Jadwiga – the symbol of the dignity of the office allowed by the popes to the ordinaries of only four dioceses in the world. His sermon fully corresponded with the symbolic splendor of his dress. He started with the words: "Man cannot enter this cathedral without the feeling of trepidation and apprehension since it is permeated, as hardly any other cathedral in the world, with an aura of incredible greatness, through which all our history and all our past speak to us. [...] And therefore man who enters this cathedral, even as an unsuspecting pilgrim, must stop in front of this greatness. And so much more is this true of man, who enters this cathedral to add some new elements to all this greatness through which the past speaks, to all the existing reality..."

Archbishop of Cracow Karol Wojtyła wanted to build on the foundation of the great past of the Polish nation and Polish faith, alive at every step in the Wawel Cathedral. And he added new elements to it, maybe even more splendid than the ones he was wearing on the day of his magnificent ingress.

Nave of Wawel Cathedral: the confession (tomb) of St Stanislaus in the center

John Paul II at Wawel Cathedral in 1999 (behind him the confession of St Stanislaus and diadem cross of Bolesław the Chaste and St Kinga)

CHAPTER V
Second Vatican Council and the world

The Cracow bishop served not only his archdiocese. John XXIII reminded bishops that they were called by their ministry to serve also the universal Church. Elected on 28 October 1958, the new pope initiated the General Council in the third month of his pontificate. In the whole history of the Church there had been but twenty Councils – called with a view to fighting heresy, defining the dogmas of faith and providing their interpretation. A new Council, the first and the only one in the 20th c. was intended to center on pastoral concerns. This gathering of the bishops from all over the world was to start spiritual renewal inside the Church, bring it up to date with the challenges of contemporary civilization, and, finally, pave the way for restoring unity among Christians. Acting in the world, which changed so quickly and dramatically, the Church had to look for a new language of dialogue with man of this world. John XXIII wanted to draw on his brothers in bishophood to support him in the fight for the soul of contemporary man.

The invitation to participate in the Council as its full-fledged members (the "Council's Fathers") was extended to the cardinals, patriarchs, archbishops, bishops-ordinaries as well as abbots and superiors general of men's orders. Advisory opinions were to be given by the theologians and experts at canon law. In addition, the representatives of non-Catholic Christian religions were invited to the Council as official observers. It was a tremendous undertaking, the most ambitious in the twenty centuries of the Church's history. Karol Wojtyła took an extremely active part in it.

His involvement started in October 1959 with an extensive answer he provided to the inquiry of the Preparatory Commission appointed by the pope. The main aim of the Commission was to gather the opinions of all the bishops on the proposed topics to be covered during the Council. The Cracow bishop suggested that the discussion should center on man and should lead to formulating a new, modern definition of Christian humanism. In the century of despair, caused by mass killings and empty promises of various ideologies, the Church should learn how to most effectively bring hope to all who despair. The Cracow bishop, among others, believed that to reach more people with the Good News, the gospel message should be preached in national languages (till then Latin had been the language of liturgy) but he also wished to imbue culture (also mass culture) with the Christian spirit.

By the decree of Providence, the future pope was able to present his opinions and share his experiences not only indi-

Cardinals and bishops gathered in front of St Peter's Basilica

Bishop Karol Wojtyła (bottom row, first from the right) during the first session of Second Vatican Council – still far from the altar...

rectly, in writing, but also verbally, by attending all four sessions of the Council. The first session of the Second Vatican Council was called for October 1962. Had Karol Wojtyła been only an auxiliary bishop (not an ordinary), he could not have been invited to participate in the Council. However, just in mid 1962, as mentioned before, following the death of Archbishop Baziak, he was elected vicar general of the diocese and became its canon and actual administrator, which opened the door for him to be invited to the Council.

On 11 October 1962, together with other 15 bishops from Poland, under the lead of Primate Stefan Wyszyński, he entered huge St. Peter's Basilica in Rome. The most famous Christian church was temporarily adapted to the needs of the Council. In the middle of the enormous nave, on either side of the main altar were placed rows of seats, as in an amphitheater, rising almost like gigantic stairs row upon row towards the basilica roof. Two thousand "Council Fathers" were seated in them. Seats were assigned according to the hierarchy of the Council participants. Thus, during the first session, the Cracow vicar general's seat was next to

the entrance of St Peter's Basilica. During the third and fourth session, in 1964 and 1965, after he had been appointed Archbishop of Cracow, he was moved much closer to the altar.

Participation in the Second Vatican Council affected him deeply. He gave vent to his emotions first in poetry. In 1963, he published in the *Znak* monthly (under his pseudonym Andrzej Jawień), an extensive poem *The Church: the Shepherds and the Spring,* referring explicitly to his experience of the first Council session. He conveyed in it his fascination with the opportunity of meeting Christians from all over the world, and with the spiritual unity of their convictions, though expressed in the diversity of cultural forms (a poem *A Black Man*). He tried to render the atmosphere of the disputes held under St Peter's Basilica roof. He stressed that the Council participants did not contend for power but were motivated by a deep desire to best serve the Church. He beautifully captured the essence of the spiritual battle of the "Council Fathers" in his poem *Synodus:*

*We will remain poor and naked and
yet transparent like glass,
Which does not only reflect the light
but cuts:
And let the wound of such a dissected
world heal up under the
lashes of conscience,
With the enormous church
as a background.*

The meetings began with the Mass and went on until 1 p.m. The rest of the time was spent on preparations for the next day. Each participant could deliver a speech, the so-called intervention, presenting his conclusions and suggestions. The meetings, led by four cardinal moderators, were devoted to the discussion and voting on the drafts of the Council documents – new „decrees" of the Catholic Church. The language of the debates was Latin. And that's where the Cracow bishop could be thankful for his fluency in Latin, which he had gained in his Wadowice gymnasium. It was easier for him than for many other "Council Fathers" to find the arguments supporting his addresses, to formulate his thoughts clearly and to follow the progress of debates.

His knowledge of Latin but also of all the major Western languages (he was most proficient in Italian and French, as well as a fluent speaker of German, English and Spanish), helped him tremendously to make friends with the Council members from all over the world. The venue of these informal contacts, meetings and longer talks was naturally not the Council aula but its lobbies, with two coffee bars opened during the sessions in St Peter's Basilica itself, along with various cloisters, seminars and hotels serving lunches and dinners to the participants. An invaluable helper of the Cracow bishop, guiding him through the corridors of the Roman Curia, as well as introducing him to many of the Council guests, was Prelate Andrzej Maria Deskur, his friend from the seminary, with whom he had worked closely in the Fellowship of the Students of the Jagiellonian University in 1945-1946. Employed in the Vatican offices for many years, and in particular in the Secretariat of State, which coordinated the foreign policy of the Holy See, Prelate Deskur indefatigably organized the meetings of his friend with the more important and distinguished personages of the universal Church. He himself had no doubt that the Cracow bishop should be included in this elitist circle as quickly as possible. He was joined in his opinion by another Polish resident of the city on the Tiber – Prelate Władysław Rubin, who in 1962 was Rector of the Polish College on Piazza Remuria on Aventine Hill, where Bishop Wojtyla stayed during most of his visits to Rome. Prelate Rubin, who – like Prelate Deskur – was later elevated to Bishop and Cardinal, worked hard and competently to break a trail for the future pope through the Vatican thicket.

But first of all it was the young "Council Father" who was able to break a trail with his personal talents – as best attested to by his speeches ("interventions") delivered during the subsequent sessions of the Council. Already at the first session (October-December 1962) he spoke on several occasions addressing e.g. the issue of the responsibility of both the priests and the laity for the Church. Also, together with other Polish bishops, he proposed to publish a special Council document on the Virgin Mary. During the second session, a year later, the Cracow bishop participated several times in a great debate on the Church, emphasizing again that all its members, not just priests and monks, are called to holiness. He also spoke on this topic in a Vatican Radio broadcast: "Catholics living in the world must, on all accounts, regain the awareness of their share in Christ's priesthood – that is, they must give the deepest consid-

eration to the meaning of their baptism and confirmation." Owing to the invitation to speak on the Vatican Radio, he was able to draw attention of the listeners from all over the world to the approaching 600th anniversary of the foundation of his beloved Jagiellonian University.

His speeches during the next sessions carried even more weight since he delivered them in his new capacity as Metropolitan Archbishop of Cracow. His friend, Father Mieczysław Maliński, who viewed the third session (September-November 1964) from behind the scene, has this to say: "I remember a sensation he created

in the Aula when in the beginning of October he spoke on the apostolate of the laity. He started his speech with the words: *Venerabiles patres, fratres et sorores* (the venerable fathers, brothers and sisters). This was the first time that women were mentioned at the Council. By the way, on account of the topics discussed, they happened to be present in the Aula." During this session, the Cracow archbishop also

John XXIII receives the delegation of the Polish Episcopate for the first session of the Council (Cardinal Wyszyński standing next to the Pope, Bishop Wojtyła at the back)

Archbishop of Cracow at the tomb of John XXIII in a vault of St Peter's Basilica

emphasized the importance of the young in the mission of the Church as well as the necessity of engaging people of culture, writers and artists in the task of a new evangelization. He contributed greatly to the Council documents on ecumenism and on the Church in the modern world.

On the topic of the latter, extremely important, document known from its first words as *Gaudium et Spes* (Joy and hope…), Archbishop Karol Wojtyła made an emphatic speech at the session of 21 October 1964. Acting as chief spokesman for the Polish Episcopate, he stated that the dialogue between the Church and the world had to allow for the differences of circumstances among the faithful in various countries. There were countries where the gospel could be freely preached, but there were also others where religion was brutally suppressed. Therefore, the Church could not address its faithful in the same language as its persecutors. It could not agree, either, to have "its program dictated" by the contemporary world. In order for a dialogue to take place the world should also listen to the voice of the Church. The speech of Archbishop of Cracow called everybody's attention and restrained the impulses of the most radically oriented "reformers of the Church," who were aiming at its complete dissolution in the contemporary world. It also led to Wojtyła's appointment to the committee of eight bishops which was to prepare a detailed draft of the pastoral constitution on the Church in the contemporary world.

Archbishop Wojtyła also played a significant role in shaping the Council's declaration on religious freedom (*Dignitatis humanae*). In it, he followed the precepts of the 15th-c. school of thought of Paweł Włodkowic, professor of the Jagiellonian University, who already then, 550 years before the Second Vatican Council, demanded the right to religious freedom and protested against forcible conversion of the pagans. (Many times did Karol Wojtyła refer to the significance in the history of the world thought of the 15th-c. pioneer Polish concept of freedom – also as the pope, e.g. remembering the person of Paweł Włodkowic during his address in the UNO in October 1995.) He called for religious freedom but at the same time he underscored the necessity of relating freedom to truth and responsibility. It was this line of thought to which he remained faithful: in his next philosophical work, *The Acting Person,* in all his priestly activities, and finally, in his papal encycli-

cals, in particular in the encyclical *Veritatis Splendor* (The Splendor of Truth), devoted to the limits of freedom.

The Archbishop of Cracow capitalized on the opportunities presented by his participation in the Council to help his diocese. With his new acquaintances in the Roman Curia he first of all spoke of the causes of beatification of the saintly Poles. During the second session of the Council he mobilized all the Polish bishops to sign a letter in support of the beatification of Brother Albert, and intervened personal-

ly with the Cardinal-Prefect of the Congregation for the Causes of Saints, which prepared the ground for the final decisions of the Holy Father on the new blessed and saints of the Catholic Church. During the next two sessions he intensified his efforts to have Queen Jadwiga, the "Wawel Lady," beatified and he also started to pave the way for declaring blessed Sister Faustyna Kowalska, the

In the Council Auditorium during the third session (1964)

Among the Council Fathers at the official meeting in 1962 (Bishop of Cracow is in the front row, third from the left)

apostle of the Lord's Mercy from the Łagiewniki sanctuary in Cracow.

As – due to his Council involvement – the communist regime "magnanimously" agreed to give him a passport, the Cracow bishop was finally able to make his pilgrimage in the footsteps of the other great saints – the first Apostles and their Lord. Just after the closing of the first session, in December 1963, together with a dozen other Polish bishops, he went on a pilgrimage to the Holy Land. It started in Egypt in Moslem Cairo and followed the path of the chosen nation to the Promised Land: across the Red Sea, across the dessert and up Mount Sinai. He described its impact both in a letter to his priests and in his poetry – in the cycle *A Pilgrimage to the Holy Places* – relating how deeply moved he was by coming to the same places which the Lord had visited two thousand years before. He said Masses in the Basilica of Christ's Birth in Bethlehem and on Mount Tabor; he followed the Way of the Cross, and prayed at Golgotha – in the Church of Holy Sepulcher. He stopped by Lake Gennesaret by Peter's Primacy Rock. A photo documenting this pilgrimage shows him sitting deep in thoughts on the rock. Could he have already sensed that one day he would be called to become a successor of St Peter? During this pilgrimage he was also able to step on the trail of the second great Apostle, St Paul – he visited Athens. Here, close to the Acropolis, on the former Areopagus, where the Apostle of the Nations tried to teach the pagans about God, the young Cracow bishop could have pondered again over his personal vocation…He was to come back to Jerusalem after 37 years and to Athens – after 38. But this time he came as John Paul II.

On 8 December 1965, when the fourth and last session of the Council was drawing to an end, he was no longer an "anonymous" bishop from the back row. He was a recognized participant of the most important debates of his Church, known among the highest hierarchy and the most eminent contemporary theologians. He had a chance to meet in person not only many of his colleague priests, the "Council Fathers," but also or, maybe, first of all, the two popes. The initiator of the Council, the good-natured "Parish Priest of the World," John XXIII, was just able to launch his great project. The second session of the Council was already opened by his successor, Giovanni Battista Montini, who took on the name of Paul VI. In the course of the next ses-

Delegation of the Polish Episcopate for the third session of the Council with Archbishop of Poznań Antoni Baraniak (fourth from the right), Primate Stefan Wyszyński (sixth) and Archbishop Karol Wojtyła (eleventh)

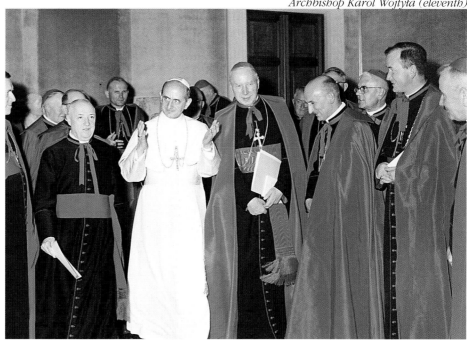

Bishops of Poland meeting the new Pope Paul VI (as usual, Archbishop Wojtyła stands in the back, behind the Holy Father)

sions he could fully appreciate the contribution made by Karol Wojtyła not only to his local Church but to the universal Church as well.

The acquaintance of Bishop Wojtyła and Cardinal Montini dated back to the time of the first session. During the second session, in October 1964, the latter – acting already in his capacity as Paul VI – ceremoniously invested a new Archbishop of Cracow with the pallium (a narrow woolen band worn on the chasuble whose use is reserved to the pope and the metropolitans as a sign of their jurisdiction in the Church). On having closed

the session, on 30 November, he granted the first private audience to Karol Wojtyła. For the Cracow Metropolitan it was a chance to thank the pope for the initiative he had taken while still being Archbishop of Milan, of mobilizing one of his parishes to offer the new bells to St Florian's church in Cracow. The pope was very interested in his guest's experiences, especially of pastoral work among the young and the workers. Paul VI also great-

Bishop of Cracow among Arab youths in front of the Alabaster Mosque in Cairo (December 1963)

Bishop Karol Wojtyła poses for a photograph at the Red Sea together with other pilgrims to the Holy Land

In Jerusalem, at the foot of the Mount of Olives (Karol Wojtyła is the first from the left)

ly appreciated the illuminating reflections of the Cracow Metropolitan on marital ethics as the archbishop saw more of the lay world than any other bishop. Paul VI wanted to make the best use of this experience in helping to implement the Council's ideas.

In April 1967 the Archbishop of Cracow was nominated Consultor of the Pontifical Council for the Laity. By that time Paul VI had already decided to appoint Karol Wojtyła cardinal, a member of the – most exclusive in the Church – assembly of the assistants of the pope. The nomination was announced on 29 May 1967. A month later, on 28 June, in what is probably the most beautiful room in the world, frescoed in the most spectacular way by Michelangelo – the Sistine Chapel – Archbishop of Cracow received his cardinal's hat from the pope. For the record, Karol Wojtyła's scarlet vestments, which symbolized the sacrifice of blood the cardinals should be ready to offer in defense of the Church and the pope, were incomplete: the red socks were unavailable in Rome (he had to wear the black ones)... This minor breach of the protocol did not interrupt the solemnity of the occasion. Here, for the tenth time in the Church history, the Cracow bishop was numbered among the princes of the Church – closest to the Holy See. Like other cardinals, Karol Wojtyła received a titular parish church in Rome – his was to be a tiny Church of St Cesareo on the Palatine. This nomination was a tangible proof of trust Paul VI had in the Archbishop of Cracow. The nominee had also the distinction of being asked by the pope to address him during the audience after the cardinals' nomination in his mother tongue – Polish.

On the way back from the consistory (the formal meeting of the cardinals), the nominee from Cracow stopped in a few symbolic places. The first one was Osjak in Austria, where – according to the legend – King Bolesław the Brave died and was buried. Karol Wojtyła played the part of this King, expiating for murdering St Stanislaus, in the performances of the underground Rhapsodic Theatre. Now he prayed at his grave as the successor of the bishop-martyr. The next station of his pilgrimage was Mauthausen, the Nazi concentration camp, where nearly 30, 000 Poles died – a symbol of the martyrdom of the whole nation. And, finally, he came to the place of triumph: Kahlenberg near Vienna. On the hill from which King Jan III Sobieski commanded the victorious Battle of Vienna of 1683, the newly nominated Cardinal celebrated the Thanksgiving Mass.

Another reference to the tragic and great pages of the history of the Polish nation and the Church was the pilgrimage, made three years later, of 220 priests, the former inmates of the German concentration camps. Cardinal Wojtyła joined the pilgrimage in the most symbolic place, at Monte Cassino. Here, at the graves of the soldiers of the Polish I Corps, who, under General Władysław Anders, had stormed the monastery hill 25 years before, the Metropolitan of Cracow said Mass on 27 May, 1970. Addressing the pilgrims gathered at the site he said that this war cemetery of the Poles bore "a testimony of truth, professed by many generations of Poles that Poland has not perished yet! And also the testimony of the Polish struggle […] for freedom ours and yours; this is the joint testimony of the soldiers and of the prisoners, like two even branches growing out of one trunk […] A Polish priest spared no costs in trying to unite – in various ways – the earthly homeland with the heavenly homeland. That is why his relationship with his earthly homeland became so deep rooted and secure – so that he could lead all the people to the heavenly homeland and lift them all." The focal point of this pilgrimage was the Mass held, two days later, by Cardinal Wojtyła in St Peter's Basilica for Paul VI celebrating the 50th anniversary of his priesthood. Together with other priests, former inmates of the Nazi concentration camps, the Metropolitan of Cracow gave the testimony of the loyalty to Rome of the Polish Church, the loyalty that passed the "test of blood and the test of faith." The pilgrims from Poland were warmly received by Paul VI at a special audience. As always during his visits to the Vatican, the cardinal from Cracow was singled out with being invited to participate in the Mass in the papal chapel.

The honors and favors bestowed on Archbishop of Cracow were tied to the new responsibilities. Soon after receiving the cardinal's hat he was nominated a member of the Sacred Congregation of the Council (later to be transformed into the Congregation for the Clergy), and of the Congregation for the Oriental Churches. From 1970 he was also a member of the Congregation for God's Cult. His participation in the work of these "Ministries" of the universal Church gave the Cracow cardinal an excellent insight into the problems extending far beyond the Vistula horizon, preparing him for his future role

Bishop of Cracow sitting on Peter's Primacy Rock on the bank of Lake Gennesaret

First visit to the ruins of the Acropolis in Athens – pilgrimage in the footsteps of St Paul (Karol Wojtyła is the second from the left)

Audience for members of the Secretariat of the Council of the Synod of Bishops in 1971 (Archbishop of Cracow second to the right from Paul VI holding a folder with documents)

Paul VI places the cardinal's hat on Karol Wojtyła's head (1967)

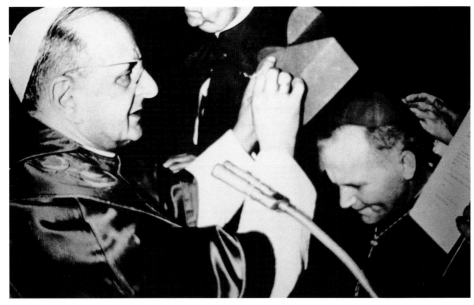

Cardinal Wojtyła celebrates Mass at the Monte Cassino military cemetery (standing next to him the indispensable Fr. Stanisław Dziwisz)

as the world shepherd. Particularly fruitful was his involvement in the work of the Synod of Bishops. This Church structure was established in 1965 by Pope Paul VI who wished to set up a permanent council of the bishops from all over the world to continue the work of the Second Vatican Council. Cardinal Wojtyła did not take part in the first meeting of the Synod, held in autumn 1967, as a sign of solidarity with Primate Stefan Wyszyński, whom the Communist regime refused a passport. In the next meetings of the Synod, held in autumn in 1969, 1971, 1974 and 1977, Archbishop of Cracow played already a crucial role. He shared his thoughts on the collegiality in the Church; he consequently supported the cause for the celibacy of the priests; he emphasized the role of freedom of conscience as the basis of political justice; he presented his vision of universal evangelization, viewed not only as a preparation for eternal life but as a chance to change man's earthly life and to protect his dignity. From 1971 he was a member of a twelve-person Permanent Council of the General Secretariat of the Synod of Bishops, which supervised its work in the period between the sessions.

In Cardinal Wojtyła's opinion, the problems that the Synod had to face resulted from the crisis of the Church's growth. The Church's opening to the world allowed it to reach millions of non-believers with the Good News. For all that, the Council became a pretext for further secularization and for the attempts to "convert" the Church to the modern lifestyle, especially in the most developed countries of the West. The principle of collegiality was read as a simple transfer of lay democracy to the Church. In its name the right of the pope and of the Church hierarchy to interpret the faith dogmas and the principles of the Catholic ethics was being seriously undermined; with the development of the modern concept of equality of sexes came the growing demand for the right of women to be ordained priests. As a result of watering down the traditional moral values, increasingly more people demanded that the Church should re-examine its sexual teaching and approve of contraceptives and, even, of abortion. For those who shouted the battle cry of Freedom the enemy was Truth. Watching these trends in the countries of Western Europe (particularly in Holland, Belgium, France and Germany), Cardinal Wojtyła desired passionately to defend the teaching of the

Council of which he truly felt one of the "Fathers." He wished to actively implement its decisions in his diocese and at the same time to defend it against over-interpretation.

When Paul VI decided to cool the heated debates about the moral principles of family planning and responsible parenthood, the Archbishop of Cracow – the author of *Love and Responsibility* – took on the task of drafting a new papal encyclical. Paul VI was not satisfied with the findings of his own commissions, some of which favored the use of artificial contraceptives while others strongly objected. Relying on the Archdiocese Institute of Family Theology, Karol Wojtyła instituted his own commission, which consisted of both the priests and the lay people. The documents submitted by this commission became the basis for the cardinal's own proposal which he put forward to the pope. The starting point of the document was the definition of human dignity and marital love. The use of mechanical or chemical contraceptives was described as being contrary to the dignity of the married couple. "Family planning through obeying the natural biological rhythms is the only method of birth control which respects – on the personal level – the dignity and equality of the partners in marriage" – this was the essence of the "Cracow" proposal, as summarized by one of the commentators of Karol Wojtyła's thought. Paul VI appreciated this proposition, making it one of the foundations for his encyclical *Humanae Vitae,* announced finally in 1968. John Paul II was consequently upholding this teaching throughout his whole pontificate.

In 1969 Cardinal Wojtyła had the first opportunity to confront his ideas with the reality of the country which was becoming the symbol of moral and sexual revolution. In August, the Metropolitan of Cracow left, via Rome and Paris, for nearly a five-week visit to North America. First, as part of the celebrations of the 25th anniversary of the Congress of the Canadian Polonia, he visited Montreal, Toronto, Quebec, Ottawa, and Edmonton, reaching in the end the Niagara Waterfalls. Then his route took him through the north-western and central states of the USA. He stopped off in Buffalo, Cleveland, Detroit, in the Polish Seminary in Orchard Lake, Boston, Baltimore, Washington, St. Louis, Chicago, Philadelphia (where he was hosted by Cardinal John Krol – of the Polish origin), and, finally, in New York.

For the first time on the American soil: arrival in the United States in 1969 (Fr. Franciszek Macharski and Fr. Stanisław Dziwisz standing higher on the stairs)

Under the monument to Tadeusz Kościuszko in Boston (August 1969)

The program of this extremely lengthy journey included the meetings with Polonia but also the talks with the hierarchs and the believers from the Canadian and American Churches; it impressed with its scale and heralded the future pilgrimages of John Paul II. And already then – as in all future pilgrimages – his closest assistant was Father Dziwisz, who from 1966 served as his chaplain.

In February 1973 Cardinal Wojtyła headed the Polish delegation at the Eucharistic Congress in Melbourne. The discussion centered on practical ways of implementing the teaching of the Second Vatican Council. For the future pope it was one of the first occasions to recognize the pressing need of the Church's involvement in bringing relief to the Third World countries. The symbol of such an involvement was Mother Teresa from Calcutta, devoting her life to helping – materially and spiritually – the poorest in India. During this distant trip to the Antipodes the Cracow cardinal visited numerous Polonia circles, both in Australia and in New Zealand. He called on the Polish missionaries working among the Papuans and Melanesians in New Guinea. Here he got a glimpse of the problem of the Church's "enculturation" i.e. modifying the external forms of the rituals to the mentality of the natives. He was happy to listen to the beautiful singing of the Melanesians and gratefully accepted their original gifts; in his journey diary he just observed delicately that "their attitude towards clothes is different than ours …" On the way there, he also stopped in the capital of the Philippines, Manila, where 22 years later, as a pope, he was to celebrate the World Youth Day – the greatest gathering in the history of the world (estimated to be attended by five to seven million people).

In August 1976 he headed another Polish delegation at the Eucharistic Congress in Philadelphia. On this occasion he visited Harvard University (e.g. the Ukrainian Institute), revisited Washington, Baltimore, Orchard Lake, Buffalo, Chicago, New York, but also, for the first time, stopped off in the cities of the West Coast: San Francisco, Los Angeles and even Montana. Other Polish participants of this great tour observed that the cardinal was disappointed with the "shallowness" of the American mass culture and disturbed by the prevailing tendency to abuse the slogan of freedom. He was to face the same problem again – on a global scale – as the shepherd of the universal Church.

Archbishop of Cracow and the symbol of Australia – the kangaroo (relaxing during the Eucharistic Congress in Melbourne in 1973)

Natives from New Guinea offering their gifts and presenting their outfits to Cardinal Wojtyła

In front of St Patrick's Cathedral in New York, next to his host, Cardinal Terence Cook (September 1976)

New honors and responsibilities resulting from the participation of the Cracow Metropolitan in the Council expanded his horizons and opened his eyes to the world problems. Yet, he continued to come back to his archdiocese, to Poland – his homeland. On return from his first visit to America he beautifully expressed his feelings: "When I was overseas I often saw with the eyes of my soul a tree. The tree does not ask for its roots, it simply has them. Man, however, must ask. Therefore we, the Poles living in this country on the Vistula, and the Poles living overseas, are bonded with each other by the roots from which this common tree grows out […] Through our work, through our suffering, through our spiritual achievements, through our history, through our testimony, through our culture we bring new vitality, new contents and values into this great spiritual tree. And this is our place in the human family […], in which we, the Poles, play special part, in which «Polishness» carries unique values." This was also a lesson the Cracow bishop learnt from his opening to the world. Poland had much to offer to the world and to the universal Church.

CHAPTER VI
Fight for the dignity of the nation (1965-1978)

An excellent occasion to evoke the great tradition and the spiritual culture of the nation, rich with a history of centuries, was the 1000th anniversary of the baptism of Poland. The culmination of the celebrations was planned by Primate Stefan Wyszyński for the Millennium Year – 1966. Towards the end of the Second Vatican Council all the Polish bishops present wrote 56 letters to the episcopates of various countries inviting them to this very special jubilee. Among them there was also *The Proclamation of the Polish Bishops to their German Brothers in Pastoral Office* of 18 November 1965. The letter to the German bishops was not just a curt invitation. It was written with the intention to start a reconciliation process between the Poles and the Germans. The letter's initiators – Bolesław Kominek, Archbishop of Wrocław, Primate Wyszyński and Archbishop Wojtyła – desired to help to heal the wounds of the past. Thus, they did not only address the horrible wrongs suffered by the Poles at the hands of the German occupants during the World War II, and, earlier – for 123 years – during the Partitions, initiated by Prussia. Underlying the fact that the Polish right to the Western Territories, incorporated into Poland after the World War II, was "to be or not to be" for Poland, they were also ready to admit the suffering experienced by millions of Germans expelled from their homes. The words: "we forgive you and ask your forgiveness" became the best symbol of the spirit ingrained into the Polish culture after a thousand year of Christianity. They also helped to establish a new framework for the future Polish-German relations.

This proclamation was like a red rag to a bull to the Communist regime. The then First Party Secretary Władysław Gomułka, saw in it an impertinent attempt of the Polish bishops to trample on the territory of foreign policy reserved for

Icon of Our Lady of Częstochowa, whose copy shook the foundations of the Communist regime in 1966

Parade of the Millenium: tanks and armored vehicles as symbols of the power of Gomułka's regime

him and his party. The situation was further aggravated by the reply of the German Episcopate, interpreted as the support for the German revisionist attitude towards the western border of Poland. Gomułka, who, up till then, had conducted guerilla warfare against the Polish Church, went to open war. An unprecedented campaign against the bishop-authors of the proclamation was unleashed in the media. The newspapers and radio propagandists accused them of "high treason," "acting against Polish national interests," "a profanation of the memory of 6 million Polish victims of Nazism." The letter of the Polish bishops was criticized even by the parliamentary circle of the Catholic MPs. The authorities organized meetings in the workplaces to dictate special resolution condemning this proclamation. One of such propaganda hatred séances was held in the Solvay chemical plant in Cracow, only to rebuke their former co-worker – now Archbishop Karol Wojtyła. The workers wrote an „open letter" to the Metropolitan of Cracow, expressing their "great indignation" at his "action which was not like that of a good citizen." The archbishop responded with a lengthy letter in which he explained the true intentions of the proclamation. As a final point, he invited his former co-workers from the Solvay plant and their families to Christmas Mass in the Home Chapel of the Archbishops' Palace.

The communists tried to use also this occasion to create a rift in the Polish Church and to undermine the leadership of Primate Wyszyński. In January and February 1966, the bishops of all the dioceses were summoned for questioning by the authorities over the proclamation to the German Episcopate. Archbishop of Cracow blighted the hopes of the communists: he stood firmly by the Primate and by his own interpretation of the proclamation as "a great gesture towards improving Polish-German relations." However, the Communist regime continued its pressure on the lower levels of the Church hierarchy. In April 1966, in the Operation Parish Priest, 3774 priests were interrogated by the political officers of the army who tried to make them rebuke the proclamation. In an attempt to disrupt the celebrations of the 1000th anniversary of Christianity in Poland, the authorities summoned the bishops for the second round of "consultations," presenting them with the demands to introduce changes to the Millennium program and to limit the number of its participants. The Poles were to be deprived of the occasion to express publicly their attachment to Catholicism and to the Church hierarchy.

The biggest eyesore to the communists was the form of the popular devotion chosen by Primate Wyszyński to enliven the Polish piety – a pilgrimage of the copy of the Black Madonna of Częstochowa through all the parishes in the country. What caused fury among the authorities was the crowds gathering along its route and greeting the icon in their dioceses and parishes. They saw in it the key threat to their fight for the souls of the Poles. Therefore, they organized rival lay celebrations of the 1000th anniversary of the nation, often in stark opposition to the Church events planned beforehand. Such was the case, for example, on the occasion of High Mass in Gniezno, held precisely on the 1000th anniversary of Prince Mieszko's baptism, on 14 April 1966. The Mass, celebrated by the Archbishop of Cracow, was drowned by the mortar salutes, announcing the arrival of the Minister of Defense for the national manifestation...On a smaller scale the same scenario was repeated everywhere. Its most poignant expression was the authority's refusal to allow the Holy Father Paul VI to take part in the central Millennium celebrations in Częstochowa. On 3 May 1966, over 300, 000 people gathered in

Cardinal Karol Wojtyła – greatly exercised
Metropolitan of Cracow as a powerful preacher

front of the bulwarks of Jasna Góra, faced an empty papal throne.

The main Millennium celebrations in Cracow were held on 7 and 8 May and included a visit of the icon of the Black Madonna of Częstochowa. A group of "demonstrators," mobilized by the local committee of the PZPR, marched off against the bishops gathered at Wawel. They carried banners that read: "We do not forgive!", "Poland will never be the playtoy of the foreign powers!" An answer came the next day when the densely crowded procession was seeing the icon off to the tollgates of Cracow. People shouted to the surrounding policemen: "We forgive you!", "Come with us!", "Freedom for religion in schools!" In Warsaw the police used clubs to disperse the procession of Corpus Christi in order to clear the way for the rival "procession" – of the party action group, demonstrating against Primate Wyszyński. In September the police "arrested" the peregrinating icon and sent it back to Jasna Góra.

And yet, the Communist regime lost this battle. Summing up the actions of 1966, the Ministry for Church Affairs expressed its regret that "Wyszyński and his devoted ordinaries" (with the Archbishop of Cracow top of the list) were not intimidated and continued to organize "illegal processions, pilgrimages, and mass greeting ceremonies along the route of the peregrinating Częstochowa icon, turning these events into political manifestations."

Archbishop Wojtyła implemented the pastoral program of the Millennium with indefatigable energy – not only in his own archdiocese. He traveled widely, visited parishes, encouraged and preached sermons in which patriotic pride mixed with the reflection on the Christian meaning of the Millennium. After the celebrations in Cracow were concluded with a scientific session with the whole episcopate present (during which the Metropolitan of Cracow remembered his great predecessor – Cardinal Sapieha), the millennium route took him through Szczepanów, Kęty, Katowice, Częstochowa, Piekary Śląskie, Żywiec, Gdańsk, Bydgoszcz, Lublin, Olsztyn, Frombork, Halcnów, Wiślica, Tarnów, Stary Sącz, Łomża, Ludźmierz, Opole, Kalwaria Zebrzydowska, Przemyśl, Myślenice, Orawka, Radomsko, Siedlce, Drohiczyn, Wrocław, Trzebnica. This was merely a 4-month fragment of the great millennium route which had started nine years before and was to last for another few months. An indefatigable Pilgrim-Archbishop of Cracow paved

the way for the Pilgrim Pope. The concept of pastoral care based on the meetings with the masses and on finding common ground with the crowds of the faithful was actually forged in the school of Millennium celebrations.

At the same time he attended to his routine duties of the shepherd of the Cracow archdiocese. Its center was the Archbishops' Palace in Franciszkańska Street, where he moved from his flat in Kanonicza Street. Here was his new home and his "office" – the Cracow Curia. The archbishop got up early in the morning at 5.00 a.m. and started his day with a long prayer in his private chapel. At 7.00 he said Mass. After breakfast he read, wrote correspondence or prepared his texts – sermons, articles, announcements, and pastoral letters. From 11.00 until early

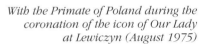

At a meeting of Oasis movement at Olszówka with a group of priests

afternoon he received various clients. Lunch, which he always shared with the Curia workers or guests, was an introduction to a more "relaxing" part of the day. When he was in Cracow and had a free afternoon, he liked to go for a walk (e.g. to the forest complex of Lasek Wolski or Sikornik). After dinner, which was at 7 p.m., he received guests or worked on his own. He did not have a television set. He spent the last part of his day praying in the chapel – usually until midnight.

With the Primate of Poland during the coronation of the icon of Our Lady at Lewiczyn (August 1975)

The cardinal hands in prizes to the winners of Sacrosong Contest in Cracow (September 1972)

Bishop's ring of Karol Wojtyła (now stored in the cathedral treasury at Wawel)

The routine pastoral work in the diocese required also his frequent trips, in particular to the priests' ordinations, confirmations, parish visitations, retreats, celebrations in the parishes and jubilees of religious profession, to see to the building of new churches (building permits for the "cult objects" were granted most reluctantly and after much struggling), and to consecrate the newly built churches and altars. To make the best use of his time, the Cracow archbishop had in his car (first an Opel and then a Wołga), a writing desk and a lamp installed so that he could write and read while traveling It was the only way he could reconcile his increasingly heavy load of duties with his research work and…poetry.

The highlight of his research work conducted after receiving the cardinal's hat was the philosophical study *The Acting Person,* published in 1969. In it, he engaged in the analysis of the human person and his growth through moral actions. Though it made difficult reading, the message of this book was simple: it was neither individualism nor collectivism but solidarity that allowed man – through serving others – to lead the life of moral self-fulfillment. The same message, expressed through the same word, SOLIDARITY, was to become, 11 years later, the signal for a peace revolution, prepared – through his moral actions – by the same author: Karol Wojtyła – John Paul II.

The same flow of thought can be seen in the poetic cycles of the Cracow Metropolitan: *Easter Vigil of 1966, Reflections on Death, Stanislaus* or, finally, maybe the most important – *Thinking Homeland* – dated for 1974 but published only after his election to the papacy. This penetrating insight into the Polish history was accompanied by a sort of poetic and moral program: "Freedom has to be conquered every day; you cannot possess it. It comes as a gift but it has to be defended to be maintained […] History covers up the struggles of conscience with the strain of events. […] Can history flow against the current of conscience?"

Karol Wojtyła tried to find an answer to this dramatic question through his enduring work to awaken the conscience of the Poles. He knew that culture could be a powerful ally in this effort. Therefore, he did not seal it off from his palace; on the contrary, he tried to participate in it and draw it to the Church. He organized and patronized tens of sessions and conferences which brought together lay scientists and writers. He turned to them as his allies in the struggle for conscience of Poland. He also looked for help among the young people who expressed their cultural fascinations through other forms, pertaining to the language of the youth. He committed himself to this search by assuming patronage over the Sacrosong, an annual festival of the young religious music, initiated by Father Palusiński. The first contest was held in 1969, the next ones were organized illegally (e.g. in the Nowa Huta church). The last time Cardinal Wojtyła visited Sacrosong was precisely one month before his election. On this occasion, on 16 September 1978, he recalled with a smile the alarm with which he looked in the beginning at all the instruments of the young music being brought into the church. Now he appealed to the young

to take delight in culture – and to take delight in moral self-improvement. "There must be this feeling of delight because it brings beauty into the life of an individual, of a society, of a nation. And it is beauty that inspires and animates culture." At the same time he warned the authorities against using mass media to create a sort of "anticulture," culture against religion: "You cannot produce culture with administrative measures! With administrative measures, you can only destroy culture!"

He himself did not have many occasions on which he could enjoy – as a recipient – the greatest achievements of the Polish culture of the period. His beloved Rhapsodic Theater, with the artists of which he maintained close contact, was closed by the authorities in 1967. Cardinal Wojtyła immediately wrote a letter to the Minister of Culture asking for the annulment of this decision. Unfortunately – to no avail. He did not, however, give up his interest in theater. It manifested itself, for example, during his talk with Konrad Swinarski at the beginning of 1975. Swinarski, the most eminent director of the time, was the author of the greatest performances in the Old Theater, in which he interpreted anew the repertory that was also close to Karol Wojtyła's heart: *Forefather's Eve* by Mickiewicz, *Liberation* by Wyspiański, *Non-Divine Comedy* by Krasiński. In connection with the planned staging of the *Forefathers' Eve* in one of the London churches, the director asked – through the cardinal's close theater friend Halina Królikiewicz-Kwiatkowska – for the permission to use for rehearsals the Dominican monastery, which had a similar acoustics as the London church. The cardinal invited Swinarski to the talk in the palace. They chatted like two people of the theater – about the drama (the cardinal had already seen the staging of *Forefathers' Eve* in the Old Theater), about romanticism, about Polish culture. Needless to say, the rehearsals were held in the Dominican monastery.

The cardinal did not give up, either, his favorite forms of holiday recreation. In summer he continued to go kayaking although in October 1970 he was touched by a great personal loss. The initiator of the trips and one of his closest friends Jerzy Ciesielski, the senior lecturer at Cracow University of Technology, drowned together with his two children in the ship catastrophe on the Nile near Khartoum. To the Cracow Metropolitan he was an example of how a lay person could pursue holiness in everyday life. Today he is awaiting beatification. Cardinal Wojtyła made his last kayak trip – to Lake Krępsko – about ten weeks before his election to the Holy See, in the end of July 1978. As a pope he did not pursue this form of recreation and spiritual reflection in the circle of his friends. However, he maintained, at least for some time, his other habit – of taking skiing holiday. As a cardinal he made such short escapades (often with his friends from the Catholic University of Lublin, Father Professors: Styczeń, Nagym or Marian Jaworski), during which – free from the hassle of everyday activity – he could think over some scientific, theological or pastoral problem. He skied down Kasprowy Mountain or the lower mountain peaks in Beskidy. He also liked mountain hiking. But even during his hikes he could not escape the shadow cast on his pastoral work and his fight for the dignity of Poles by the Communist regime. Father Nagy remembers when, on the way back from one of the skiing expeditions in the Western Tatras, "the cardinal suddenly turned round and looking thoughtfully at the beautiful view interrupted his deep meditation to say with a surprising strength and a deep sadness in his voice: and they – everybody knew who "they" were – want to destroy this Nation."

"They" haunted him also in the mountains. Sometimes – literally. Such was the case, for example, when President of France, Charles de Gaulle, visited Poland in September 1967. Gomułka brought pressure on the French delegation to cancel the meeting with Primate Wyszyński. Once again did the authorities try to set

With Primate Stefan Wyszyński – blessing for the Polish nation

Moment of relaxation at a kayak trip (with Jerzy and Danuta Ciesielskis)

Cardinal Wojtyła and Fr. Franciszek Macharski in the mountains "hiding" from Gen. de Gaulle

Demonstration at the Regional Police headquarters in Szczecin in December 1970

Monument to the Poznań Riots of June 1956 commemorating all the Polish attempts to fight the Communist regime

the newly-nominated Cardinal Wojtyła against the hated Primate and to have the Cracow Metropolitan do the honors of the house – at least in his own diocese (the French guest was to spend the night at Wawel Castle). With a group of his friends, Archbishop Wojtyła managed to get away from the police guard, slipping out by car to the mountains. He did not want to meet de Gaulle – to express his solidarity with the Primate. As a result, there is no entry in the official biography of Cardinal Wojtyła between September 11 and September 12, 1967. It was the sacristan of the Wawel Cathedral who did the honors of the house to the French President …

As a result of the Baltic Riots of December 1970, which brought the second – after the Poznań Riots of June 1956 – wave of mass workers' protests against the Communist system, Gomułka was dispatched from his office. A new team, led by Edward Gierek, made some initial conciliatory gestures towards the society and the Church, e.g. increasing the number of building permits for new churches. The authorities also attempted to establish the regular diplomatic relations with the Holy See – behind the back of the Polish Episcopate. Normalizing the relations with the Vatican did not, however, produce the results the communists had expected. The authority of the Church and of her hierarchy in Poland was not to be undermined. Gradually, the regime softened their attitude towards Primate Wyszyński. Now another member of the episcopate was becoming the public enemy number one – the Cracow cardinal. Why?

The answer to this question is to be found in his sermons, preached on various occasions, such as the traditional processions on the Feast of St Stanislaus from Wawel to Skałka, a site of the martyred death of the bishop from the hand of the king, the processions on Corpus Christi Day, systematically repressed by the local government, or the pilgrimages of men to Piekary

Śląskie, to which the Cracow Metropolitan was invited every year by Bishop of Katowice Herbert Bednorz. Let us look at some of the subjects of Cardinal Wojtyła's sermons delivered in Piekary. In 1973 he called on the authorities to create – in the country where the majority was Catholic – public space for the Catholic citizens. In 1974 he warned them that "education should not be a method of spiritual separation of the children from their parents." He mentioned a new host of restrictions imposed on building new churches. Finishing his sermon, he challenged the Communist regime: "And we ask all these questions to learn the true meaning of the word «socialist.» Does it mean the respect for the rights of working people or something else?"

But what really aggravated the authorities was that in the same sermon the cardinal remembered the Catholics in the neighboring Czechoslovakia experiencing even greater hardships than the Polish Catholics. A few weeks before his pilgrimage to Piekary, in the middle of April 1974, he attended the funeral of Cardinal Trochta from Litomerice, who had spent nine years in a Communist prison, and eight years doing physical work. The Czechoslovakian secret police did not allow the Cracow cardinal to co-celebrate Mass. Nevertheless, he managed to say a few words over the coffin of the heroic cardinal.

The next year, his sermon in Piekary was even more powerful. "You mustn't fight with religion! […] We have to demand that no man should be persecuted or threatened with losing his job because of his religious convictions." In 1976 he repeated the same demand, playing on the fact that, in the meantime, the Communist government signed the international Convention on Human Rights. Finally, in 1978, he talked about the right of man to observe the Sabbath rest. This right was abused by the authorities who – in the name of the screwed up plans –

made the miners work on Sunday. "Man who has been created to work has been also created to l i v e   a b u n d a n t l y […] Let us ask if, by any chance, the new generations of Poles are not threatened with frustration? With the feeling that work is futile and life is meaningless?"

The Cracow Metropolitan did not espouse the political cause. He spoke out of concern for the dignity of the people whom he was called to serve. In the Communist system, however, everything carried political connotations – especially the issue of the dignity of workers or simply of people in general. Already in 1973-1974 the general prosecuting attorney of the Polish People's Republic thought of bringing Cardinal Wojtyła to justice – for the sermons preached e.g. at the processions of St Stanislaus in Cracow, at the 300th anniversary of the death of Father Kordecki on Jasna Góra (5 May 1973), or on a building site of the church in Nowa Huta. He wanted to charge him with penal code violation for propagating "anti-state contents" during the religious ceremonies, which carried a penalty of one to ten years. However, the high international position of the cardinal saved him from open persecution.

Stanisław Kania, a member of the Political Bureau of the PZPR, who in the 70s was in charge of the relations with the Church, could only report in helpless fury on the Cracow Metropolitan's stance of support for the growth of resistance in the society. When in summer 1976 the authorities attempted to increase food prices, it was met with an outburst of rioting, notably at the factories at Radom and Ursus. To help the persecuted workers the Committee for the Workers' Defense (KOR) was set up. During his talk with Secretary of Episcopate, Archbishop Dąbrowski, Kania accused Cardinal Wojtyła of "meeting with a group of political rascals" (he meant the co-founders of the KOR: Father Zieja and Józef Rybicki), of "encouraging them and collecting money among the priests at their request." A year later, in May 1977, the SB treacherously murdered Stanisław Pyjas, an activist of a growing student opposition in Cracow. The Metropolitan obligated the Curia lawyer, Andrzej Rozmarynowicz, to take action to apprehend the perpetrators of the crime. Kania thundered forth: "The Cracow cardinal went beyond the bounds; with his rabble-rousing sermons he is asking for trouble…"

The Communist secret service reacted quickly. The cardinal's trusted "political informer" was his old friend, Father

Visitation of the Metropolitan of Cracow in one of the parishes in Nowa Huta
Primate Stefan Wyszyński blesses the faithful during the Corpus Christi procession

Andrzej Bardecki, the church assistant of *Tygodnik Powszechny*. Once a week he updated the Cracow Metropolitan on the recent events in the country and their coverage in the official press. On 21 December 1977, after the meeting with Cardinal Wojtyła, Father Bardecki did not manage to make it to his flat, located merely a few hundred yards from the Archbishops' Palace. Outside his house he was confronted by the two masked men… Kicked black and blue, the priest owed his life only to a chance passerby, who happened to be walking his robust dog in the area. The cardinal visited Father Bardecki the next day. He had no doubts: "This battering was meant for me."

Neither of them knew that they became an object of interest not only for the Polish Communist secret service but also for the Moscow "headquarters." The recently revealed KGB files describe the details of the operation "Progress," begun in 1971. After the Baltic Riots of December 1970, the KGB decided to conduct an independent investigation in order to ascertain the position of the Church in Poland and the political leaning of its hierarchs. In the beginning, "the Moscow comrades" examined the characteristics supplied by their colleagues from the SB. Cardinal Wojtyła was an obvious candidate for thorough investigation. "His political views are radically anti-Communist; he criticizes the authorities of the Polish People's Republic accusing them of violating the basic human rights of the citizens of the Poland and of the unacceptable exploitation of the workers whom *the Catholic Church has to protect against the workers' government…*" A list of accusations the Cracow Metropolitan brought up against the Communist system, quoted in detail in the SB report forwarded to Moscow, was much longer. But even a cursory look was enough to send the best KGB agents to Cracow. The first to come was an agent codenamed "Bogun," pretending to be a photo reporter from West Germany. He was followed by "Fiłozof," a citizen of France of Ukrainian origin, who published his books in Paris with the money he was receiving from Moscow. They both tried to strike acquaintance with Father Bardecki in the hope of winning his trust and finding out as much as possible about the Cracow Metropolitan's views, contacts and "weak points." In 1977 "Fiłozof" reported to the headquarters that he "established a contact," while actually he was meeting Father Bardecki in the editorial office of *Tygodnik Powszechny*, which was open to all the foreigners. The former archivist of the KGB, Wasilij Mitrochin, ascertained with pride that in trying to hem in the Cracow cardinal his "organization" proved to be very insightful. Wasn't he going to be a pope in a year time? The head of the Catholic Church… And the rulers of the Kremlin were always curious how many divisions the pope has.

The Cracow Metropolitan's "divisions" were not formed in confrontation with the KGB or SB, nor were they formed in confrontation with the Communist system. They were formed in the course of everyday pastoral work. It was into this work that Cardinal Wojtyła put most of his indefatigable energy. He devoted a lot of attention to the ministry of families, to the ongoing dialogue with the intellectuals, to the ministry of the sick and the poor (one of his first action on becoming archbishop was to set up in Curia a separate Department for Charity Work; he also introduced the annual Day of the Sick). He particularly enjoyed his work with the young. A way back when he was vicar of St Florian's he set an example for how to organize a lively ministry for students which would attract people of worth. His work in that field was carried on by St Ann's academic church and by the students' "Barrel" ministry of the Dominican church.

Cardinal Wojtyła returns from a vacation

1 of May parade – one of the main "rites" of the Communist regime

On a larger, national scale the Cracow cardinal's ideas were embraced by the "Light and Life" Movement, initiated by a charismatic leader of the young, Father Blachnicki, Professor of Sociology at the Catholic University of Lublin. As an antidote to atheistic propaganda and moral indifference Father Blachnicki proposed "oases" – the summer camps organized in beautiful locations, where the secondary school pupils could meet, sing at the fireplaces, pray and discuss things together. Cardinal Wojtyła gave his hearty support to a mass Oasis Movement. He often visited the camps, said Masses for the participants, and tried to shelter them from the increasingly frequent interventions of the authorities who did not appreciate Father Blachnicki's idea of education. A highlight in the history of the Oasis Movement was the meeting at Mount Błyszcz near Tylmanowa on 16 August 1972. Together with 700 hundred young people, the cardinal hiked up the mountain – in spite of the coming storm. On the way up he joked: "I know three daredevils: the first one is me, the second one is my secretary [Father Dziwisz], and the third one [Father Blachnicki] is waiting at the top." The storm caught up with them at the summit. Nevertheless, the sky echoing with the peals of thunder, the Mass was celebrated, leaving a lasting impression on the young participants. Equally unforgettable were the cardinal's words in which he vividly characterized the situation of religion in Communist Poland: "I am afraid that if there is an "oasis" there is also a desert because the oasis can exist only in the desert. However, the desert cannot discourage us; on the contrary, it should encourage us to create as many oases as possible because only the desert without oasis is frightening. The desert is frightening. Or let us put it differently: the desert would be frightening if we did not create oases."

The cardinal also looked after the education of the young priests. He took special care of the Theological Faculty expelled from the Jagiellonian University and helped it to survive as a section of the Priests' Seminary. In 1974 he managed to secure its official status as the Papal Theological Faculty. He encouraged the Faculty to develop postgraduate studies for priests, offering various courses, not only in theology. He worked on bridging the distance between the young priests and the lay scientists to whom he was authority. The meetings in the Archbishops' Palace in Franciszkańska Street

Two cardinals from Poland in Rome: Primate Wyszyński and Metropolitan of Cracow

First Secretary of the Communist party Edward Gierek with his wife search political support with Paul VI (December 1977)

Queuing for bread – one of the typical images from Poland in the late 1970s

Silver miter prepared for the Metropolitan of Cracow for the Synod

were frequented by Professors: Stanisław Pigoń, Adam Vetulani (the law historian), the historians Henryk Wereszycki and Józef Mitkowski, the physicist Henryk Niewodniczański, the psychiatrist Antoni Kępiński, the art historian Adam Bochnak, and obviously by the editors and co-workers of *Tygodnik Powszechny* and the *Znak* monthly.

Wojtyła was not only the cardinal of intellectuals or of the young. He wished to touch all his diocesans with his pastoral care. The most ambitious initiative which was to help him to fulfill this task was the Synod of the Cracow Church Province. It was called on the occasion of the 900th anniversary of the appointment of St Stanislaus to the Cracow diocese. Declared on 8 May 1972, the Synod encouraged all the faithful to participate in order to "enrich and deepen our faith, make it well-grounded and mature – adequate to our times – so that it could influence our life and shape our morality." Helped by his auxiliary bishops, Jan Pietraszko, Stanisław Smoleński and Albin Małysiak, the cardinal mobilized both the priests and the lay people of the whole archdiocese for a colossal effort. Almost 500 working groups were organized: students', priests', monastic orders', the groups of fathers and mothers… We can get some idea on the topics covered during these meetings, meant to rekindle the spirit of cooperation and Christian unity, from the titles of the documents devised as a result of the seven-years' work of the Synod: *The Transmission and Growth of Faith in a Family, A*

Christian Marriage, A Child in the Community of the Church, A Christian in His Job, Sanctifying the Time, Infusing Modern Culture with the Spirit of the Gospel, Responsibility of a Christian for Shaping and Renewing the World…

The Synod was called with the view to implement the teaching of the Second Vatican Council. It fostered awareness of the role of the laity. It was not a political act but it taught priests and lay people, workers and intellectuals, those seeking truth and those who have already found it how to live in a community. Its closing session was originally planned for May 1979 to coincide with the 900th anniversary celebrations of the martyred death of Bishop Stanislaus. It ended one month later. The Synod architect was not able to carry it through till the end. Eight months before the intended closing celebrations he was called from the throne of St Stanislaus to the throne of St Peter. The Communist regime did not dare not to invite the then most famous Poland's son. They decided, however, to delay the visit from May, when it would have fallen on the Feast of St Stanislaus – as so many times in the past it had provided the Cracow Metropolitan with a pretext to talk on the limits of power of any human government. John Paul II was to come to Poland, to his archdiocese, to his beloved Cracow in June 1979. As a result, the Church hierarchy decided also to delay the closing ceremony of the Cracow Synod. On 10 June, looking at two million people assembled on Cracow's common for the High Mass, John Paul II could, at least in part, recognize this seed which he had sown on this land…

Chapter VII
Election

"*Annuntio vobis gaudium magnum – Habemus Papam.* I announce to you a great joy – we have a Pope". All those who reach back in their memory to 1978 will certainly never forget this joy, this emotion. On 16 October at 6:44 p.m., Cardinal Pericle Felici appeared in the loggia of St Peter's Basilica to announce that Rome and the world had a new Bishop. "The most Eminent and Reverend Lord of the Holy Roman Church, Cardinal Karol Wojtyła, who has taken for himself the name of John Paul II."

A bishop from Poland, the first non-Italian from 1522, as the successor of St Peter. How did it come about? The Holy Spirit "blows where it wills" – this answer should in theory be sufficient for the faithful. But it does not satisfy our human curiosity. That is why we always look for some hints, reasons, signs which would predict or explain the choice made by the congregation of cardinals. We have already hinted at Wojtyła's previous choices which were preparatory to this one and marked certain stages towards it. And so first was his priesthood – and the decision not to respond to the actor's calling as well as not to enter the Carmelites' Order. The nomination for bishop and archbishop of the Cracow Diocese followed, which allowed him to participate in the Second Vatican

Council. As a consequence, he was elected to the College of Cardinals and thus entered the group from which the Pope emerged. In this body, which at the time of Paul VI usually numbered some 100 cardinals, the Metropolitan of Cracow made himself known as an outstanding figure thanks to both his involvement in the Synod of Bishops and his relatively frequent foreign trips and international contacts.

One more important event should certainly be added to this. In March 1976 Cardinal Wojtyła, invited by Pope Paul VI, presided over the Lent retreat for the Pontiff and the entire Roman Curia. As Bishop Andrzej Deskur, the Polish curialist, claimed much later, the Pope clearly "wanted to show Roman cardinals how knowledgeable and pious Cardinal Wojtyła was." In the five-day spiritual exercise, the Cardinal of Cracow reached not only for the wealth of the Gospel and theological reflections, but also for the testimony of belles lettres – Saint Exupery's *Night Flight*, Milton's *Paradise Lost* – as well as that of contemporary secular thinkers, such as Martin Heidegger or Paul Ricoeur. He did that not in order to show off, but rather to emphasize the message of the retreat: the Church must stand by the Truth, even when the world opposes it. Only then will it retain its ability to defend human dignity, which consists in the responsible use of human freedom. The retreat sermons, which were published later under the title *Sign of Contradiction*, made a great impression on the congregation. John Paul II himself, a year after his election, regarded them as his "main identification for the world."

Indeed, from the time of the Vatican retreat, his name started to circulate among the journalists who speculated about possible successors of Paul VI, ill and tired with his difficult pontificate. The Pope himself could have foreseen Karol Wojtyła in this role, as testified by numerous gestures of recognition, including that of offering a numerous group of Vatican cardinals an opportunity to get to know the Metropolitan of Cracow closer during the retreat in March 1976. The Pope does not nominate his successor though. It is the cardinals who elect him. And among those Karol Wojtyła had devoted followers already in the mid-1970s. The most influential among them was the Archbishop of Vienna, Franz König. 13 years his superior, he had been a member of the College of Cardinals since 1958 and had played an important role during the Second Vatican Council. Always interested in the fate of the Church in East-Central Europe, he quickly noticed in Wojtyła the pastor who was able to meet the challenge of the anti-religious Communist system in the most appropriate way. He was hosted in Cracow for the first time in 1963, and then the two met many times – in Vienna, Cracow or Rome – developing mutual trust and respect. Cardinal König, who in the 70s was recognized as the informal leader of German-speaking cardinals, spread among them the conviction of the exceptional charisma of the Metropolitan of Cracow. Karol Wojtyła had an opportunity to present himself to this group on many occasions, also personally, starting with his contribution to the Address of the Polish Bishops to the German Bishops in 1965. The last such opportunity was his participation in the official delegation of the Polish Episcopate when they visited

the Federal Republic of Germany on 20-25 September 1978. The natural leader of the delegation was of course Primate Wyszyński, but the Archbishop of Cracow, both in the talks with German bishops as well as in official speeches and sermons e.g. in Fulda, Cologne, Munich, and Dachau, could again show his skill as an excellent spokesman for dialogue and reconciliation.

The visit in Germany took place during the short pontificate of John Paul I. Wojtyła had already taken part in the conclave. The news of the death of the 81-year-old Paul VI reached the Metropolitan of Cracow on 6 August, when he was on vacation with his friends in the Bieszczady Mountains in southeastern Poland. On 11 August he traveled to Rome, together with Cardinal Wyszyński, to celebrate the burial of the Pope and to elect his successor. On 25 August, together with 110 other members of the Cardinals' College eligible to take part in the conclave (Paul VI had barred the cardinals who were over 80 from electing the Pope), Wojtyła entered the Sistine Chapel. Now, cut off from the world, they were to pray for the inspiration of the Holy Spirit and vote. Unexpectedly quickly – already in the fourth round of voting – one candidate received the required majority of two thirds of the votes. He turned out to be the very modest, shy and inconspicuous (just 160 cm tall) Patriarch of Venice, Albino Luciani. As a sign of respect for two of his predecessors, John XXIII and Paul VI, the new Pope took the name of John Paul I. Due to his cheerful disposition, he was nicknamed the "Smiling Pope", from the very first hours following his election.

Although according to the internal rules the conclave participants have to keep the details of the Pope electoral process secret, the unofficial report of the Dean of the College of Cardinals, Carl Confalonieri, revealed that already this election brought the Cardinal of Cracow several votes. When he returned to Poland from the conclave, he felt a relief. He wanted to complete the Synod of the Archdiocese, as well as prepare the jubilee celebration of 900 years of the martyrdom of St Stanislaus. He was to return to his regular duties for good following the visit in Germany.

On 28 September 20 years had passed from his nomination for bishop. He did not organize any official celebration of the anniversary. He traveled to the Shrine of Kalwaria Zebrzydowska, and in the evening he said mass at Wawel Cathedral in front of the miraculous crucifix of Queen Jadwiga. After the mass he managed to open the new Cathedral Museum. The next day, after the mass which he had celebrated at 7 am as usual, he went down to breakfast only to see his driver rushing into the dining room with the news just heard on the radio – John Paul I had died. In human terms, this Pope, not even 66 years of age when elected, could have run the Church for a long time, leading it to the threshold of the new millennium. We do not know what the Church would have been like when led by his hand. We do know that then there would have been no John Paul II. Providence apparently decided otherwise. Following 33 days of the pontificate, the ill heart of the Patriarch of Venice did not endure the burden that had been put upon him so unexpectedly.

It was a great shock to Cardinal Wojtyła, but he also received this as a sign of Providence. It was clear to many observers in those days that the future Pope was internally moved. Did he realize back then that this sign concerned him personally, that it was him who was to lead the Church into the new millennium? 15 years earlier, when talking to his friends still at the Kanonicza flat, in response to Professor Mitkowski's comment that the friends saw in their bishop a legal successor to one of the Apostles, Karol Wojtyła smiled and said: "This is true, but I don't know which one." Several months later, in December 1963, he had an opportunity to meditate and pray on the Rock of St Peter's Primacy overlooking Lake Gennesaret. Could he then have imagined that he would be called to follow in the footsteps of the first among the Apostles? He started receiving such wishes af-

The Metropolitan of Cracow bids farewell to his collaborators before departing for the conclave

Before departure for Rome, Cardinal Wojtyła consecrates the newly opened Cathedral Museum at Wawel

After the opening (28 September 1978) he meets the nestor of Cracow museologists Karol Estreicher (in the center)

*Cardinal Wojtyła talking to the "smiling Pope"
– John Paul I*

*Metropolitan of Cracow accompanied by his Vatican friend, Bishop
Andrzej Deskur (in the church at Mistrzejowice, 1974)*

ter he had been nominated cardinal. Again, in human terms it was totally unlikely – how could a young bishop "from a far country" have counted on becoming the Pope? To the scholars and experts in Church matters, this kind of expectation could only have seemed an expression of great naiveté, just like the wish that he would become Pope, which the cardinal heard on the Assumption Day, 15 August 1967, during his visit to the Shrine of Our Lady at Ludźmierz, from a young girl who handed him flowers.

Eleven years later, some friends of the Metropolitan of Cracow took this possibility into account quite seriously. One of them, Fr. Mieczysław Maliński, told Cardinal Wojtyła about it just before the August conclave. They met at the Polish College in Rome. He put forward quite rational arguments in favor of Wojtyła's election: "If the Italians do not have their own candidate, then the cardinals are going to vote for a foreigner. And if it is to be a foreigner, then he will surely not be American, since Italians do not want the Vatican to become another American state. He will not be German as the history is still too vivid for anyone to dare to vote for a German. He will not be French, as Italians would be afraid of the Vatican becoming too French. It may only be a cardinal from a small country." When the future pontiff still objected: "Why does it have to be Wojtyła?", his persistent friend continued to argue in this manner: He is a pastor, not a Church official. He is the man of the "golden middle" – does not represent either of the extreme wings of the world's episcopate, which struggle with each other, he is neither a progressive nor a conservative "integrist." He was a representative of the Polish Church,

which under the lead of Primate Wyszyński had shown the great capacity to withstand the Communist challenge, and at the same time had not experienced the post-Council crisis, unlike many other local Churches. "Americans like you, for example through Cardinal John Król from Philadelphia. Germans like you through Höffner from Cologne and Austrians like you through König from Vienna. African bishops flocked to you at the Synod. Latin American bishops like you too. What else would you want?"

The Metropolitan of Cracow did not want anything, and in August 1978 he did not believe in these auguries and arguments. It was not Fr. Maliński who was right, but rather Primate Wyszyński, who consistently believed that the Pope would traditionally be Italian. When John Paul I unexpectedly died, however, both the speculations presented by Fr. Maliński and the tangible evidence of the votes Wojtyła received at the conclave in August must have made the cardinal wake up to the possibility of his new calling. On 30 September, when he visited the parish of Divine Providence in Bielsko-Biała, a terrible thunderstorm broke out. He must have experienced something unusual then – he even mentioned that when in Rome, just before his election. When in the evening of 1 October he celebrated the mass for the soul of John Paul I in St Mary's Basilica in Cracow, he was visibly moved. Krystyna Litewkowa, daughter of Wojtyła's mathematics teacher back in the Wadowice secondary school, had brought a letter from her father to the cardinal and wondered if she should not postpone delivering it until the cardinal returned from the new conclave. After the mass she had no doubt any longer – the

Last photograph of Cardinal Wojtyła at Wawel
(28 September 1978)

Primate Stefan Wyszyński pays homage to John Paul II during
the inauguration of the pontificate

cardinal was clearly bidding farewell to Cracow and Poland and she had to hand in the letter right away. Fr. Andrzej Bardecki had a similar impression. He met the Metropolitan after the mass, in the sacristy of the basilica. Just like his friends from the Catholic weekly *Tygodnik Powszechny*, he did not even dare to think that the cardinal of Cracow could be elected Pope. It seemed to him that he knew the life of the Church too well to delude himself with such dreams. But he too, when asked by the cardinal to say goodbye on his behalf to his close friends whom Wojtyła had failed to meet before his departure for Rome, sensed something unusual in his behavior.

On 2 October Cardinal Wojtyła and Primate Wyszyński flew to Rome again. The Cracow Metropolitan stayed at the Polish College again. Here the tension was relieved by the then Rector of the College, Fr. Józef Michalik, who tried to persuade his guest from Cracow: "Can you please allow them to elect you, Cardinal?" Wojtyła would jokingly reply: "You see, our Primate does not agree" (Cardinal Wyszyński was convinced that the Pope could only be Italian). Rector Michalik would insist: "If you allow them to elect you, we will finally have the elevator installed in our College." When 12 months later, on the first anniversary of his election, John Paul II visited the Polish College, he was quick to remind the priests who gathered to welcome him of this conversation: "Your Rector had told me to allow them to elect me. I did, but in your College there is still no sign of the elevator." Fr.

Michalik then asked him directly, and quite seriously, whether he had had any premonitions before the conclave. John Paul II replied: "When Andrzej was hit so suddenly, I shuddered." He referred to his closest friend at the Vatican, Bishop Andrzej Deskur. On 13 October, one day before the cardinals were locked *cum clave*, Bishop Deskur had suffered an extensive stroke. Some of the media even prematurely claimed that he had died. Until that day Bishop Deskur, the influential Chairman of the Pontifical Council for Social Communications, had indefatigably organized a long series of meetings of important cardinals from the Roman Curia, as well as those from outside Italy (e.g. American cardinals) with the Metropolitan of Cracow, running a kind of election campaign. The sudden grave illness of Bishop Deskur, who had attempted to bring about the election of the Cracow Metropolitan using "human means," might have been interpreted by Cardinal Wojtyła as a sign of Providence that it regarded the decision of the conclave as part of its own jurisdiction.

He was aware of the fact that the raising to the highest position in the Church was also the most difficult service, incomparable with any other, a kind of imprisonment for the sake of immense obligation. He expressed this conviction in the stirring sermon delivered at the mass for John Paul I which was celebrated in the Polish church of St Stanislaus in Rome, a week before the conclave. Referring to the text of St John's Gospel on the calling of Peter, he made clear his nearly mystical understanding of the nature of the Papacy: "Christ asks the man he wants to follow him the way he had asked Simon: 'Do you love me more than these?' Then the human heart must shudder. And so shuddered the heart of Peter and of Cardinal Albino Luciani before he took the name of John Paul I. The human heart must then shudder, as this question implies the request: You must love! You must love more than others if the entire sheepfold is to be entrusted to you ... The text of St John's Gospel continues. Christ then says these mysterious words and addresses them to Peter: 'When you were younger, you used to dress yourself and go where you wanted; but when you grow old, you will stretch out your hands, and someone else will dress you and lead you where you do not want to go.' ... Christ's command: 'Follow me' has a double meaning. It is a call for service and it is a call for death."

Even in the simplest understanding of this, the taking over of St Peter's office indeed meant the call for "death" – the radical loosening of the attachment which linked the Pope with his hitherto life, environment, beloved people, beloved places. This concerned the Pope "from a far country" all the more. He had to give himself completely to the new duties with regard to the entire world. He had to adopt new names – as if to signify that Karol Wojtyła had died and John Paul II was born. This was to happen on 16 October.

The conclave had started two days earlier. Cardinal Wojtyła nearly missed the official opening as he was stuck in a traffic jam on Roman streets riding from the Gemelli Hospital where he visited Bishop Deskur who was still in a coma. After the voting on Sunday 15 October which did not bring the majority as a result of the split in the Italian votes, the number of votes supporting Cardinal Wojtyła started to rise dramatically the following morning. His rector from the time of the Belgian College 30 years before and now Cardinal Maximilian de Fürstenberg approached the Metropolitan of Cracow and said: *Dominus adest et vocat te* – "The Lord is here and is calling you." John Paul II remembered these moving words and recalled them years later in his personal recollection of that day. Soon Cardinal Wyszyński came to him. Now he believed that his younger fellow bishop from Cracow could indeed be elected Pope. He reminded Wojtyła of the scene from the novel *Quo Vadis* by Sienkiewicz, when Christ stops Peter who is fleeing from Rome. Wyszyński called upon Wojtyła:

John Paul II, strongly holding the cross, calls on the world to "open the doors for Christ"

Cardinals line up to pay homage and express their allegiance to the new Pope

John Paul II

"Accept this election and this cross which goes along with it!"

After the results of the eighth round of voting were counted (the press speculations had it that Cardinal Wojtyła received 99 out of 111 votes) around 5:15 p.m., Cardinal Jean Villot, who was in charge of the conclave, stood in front of the pulpit of the Cracow Metropolitan and asked him: "Do you accept your canonical election as Supreme Pontiff? Cardinal Wojtyła answered: "In obedience of faith to Christ my Lord, trusting the Mother of Christ and the Church, aware of all difficulties – I accept. "

One hour later the white smoke rose above the Sistine Chapel. The Church was to discover that it had a new shepherd. The choice of the Holy Spirit, who had spoken through the conclave, and the name he had adopted were revealed to the faithful gathered at St Peter's Square by Cardinal Felici. At the same time Karol Wojtyła tried on the largest of the three white robes prepared for the new Pope. At 7:20 p.m. he appeared before the Romans and pilgrims from across the globe who waited for the new Holy Father. He

was already John Paul II – these names he adopted out of respect for his predecessors, John XXIII and Paul VI, as well as "to fulfill the inheritance of hope" left by the short pontificate of John Paul I.

Agencies of the entire globe had been reporting the news of his election for the last hour. Not all of his closest associates reacted with joy. They were worried about their beloved friend, whose new burden could crush him like it had crushed his predecessor. Professor Stanisław Nagy was in Lublin at the time. Fr. Tadeusz Styczeń, the successor of Karol Wojtyła as head of the Chair of Ethics at the Catholic University, rushed into his room and embraced him sharing the information he had heard on the radio and weeping. In Warsaw, in the flat of Professor Stefan Świeżawski, who had predicted Wojtyła's election back in 1974, the family were worried: "This man is now going to struggle!" spontaneously cried out Maria Świeżawska.

A completely different kind of worry crept into the minds of the then rulers of Poland. Indeed they heard the news earlier then others. Halina Królikiewiczówna-Kwiatkowska recollects that she had learnt about the election of her friend from school and underground theatre before the news

was broadcast by the Polish Radio. She was then doing something in the kitchen. Telephone rang and the great actor, Tadeusz Łomnicki called: "Listen, my congratulations. Your friend has become Pope." Łomnicki was then a member of the Central Committee of the Polish ruling party – he was in the position to know. When John Paul II was walking onto the balcony of St Peter's Basilica, cars with the party's secretaries started arriving at the edifice of the Central Committee in Warsaw. "Habemus flopam" – this is how they could have paraphrased the joyful words of Cardinal Felici. They knew Karol Wojtyła well enough by now. They realized that the one they so naively and clumsily tried to set against Primate Wyszyński turned out an even more fearsome opponent for them. Some even tried to console one another that perhaps this was even better as he now had no chance to become the Primate! The prevailing mood among the Communist "elite" was best expressed, however, by the Secretary Stefan Olszowski, who said at the meeting: "Now this Wojtyła is going to make our lives hell."

The symptoms of this could be seen right away. In the evening of 16 October 1978, the spontaneous carnival of joy swept through Poland. People took to the streets, sang hymns and congratulated one another. They rushed to churches in order to thank God for the election which they universally regarded as a sign of hope for their country and confirmation of their own national and Catholic identity. Cracow lost a great Metropolitan, but the world gained the Polish Pope. And this was what most Poles were proud of. They started recalling the forgotten prophecies of the poets: the poem by Konstanty Ildefons Gałczyński of 1939, which predicted "the new papacy like an oak which spreads by the Polish oak" or an extract from *Forefathers' Eve* (*Dziady*) part 3 by Adam Mickiewicz (1832), where the poet prophesied:

Behold the Vicar of Freedom on earth!
He will build the power of
His Church!
Risen above peoples and kings,
On three crowns he stands, and no crown
he bears:
His life – pains of pains,
His title – people of peoples.

The truly prophetic poem by Juliusz Słowacki from 1848/49 gained the greatest popularity, however:

Amidst discord God rings a huge bell
For the Slav Pope he opens the throne ...
He will share love, as the mighty share arms
He will carry the power of sacraments
Having taken the world by the hand...

A new stage began in the life of Karol Wojtyła. This was a new chapter in the history of Poland too – and what is the most significant – a new chapter in the history of the Catholic Church.

CHAPTER VIII
Open the doors for Christ!

On Sunday 22 October 1978, the new pontificate was solemnly inaugurated. The very description of the Pope's office as pontificate refers to the title "*Pontifex maximus*" (Supreme Priest) used back in ancient Rome. Literally *pontifex* meant the builder of bridges, thus the pontificate is the arduous raising of bridges by the successors of St Peter which are to unite peo-

ple – the followers of Christ in one Church and thus unite them with their Master and Teacher. The new successor of St Peter, the 264th Bishop of Rome, knew well that if bridges were to be built between people and God, the walls separating them had to be demolished first. And so many of them had been built in the 20th century.

He started from eliminating the wall which separated himself from other people. During the inaugural mass he did away with the awe-inspiring custom of the Pope being paraded in a litter above the heads of the crowd. He also renounced the coronation with a triple crown – the tiara, symbolizing the triple power of the Pope: the pastor, the teacher (prophet) and the king. By no means did he renounce the service of the pastor, teacher and ruler of the Church; he wanted to emphasize clearly,

however, that it is a service and not a proud elevation.

Following the prayer at the tomb of St Peter he led the procession of 112 cardinals to the square in front the Basilica. The Holy Mass began with the act of homage paid to the new Pope by the cardinals – his closest aides. Following the oldest cardinal, Carlo Gonfalonieri, the Pope was approached by the Primate of Poland Cardinal Wyszyński. When he knelt to kiss the ring of the successor of St Peter, the Pope rose from his throne, embraced the 78-year-old Primate and raising him from his knees he also kissed his hand. Thus, he publicly paid homage to the great spiritual leader

Thanksgiving service celebrated next to Wawel Cathedral in the evening of 16 October 1978

Sistine Chapel – the election venue

of the Polish Church, so that the entire world, which then focused attention on St Peter's Square, could see it. Just like Cardinal Wyszyński in Poland tried to pull down walls behind which the Communist authorities tried to enclose the Church and isolate people from one another, now his long-lasting collaborator from Cracow wished to extend this task to his new global diocese. In the homily delivered during the inaugural mass he formulated the first appeal and "motto" of his pontificate: "Do not be afraid! Open wide the doors for Christ. To his saving power open the boundaries of States, economic and political systems, the vast fields of culture, civilization and development. Do not be afraid. Christ knows 'what is in man'. He alone knows it."

The new Pope wanted to demolish the walls of the 20th century with the assistance of his Holy Patron, the devotion to whom he showed when choosing the emblem for his pontificate. It was basically the same emblem which he had once adopted as Bishop of Cracow: the Cross and under its right beam the letter M symbolizing Virgin Mary. His motto was a brief prayer to Our Lady: "*Totus Tuus*" – "I am all yours". The only novelty in comparison with the former emblem were the keys of St Peter – the symbols of the Papal power – now placed in the background. The retaining of the emblem was not only the symbol of his Marian devotion, but also the sign of his attachment to the time of his pastoral service to the Cracow Archdiocese. He movingly referred to this on 23 October during a special audience for the Poles, who arrived for his inauguration in their numbers: "It is not easy for me to decide not to return to my homeland, to the blooming meadows, to golden wheat fields, to peaks and valleys, to lakes and rivers, to the beloved people, to the Royal City of Cracow," he shared his longing with his countrymen.

Nothing could cut him off from Poland, however. Now it was Poland that mustered what was best in it and gathered around the Pope. And he passed this on to the world. During his first Christmas in Rome, John Paul II was accompanied by a large group of friends from Cracow. They sang carols together. As Fr. Bardecki, who was present then, recalls, the Pope intoned a highlanders' carol and improvised its last stanza in verse: "And here we sit caroling, caroling, and we do not understand to what kind of cottage we have come." Indeed, the faithful in many countries of the world were soon to find out that this Pope liked singing and could improvise. Although he spoke so

John Paul II in the courtyard of the Catholic University, facing the monument commemorating the scene of Cardinal Wyszyński paying homage to the new Pope in Rome

John Paul II in the grotto of Our Lady's Revelation in Lourdes, thanking her for protecting his ministry to the Church

many languages, he sang best in Polish as was discovered e.g. by New Yorkers, who gathered for the Pontifical Mass in Central Park in October 1995 or inhabitants of Lviv in June 2001, not to mention the Poles who heard him sing so many times.

The route of his first trip outside of Rome was not selected at random – he went to the shrine of Our Lady in Mentorella. The shrine is in charge of the friars from the Order of Resurrection, founded in the mid-19th century by Polish emigrants who wanted to link the struggle for the independence of Poland with a religious revival. The sermon on the love of your country, written by the founder of the order Father Hieronim Kajsiewicz, was once recited by the young seminarian Wojtyła at the official ceremony organized to celebrate the nomination of Archbishop of Cracow, Prince Sapieha, as cardinal. Now – as John Paul II – he arrived in Mentorella in order to pray to the Holy Patron of the shrine to extend her care over his pontificate. He also wished to emphasize that "prayer is the first task of the Pope and the first condition of his service in the Church." Indeed, prayer, just like before he had assumed St Peter's office, and perhaps even more intensively, filled his life more than anything else.

The outer signs of the intensive course of this pontificate were the Pope's pilgrimages. No Pope ever before had traveled so much around the world. No Pope ever before had personally met so many millions of the faithful. From the time when Pius VI visited Vienna in 1782, nearly two centuries had passed until Paul VI decided to resume the foreign travels, now undertaken not in order to pursue political and diplomatic objectives but purely pastoral ones. He undertook nine pilgrimages stretching from the Holy Land to Australia. John Paul II much intensified his pastoral mobility. The "outing" to Mentorella by helicopter a week after the inauguration was the first sign of his mobility. This Pope did not allow himself to be locked up in the Vatican. In the years that followed he covered nearly one million kilometers in over 100 apostolic voyages. This proved to be the simplest method to shorten the traditional distance which separated the office of the Pope from the world. He traveled indefatigably in order to open the doors for Christ.

The goal of his first apostolic voyage was Mexico. Here the doors were slammed shut. Mexico, ruled for the entire 20th century by one extremely anticlerical party, had been the area of particularly ruthless

John Paul II wearing a Mexican hat during his first visit to Latin America

Preparations for the visit of the Holy Father in his homeland: construction of the altar at the Victory Square in Warsaw

John Paul II walks down to the airport in Poland (followed by Primate Wyszyński, Cardinal Casaroli and Fr. Dziwisz)

In the window of "his" Archbishops' Palace in Cracow, next to his successor at Wawel Cathedral – Cardinal Franciszek Macharski

persecution of the Catholics already in the interwar period: they were murdered in their thousands for their faith and adherence to the Church. In the 1970s the active persecutions were no longer pursued, but it was still forbidden to organize public religious meetings outside of churches, and priests' cassocks as well as the habits of the religious were banned – and the country was 90% Catholic, just like Poland! The Pope wished to visit the Shrine of Our Lady of Guadalupe, famous in both Americas; he also wanted to take part in the Conference of the Latin American Episcopate. He knew that it was here, in Latin America, that the center of world Catholicism had now shifted – it was here that nearly one in two Catholics resided. He thus wished to be with them and encourage them. The President of Mexico permitted the Pope to come, although under one humiliating condition – the Pope could not be received as head of state, but as a regular visitor who had to submit his passport and visa. John Paul II did not hesitate even for a moment.

Caesar was to comment on his great victory in Gaul with the brief words: I came, I saw, I conquered. King Jan III Sobieski paraphrased this saying after his victory in the Battle of Vienna of 1683: I came, I saw, and God conquered. It seems that John Paul II could use these famous words as the true motto of numerous among his pilgrimages, and certainly to the first one, although the motto could perhaps be slightly rephrased again: I came, I was noticed, God conquered. He knew from his experiences with hundreds of thousands of the faithful at the Jasna Góra shrine how powerful was the direct contact with crowds of people who crave for the word and testimony of a real person. Now he could

count on this power even more, as he represented the office of the Vicar of Christ on Earth.

Following a brief visit of the Pope in the Dominican Republic, on 26 January 1979 his plane of the Italian Alitalia Airlines landed at the airport in Mexico City. John Paul II knelt and kissed the ground. Millions of Mexicans took to the streets to see him pass. And the barriers collapsed. The doors could no longer be slammed to Christ in Mexico. The room for the faith in Him was found even in the public sphere. The openness, smile, and unique joy which stemmed from the sense of liberating others spiritually emanated from the Pope during the pilgrimage. He understood the folk spirit of Mexican religion, just as he understood and appreciated the Polish "folk Catholicism," both of which sought special consolation in Our Lady to deal with problems and poverty they faced every day. In contrast to many "intellectuals", John Paul II never disregarded this form of religious experience, and was able to share it, that is why he found common ground with crowds of the faithful who wished to meet him. This is what happened in Guadalupe and in Puebla, as well as during the meeting with half a million of impoverished Indians from Chiapas.

John Paul II tried to restore their dignity and self-respect which had been ruined by poverty, and at the same time he warned them against the temptation of Communist revolution – the use of violence when struggling for justice. This was his serious worry as the liberation theology movement developed rapidly in Latin America, declaring the need for the Church to become politically involved and side with socialism against capitalism. The Pope decisively rejected the vision of "Christ holding a gun." He openly condemned the unjust division of goods, which had left so many people in Latin America and the entire Third World in dire poverty. In his public messages he called for reforms which would change this state of affairs, but he firmly warned the people against a revolution as a way of seeking justice. He was well aware of the results this method would bring – he knew them from Eastern Europe. And although he was not in a position to enforce the necessary reforms in one apostolic voyage, he was not in a position to convert everyone who went astray onto the "shining path" of anarchic revolution, he left the country he visited with a new sense of hope. And the majority of the Mexicans sensed it, the evidence of which was the highly original way this largest city in the world bade farewell to John Paul II. Flying away from Ciudad Mexico, the Pope saw a strange glare – it was hundreds of thousands of Mexicans holding hand mirrors in their hands which reflected the sun rays.

Back in the plane, John Paul II already thought of his next apostolic voyage – to his homeland. There too he was to pull down walls and restore hope. Asked about it on his return flight by the only Polish journalist present there, Marek Skwarnicki, he explained that the recollection of history would be the key to the new pilgrimage: "It will be about history. Our Polish history."

The Polish authorities realized that this time they could not prevent the Pope from coming (as they did in the case of Paul VI). The growing economic crisis more and more clearly threatened with the outburst of public discontent. The refusal to let the Polish Pope visit his homeland could have turned into a spark which would have triggered the explosion. The First Secretary of the party, Edward Gierek, had to present these arguments to his Russian superior, Leonid Brezhnev, who in turn tried to persuade him through the phone that "Gomułka was a better Communist, as he did not receive the Pope [Paul VI] in Poland – and the world did not collapse." The Soviet Minister of Foreign Affairs, Andrei Gromyko, traveled to the Vatican to probe the intentions of John Paul II before his visit to Poland. The infamous "Mister Niet," veteran of the Soviet diplomacy, had met popes – John XXIII and Paul VI – before in his long career. Now, during the meeting on 23 January 1979, there was no way he could deceive this Pope with regard to the situation of the Church in the countries which were ruled by Communists. Gromyko just confirmed his suspicions that he had to deal with a really fearsome opponent.

The Kremlin monitored the consecutive gestures of the new Pope with anxiety, as they testified forcefully that he did not just want to encourage his own countrymen, but he intended to awaken faith and dignity of nations throughout the Communist-ruled East-Central Europe. The KGB noted that already on the day following his inauguration, the Pope ordered two priests from Cracow to go to Vilnius with his cardinal's cap (*zuchetto*) and leave it there as a votive offering to Our Lady of Ostra Brama. The Kremlin was even more irritated by the decision of John Paul II to nominate Fr. Audrys Backis, Lithuanian emigrant and son of the last ambassador of independent Lithuania in Paris, as Undersecretary of State responsible for the relations with Eastern Europe. The Polish Pope manifested his solidarity with the persecuted Catholic Church in Lithuania. A month after his inauguration he also met Cardinal Josyf Slipyj, the aged Metropolitan of the Byzantine-Ukrainian (Uniate) Church, made totally illegal in the

The Pope (again accompanied by Archbishop Macharski) meets the children from his former Archdiocese

The Holy Father in Warsaw before the Mass at Victory Square

John Paul II prays in the Auschwitz concentration camp

The Pope greets Polish war veterans in Częstochowa

John Paul II at home – the Błonia meadow in Cracow

Soviet Union. Created in the late 16th century as a result of the Union of Brest, the Church attracted those Christians who retained most of the Orthodox rite in liturgy, but they recognized the spiritual authority of Rome. Treated with particular ruthlessness by Moscow, the Church was persecuted as a rival to Orthodoxy even back in Tsarist times. In the Communist system it became victim of physical extermination as the main source of cultural and national identity for millions of Ukrainians. Cardinal Slipyj, having spent 17 years in Soviet labor camps, was a living symbol of the Church's martyrdom. John Paul II made sure to support the clandestine Ukrainian church by soon nominating Myrosław Lubachivski to the post of assistant and successor to Cardinal Slipyj as Archbishop of Lviv in March 1980.

The Pope also tried to encourage the Churches of Poland's southern neighbors to be more active. Already in December 1978 he wrote a special letter to the Bishops of Hungary. At this and other occasions he admonished them to fight more boldly for the right of the Church to run religious instruction classes. He reputedly told the Primate of Hungary Laszlo Lékai, who tended to seek compromise with Communists, that he would visit Hungary when the Primate had learned how to "bang the table with his fist." In March 1979 John Paul II sent a special letter to Czechs and Slovaks, which was on the occasion of the 250th anniversary of the canonizing of St John Nepomuk, the martyr of their Church who courageously opposed the secular authority. He now called on Poland's neighbors to remain faithful to religion with similar courage and not to yield to persecution, as was the case of the entire movement of "Pacem in Terris" priests, who actually served the needs of the Communist state. The leader of the Church in Czechoslovakia, Cardinal František Tomášek, encouraged with the unambiguous support of the Pope, drew closer to the secular anti-Communist opposition and hardened his own position with regard to the relations with the authorities.

The visit of John Paul II in Poland confirmed the worst nightmares of the Kremlin. The doors to Eastern Europe had now been opened by the Pope for good – and it was no use trying to slam them shut again. The first apostolic voyage to Poland went through Poland as air-clearing thunderstorm. Warsaw, Gniezno, Jasna Góra, Cracow, Kalwaria Zebrzydowska, Wadowice, Auschwitz-Birkenau, Nowy Targ, Mogiła

The Pope and Primate Stefan Wyszyński pay tribute to the heroes of Polish history at the Tomb to the Unknown Soldier in Warsaw

Riding the "Papamobile" through Częstochowa

Monastery in the workers' district of Nowa Huta and finally the Błonia meadow of Cracow. These stations of the nine-day-long pilgrimage (2–10 June 1979) linked the places most symbolic for the faith and history of the Polish nation with those most dear to the heart of John Paul II.

Following the meeting with Edward Gierek, the official host on the part of the state, in the palace of Belweder, the first great moment of the pilgrimage was the Holy Mass celebrated at Plac Zwycięstwa (Victory Square) in Warsaw. In his homily, the Pope defended the dignity of the nation, which he described as "a special community, most strongly connected with the family, most important in man's spiritual history." The dignity and greatness of the Polish nation is an inseparable part of its history, which is symbolized by the nearby Tomb of the Unknown Soldier. The Pope also forcibly stated: "It is not possible to understand the history of the Polish nation – so astonishing, but also so terribly difficult – without Christ." He objected to falsifying the historical identity and culture of the Poles by trying to wipe out the thousand years of Christianity from it. At the end he appealed for the revival of Christian inspiration in the life of the Poles in these memorable words: "Let Your Spirit descend! Let Your Spirit descend! And renew the face of the earth, the face of this land! Amen."

In Gniezno, the cradle of the Polish state, John Paul II broadened the goal of his pilgrimage. He did not strive at renewing the Polish land only. He emphasized the presence of Christianity in the life of the nations of the whole of Eastern Europe. He also delivered the message of reconciliation towards Orthodox Russia. He called on the three nations which inherited its tradition: the Russians, Ukrainians and Belorussians, to remember their Christian roots at the threshold of the millennium of Christianity in Kiev (in 988). He also pointed out the affiliation of "our Lithuanian brothers" with Western tradition. He did not forget about Czechs, Slovaks, Croatians, Serbs, Bulgarians, or even about the Lusatians living in the German Democratic Republic. The Slavic Pope called on all of them to "return towards the Cross and Resurrection." For the Soviet Union who fought religion and all the "devolutionary" nationalist movements, as well as for the whole Communist bloc, the sermon of John Paul II delivered in the meadow of Gniezno was an open challenge.

John Paul II referred to the great role of the Church in the life of the Polish nation again when on Jasna Góra: "here we

The Pope at Jasna Góra

have always been free." In Auschwitz he prayed in the cell of Father Maximilian Maria Kolbe, who offered his life there for his neighbor. He also remembered the Carmelitan nun – Mother Teresa Benedicta of the Cross, or the Jewish convert Edith Stein – who was tortured to death there. He was to declare both Saints of the Catholic Church as models of the Christian attitude towards death. Visiting the former Birkenau camp, John Paul II stopped at the plaque which commemorated the martyrdom of the Jews as "the nation whose sons and daughters were destined for total extermination." He also reflected on the Russian victims in this camp and during the whole Second World War. Naturally, he also stopped at the Polish plaque and took this opportunity to restate the right of nations "to exist, to enjoy freedom and independence, and to have their own culture and proper development," which "insane ideologies" attempt to take away from them.

Wadowice, Kalwaria and Nowy Targ were the places to which the Pope returned as if back home – to his beloved mountains, to the first paths he traveled along as a pilgrim. The same was true about Cracow, of course. There he was welcomed most cordially by his successor as metropolitan of Cracow, Archbishop Franciszek Macharski, the long-lasting friend and companion of his skiing trips into the mountains. There he visited the tomb of his parents in the Rakowice Cemetery, he met his friends from school and university, from the Rhapsodic Theatre, from St Florian's academic pastoral. There in an extraordinary atmosphere, which all the participants will certainly remember until the end of their days, he met young people at the Skałka Monastery. In the Cistercian Abbey of Mogiła, located in the industrial district of Nowa Huta, he could now recall the struggle for the cross, for the presence of the Church among the workers.

The last stage of the pilgrimage, which summarized its entire program and significance, was the Holy Mass celebrated at the Błonia meadow in Cracow on 10 June. It attracted the congregation of two million – such a huge gathering of Poles, concentrated, prayerful and joyful at the same time, had never taken place before (nor perhaps ever after). Referring to the final session of the Archdiocesan Synod, devoted to the 900th anniversary of the martyrdom of St Stanislaus, the Pope reminded his countrymen that moral law is more important than constraints which the secular authorities try to develop against it. He

In Gniezno Cathedral together with Primate Wyszyński

Meeting the highlanders in Nowy Targ

called for courage to defend the law, for testimony to the faith. He considered the mass in Błonia as a reminder of the Sacrament of Confirmation – the sacrament of Christian courage. He seemed to administer this sacrament to the entire nation: "Before I depart from here, I would like to ask you to accept all this spiritual heritage whose name is Poland with faith, hope and love – those Christ injected in us in the holy baptism. I ask you never to doubt, nor grow tired nor become discouraged. I ask you not to cut off the roots from which we all have grown."

Not much time was necessary for the teaching to bear fruit. Poles believed again that they might constitute a community. They believed that they can fight for dignity – without resorting to violence. When in August 1980 a large photograph of John Paul II was put up on the metal fence of the Gdańsk Shipyard, it was difficult to have doubts as to the main source of inspiration for the Solidarity movement. The Holy Father followed the events of the summer 1980 with great interest, but also with a certain anxiety. He confided to Cardinal Deskur that he was afraid that this great movement of national revival might be crushed by the Communists in the same way that they had crushed the Polish Peasants' Party of Stanisław Mikołajczyk in 1945-46.

In the early December of 1980, Poland was threatened by Soviet military intervention. The Holy Father was informed about this by Zbigniew Brzeziński, the Polish-born National Security adviser to the President of the United States. Profesor Brzeziński thus remembers this dramatic moment: "I called the Pope to warn him and possibly give him an opportunity to intervene – in a way which he would find suitable – with western episcopates, which could in turn influence their governments to intervene with Brezhnev. ... I asked the Pope to give me his private telephone number so that I would not have to use the Vatican tele-

phone exchange. It turned out that the Pope had no private telephone number." John Paul II decided to write a personal letter to the head of the Soviet State, Leonid Brezhnev. The letter, dated 16 December 1980, has been revealed only recently in the biography of the Holy Father authored by George Weigel. In the balanced but strong words he called on the Soviet leader to relieve the tension around Poland. We do not know to what extent this appeal and to what extent other pressures brought to bear by the Pope on the world public opinion influenced the decision of the Kremlin. We know that the old men who ruled the Soviet Union finally rejected the plan of direct invasion of Poland, leaving the task of crushing Solidarity to their new favorite in the Polish Party – General Wojciech Jaruzelski.

There are many indications that the Kremlin decided to do away with John Paul II in any case. In January 1981 the Holy Father hosted the delegation of Solidarity headed by Lech Wałęsa. This was a moment of great joy for the Pope. He was happy that the workers' revolution was taking place without violence and he called on them to stay the way they were – so that Solidarity could remain the movement *about something, not against somebody*. The secret Soviet policy, however, had been aimed specifically *against him* already for over a year – a special directive to that effect had been in operation since 13 November 1979. The group who had approved the directive included Deputy Head of the KGB, Viktor Chebrikov, chief ideologist of the USSR – Mikhail Suslov, as well as the young secretary – Mikhail Gorbachev. All the Soviet media, the Soviet Academy of Sciences, as well as the allied parties subordinate to Moscow were to intensify the campaign aiming at discrediting the "policy of the Vatican." The Ministry of Foreign Affairs and the KGB (using separate means) were to persuade the world public opinion, including the Catholic opin-

Sermon at Gniezno addressed to Eastern Europeans

The "New Confirmation" of Poland at the Cracow Błonia meadow (10 June 1979)

ion, how "dangerous" the leadership of the new Pope in the Church was. The "Wojtyła syndrome" in the Communist bloc had been the subject of a special meeting of Central Committee secretaries from the whole Eastern Europe summoned to East Berlin already in July 1979. The meeting focused on propaganda and administrative methods which were to be undertaken to obstruct the religious revival.

A young Turkish terrorist, Mehmet Ali Agca, declared the intention to use completely different methods against the Pope. After he had escaped from prison he sent a letter to an Istanbul newspaper in which he expressed the will to assassinate John Paul II, if only this "Leader of All the Crusades" dared to set his foot on the Turkish soil. The Bishop of Rome and Patriarch of the West indeed intended to pay a visit to the Bishop of Constantinople and Patriarch of the East as a gesture which was to stimulate the revival of ecumenical dialogue between Catholicism and Orthodoxy. He arrived in Istanbul on the day of St Andrew the Apostle, the holy patron of the East. On 30 November 1979, during the Orthodox service he exchanged the kiss of peace with Patriarch of Dimitrios I. Agca had been at large for a week then.

On 13 May 1981 at 5 p.m., John Paul II started his weekly general audience on St Peter's Square. He stood in an open jeep, which slowly drove around the square. He was about to speak to the crowd. At 17.13 shots could be heard at St Peter's Square. Those who stood farther only noticed flocks of pigeons, residing in front of the Basilica, which suddenly took flight. Fr. Stanisław Dziwisz, who stood by the Pope as usual, noticed that the Holy Father had been shot. "Where?" he asked. John Paul II answered: "In my belly." He fell onto the arms of the priest and just kept repeating with absent eyes: "Mary, my Mother! Mary my Mother!" Fr. Dziwisz took the immediate decision to transport the Holy Father to the Gemelli Hospital, where he had a special room reserved for him. In spite of heavy traffic, the car with John Paul II, by then unconscious, reached the hospital in 8 minutes. The operation lasted five hours and 20 minutes. As a result of internal hemorrhage, the Pope lost over 60 percent of the blood. The 9-mm caliber shell which slid against a finger of the Pope's right hand, only narrowly missed the main artery, it also luckily missed the spine. The team of surgeons had to treat numerous internal wounds and cut out a section of the damaged intestine. The second shell just grazed the Pope's elbow.

The assassin – a professional killer, immediately arrested, could not understand how he could fail to kill the man when shooting from a distance of under six meters. Ali Agca was amazed, while the world was in shock and Poland was horrified. Four days after the attempt, when the Holy Father still lay in hospital, the Market Square in Cracow, the largest town square in central Europe, filled with tens of thousands of young people all dressed in white. They came to pray to God to save their countryman and to protest against evil. The sacrifice of blood sustained by John Paul II strengthened them. Evil did not triumph. The time was very sad, however. When John Paul II lay in hospital, Cardinal Wyszyński was dying in Warsaw. The Pope could bid farewell to the Great Primate only through the phone. Their last conversation took place on 25 May. The cardinal spoke in a broken voice: "Father ... suffering unites us... let us pray for each other. Mother of God is between us... She is the only hope ...."

John Paul II had no doubt that he owed his life to her. His Cracow friend, Professor Gabriel Turowski, immunologist, who watched over him in Rome throughout his convalescence, brought to his attention the fact that the assassination attempt was made exactly on the anniversary of Our Lady's appearance in Fatima of Portugal in 1917 (even minutes were right). From the three mysteries entrusted by Our Lady to three young shepherds, only Popes knew the third one. John Paul II revealed it to the public only in 2000 – it mentioned the assassination attempt of "the man in white" and his sacrifice of blood. On the anniversary of the attempt, the Pope took the shell which hit him to Fatima as a votive offering to Our Lady for saving his life.

After a brief trial before an Italian court, Agca was found guilty of the assassination attempt. He admitted that he had received his gun in Bulgaria. He refused to testify, however, on the motives and instigators of the crime. Sentenced to life imprisonment, he was released from an Italian prison in June 2000 (on several pleas made by John Paul II for clemency) and extradited to Turkey. Earlier the Pope had an opportunity to meet his would-be murderer personally – he visited him in prison in December 1983. The whole world saw pictures of the Turkish terrorist sitting bent next to the Holy Father. Fr. Andrzej Bardecki, who then stayed at the Vatican, together with Fr. Styczeń, asked the Pope the next day what it was that Agca was then telling him. On television the scene looked as if Agca was con-

Shots at St Peter's Square – Fr. Dziwisz supporting the wounded Pope

The White March: Cracow prays for the health of its Pope

John Paul II meets his would-be assassin

The Pope thanks Our Lady of Fatima for his miraculous delivery

John Paul II leaves the Gemelli Hospital following his recovery

fessing his sins. John Paul II explained that this was a misunderstanding. Agca was a very superstitious man. He was absolutely convinced that the perfectly prepared attempt had to succeed and he ultimately ascribed the failure to the intervention of the "goddess from Fatima." Terrified, he asked the Pope whether the "powerful goddess" might not chase him in revenge. The Holy Father consoled him that the "goddess" does not seek revenge as she loves all people.

For the Holy Father this was the entire mystery of the assassination attempt. He was completely uninterested in the possible instigators of the crime. As he said to Cardinal Deskur "What for? It is clear that it was done by the devil, and it is completely irrelevant whom he used to assist him." Further legal proceedings with regard to the attempt were resumed in 1982, when Agca started to testify holding Bulgarian security services (and indirectly their KGB principals) responsible, but they did not bring any final resolutions, although it was clear by now that Agca had been trained in Bulgaria.

In his long testimony, Agca first accused the Bulgarian security services of inspiring the attempt on the life of the Solidarity leader during his visit in Rome. When the preparations for this "operation" failed, they were to switch their attention to the person of the Pope. It seemed obvious that Bulgaria did not have a reason to wage a "private war" with John Paul II or Poland. The inspiration from Moscow was a natural hypothesis in this case. However, the trial of the collaborators of the Bulgarian security services captured in Rome did not bring any evidence in this regard, and the proceedings were discontinued in March 1986.

Agca renounced all his previous testimonies, although he did return to the KGB link in a private conversation with the Italian prosecutor Ferdinando Imposimato in 1997. On this account, Agca was trained in 1980 to become a professional assassin in a special camp run by the KGB in Syria, and only later handed in to Bulgarian security services, which were to organize the assassination attempt. We still do not know the true story.

The devil did not stop "the man in white," although he still struggled to slam the doors of Eastern Europe shut for Christ and for the message about liberating human dignity, which was brought by John Paul II in the first months of his pontificate. 13 May 1981 was followed by 13 December 1981, and the martial law introduced to crush Solidarity was a painful blow to John Paul II. Nonetheless, he remained an indefatigable builder of bridges above evil and hatred. He continued this work in the following years of his pastoral service to the Church.

CHAPTER IX
The Pilgrim of Freedom

John Paul II outlined the program of his pontificate already in his first encyclical *Redemptor hominis* (Redeemer of Man). Following the example of the Apostles, who sent letters to Christian communities in order to advise and encourage them, Bishops of Rome resumed that practice in the 18th century in a new form – that of encyclicals, or letters addressed to the world episcopate. John Paul II signed the first of his encyclicals on 4 March 1979. He published 14 of them altogether. The first one to some extent heralds all the following ones. It started by referring to the Jubilee of 2000 years from the birth of Christ. John Paul II regarded the preparations to the Jubilee, and most importantly the preparations of the Church to enter the new millennium, as his great task. The encyclical *Redemptor hominis* could be interpreted as a catalogue of issues which the Church had to face at the turn of the millennium. And so first of all the overcoming of the division of Christianity – the ecumenical dialogue which should be patient, but, as the Pontiff strongly emphasizes, "in no way does it or can it mean giving up or in any way diminishing the treasures of divine truth that the Church has constantly confessed and taught." Reflecting further on the mission of the Church in the contemporary world, John Paul II stressed its connection with the defense of "this freedom, which is the condition and basis for the human person's true dignity." He drew attention to various threats to that freedom posed by various ideological systems, which in fact violate human dignity. The Church should remain, as the Pope has put it, "the guardian of this freedom," since only by showing the link between freedom and moral responsibility, between freedom and the truth, it may help man who is lost in the contemporary world. The Church must first of all remind people of the love God the Redeemer has for them.

Freedom to be found in the truth and dignity and built on the Christian love for man was the message which John Paul II addressed not only to his own part of the world – East and Central Europe. His diocese was Rome as well as the entire world, and therefore the Pope took this message everywhere. Answering the question about the purpose of the unprecedented number and scope of his pilgrimages, he referred to his earlier experiences. Visiting parishes had always been high on his agenda. By receiving their bishop, the parish could better experience their unity and also develop a sense of belonging to a larger entity – the universal Church. In a conversation with a French journalist he expressed the opinion: "the more difficult the life of people, families, the world, the more important it is for the figure of the Good Shepherd to be

John Paul II talking to Sister Lucia dos Santos, the only surviving one of the three children who witnessed the revelation of Our Lady at Fatima in 1917

The Pope visits Zaire on his pilgrimage to Africa in 1985

John Paul II leans over the vision of the future created by the Japanese

John Paul II in New York's Central Park during his first pilgrimage to the United States

Cruising on Lake Togo during the Pope's pilgrimage to Africa in August 1985

present in the minds." The Pilgrim Pope resembled that figure: he gathered the sheep which were entrusted to him, and looked for those which had been lost. He also repeated the words of the greatest pilgrim among the Apostles, St Paul: "I long to see you, that I may share with you some spiritual gift so that you may be strengthened, that is, that you and I may be mutually encouraged by one another's faith, yours and mine." Everyone who observed the apostolic voyages of John Paul II understands how true these words are. The very presence of the Pope, the testimony of his faith obviously strengthened the con-

gregations. And at the same time, it was visible that the Holy Father himself was strengthened when meeting communities of the faithful that he visited. This was all the more the case when he was old and frail, and frequently tired, than at the beginning of his pontificate. Suffice it to mention his voice, which suddenly became strong and joyful when he engaged in a conversation and singing with young Ukrainians in the city of Lviv.

Mexico and Poland were followed by two other destinations of his pilgrimages – Ireland, one of the cradles of European Christianity, and the United States. The latter was one of the world's poles which the Pope addressed in his teaching – the pole of consumerist civilization, of man's over-

confidence in the possibilities offered by material goods and at the same time of the fear that the consequences of that attitude would turn against man. On the other hand, the North American Church displayed lively and spontaneous spirituality. In Boston, two million people turned out for the pontifical mass, the meeting in Philadelphia drew the crowd of one million, while in Chicago – half a million. In New York, the Pope, who rode into the Madison Square Garden meeting with young people to the accompaniment of the music from *Star Wars*, captivated all the hearts not only due to his charisma of a born showman, but also to the credibility of his unchanging message: you will reach maturity when you observe Christ and try to imitate him. In the homeland of the sexual revolution, the Pope did not hesitate to defend marital chastity as well as the life of the unborn which was destroyed by abortions.

As the pole of modernity, the North American Church was the place of unrest, which various secular ideologies tried to use to their own aims. During a meeting with nuns in Washington, John Paul II had to face demands of radical feminists. The advocate of this ideology, Sister Teresa Kane, worshipped by the media, demanded that John Paul permit women to be ordained. The Pope reminded her then that "Christ's love for you is far more important than your love for Christ." Love cannot be a slogan for the ideologies which in fact are hostile to other people or communities. Large American media companies, dominated by anti-religious attitudes and particularly unfriendly towards Catholicism, did not understand the Pope's words. In his defense of fundamental truths of the faith and Christian ethics, they saw "doctrinairism" and reproached the Pope for his lack of understanding for the demands of "progress." At the same time, however, they admitted that the visit was a great success of John Paul II. His direct contact with crowds of the faithful showed the power of the "pilgrimage" ministry of the Pope, even in modern America. This was confirmed by the next visits of John Paul II in the US in 1987 and 1995 (on the latter visit he addressed the UN in New York again, just like in 1979).

The power of papal influence became most visible during the World Youth Day celebrated in Denver, Colorado, in mid-August 1993. As usual, the media were keen to point out all possible difficulties both for the Pope and his hosts. If they were willing to write about something in positive terms, these were things like the Pope's hike in the Rocky Mountains, which he climbed in his white sneakers with golden laces offered him by a pair of teenagers. And yet, what was important was the fact that half a million people in Denver experienced something which the same media described later as the "Catholic Woodstock": a great day of joy, devoid of drugs and violence. The Pope preached what he had always preached – without any leniency. He set before the eyes of the youths, mainly coming from large American metropolises, the image of suffering Christ. His Passion is an example of "what human beings are capable of doing

The Pope in Nicaragua – struggling with the propaganda setting, in which the Communist rulers of the country tried to lock up his message

to others if their hearts are hardened and the light of their conscience is dimmed." This civilization of death, violence and cynicism, which his audience knew from television and everyday environment, should be opposed by the civilization of love. And young people from America took these words seriously and many of them put them into effect in their lives.

There is also another America, which is perhaps even more important for the future of the Church. This is Latin America, with nearly one half of all Catholics – at present almost half a billion people. Most of them had completely different problems than their rich brothers and sisters in the United States. Here the dramatic contrast between poverty and the pockets of wealth built at its expense seemed the

most urgent question to address. Hence came the temptation to treat the Church as a tool for social revolution, the temptation which John Paul II encountered already during his first apostolic voyage to Mexico. In 1983 the Pope stood face to face with the results of yielding to the temptation. In March that year he started his visit to Central America from Nicaragua. The country had been ruled by the Marxist regime of the "Sandinists" since they overthrew the right-wing dictatorship in 1979. The leader of the Church in Nicaragua, Archbishop Obando Bravo, had supported Sandinists in their struggle with the old corrupt regime until 1979. Gradually, however, he started criticizing the Marxist methods of the new government: restricting human rights and the freedom of the Church, censorship, brutal persecution of the opposition, deceitful propaganda and removing religious instruction from schools. The Sandinists, however, found supporters among the people of the Church – the fanatics of the revolutionary "liberation theology." Many priests, who frequently were members of the Jesuit Order, stood on the side of the Marxists and against their own Archbishop. A few of them even became ministers of the Sandinist government. Meanwhile, the Pope consistently maintained the ban on direct participation of members of the clergy in secular governments. The Sandinists even wanted to create their own "people's Church" and oppose it to the "Papal Church". Already during the welcome ceremony at the airport, John Paul II had to admonish the key spokesman of the "people's Church", Fr. Ernest Cardenal, who was Minister of Culture in the Sandinist government. The Pope only told him: "Settle your relations with the Church." During the Mass in the Nicaraguan capital, Sandinists showed the Pope what they were capable of. They organized a profanation of the Mass, unprecedented in all pilgrimages of the Pope. Sandinists installed a double amplifying system: one for the Pope and one for their own supporters who occupied the sectors closest to the Pope. When John Paul II started talking about the need to maintain the unity of the Church and calling on the priests in the government to resign and abandon Marxist ideology, then his loudspeakers were shut off, and the shouting of Sandinist agitators who chanted "People's power! and "People's Church!" was amplified instead. The Pope had to raise his voice in order to be heard among the faithful who were pushed to the back rows. It seemed

Enthusiasm for the Truth and its witness cannot be extinguished

A Pima Indian presents feathers of the American eagle to the Pope during the visit of John Paul II to Arizona in 1987

John Paul II at the UNO in October 1995, speaking in defense of the rights of nations

The Pope in Havana, hosted respectfully by Fidel Castro

the Sandinists triumphed as they managed to cause a scandal and jam most of the homily. The Pope's message reached this place too, however, and like in so many other places changed the reality. Lies and manipulations of the frightened regime were visible. And a few years later the "socialist experiment" in Nicaragua collapsed, just like the "people's Church."

John Paul II did not keep traveling to Latin America in order to side against the poor, who waited for bread and justice. He used his own experience from a country ruled by the Communists to teach them that the class struggle leads neither to justice nor to welfare. During each of the pilgrimages to Latin America he met the poorest, including groups of Indians, and always demanded for them not only the right to have the bare minimum, but also to enjoy relative welfare and respect for their dignity. From his first encyclical to the bull *Incarnationis Mysterium*, published at the outset of the Great Jubilee of 2000, from his first address to the UN in 1979 to the meeting with President George W. Bush in Castel Gandolfo in July 2001, John Paul II constantly appealed for a settlement to the problem of poverty on a global scale. He appealed to the richest countries of the "First World" to cancel the debts which lay heavy on poor countries of the Third World. He put forward his doctrine of social peace in a special encyclical, entitled *Sollicitudo rei socialis*, signed on 30 December 1987. There he criticized in strong terms the ongoing exploitation of Third World countries by economic powers. Too busy with the "Cold War" competition, the First and Second (Communist) World countries, the Western and Eastern blocs, were to pay more attention to the genuine problems of the countries of the poor South. At the same time, the Pope stressed that in order to enter the path of stable economic development the same Third World countries should first choose democracy as the foundation of their political system.

John Paul II visited the countries governed by Communists many times, and always took the opportunity to demand the restoration of human rights and release of opposition activists. This was particularly visible during several of his visits to Latin America, for example to Chile in April 1987. The country had been indeed saved from the Communist experiment, but from 1973 it was ruled by the ruthless dictatorship of General Augusto Pinochet. The general believed that he could run a healthy economy without the need to introduce democracy. John Paul II admonished him firmly, however: "People have the right to exercise civic freedoms, even if doing so they make mistakes." Yet, most importantly, the papal visit enabled the Chileans to acquire a new sense of community, which could again manifest itself publicly. Here too the Pope did not preach revolution but reconciliation. And again, his words, which reached millions of Chileans, soon bore fruit: 18 months after his visit the military authorities risked a national referendum – and they lost it. A year later, a civilian president, the leader of the Christian Democratic party, was democratically elected again.

In May 1988, the Pope visited the oldest dictatorship of Latin America – Paraguay, which since 1954 had been ruled by General Alfredo Stroessner. Every few years he confirmed his title to power in a fraudulent election. And so John Paul II spoke in support of the right for democratic opposition, whose representatives he wished to meet. Again he had the courage to speak in public about things which others had to be silent about: the right to freedom and justice, the need for the real participation of citizens in democratic procedures. Stroessner responded by making arrests among opposition activists and persecuting the Church. Several months later he was deposed, although true democracy did not come to Paraguay until some time later.

The last country in Latin America to host the Pope was Cuba. The visit took place only in January 1998. The Communist dictator, who had ruled the island for nearly 40 years, like many dictators before him, was ready to invite the Pope in the hope that the visit would not kill the regime in Cuba, but rather manifest its strength to the world. Taking into account the experience of Stroessner or Sandinists, however, Castro did not undertake any provocative actions against his guest. On the contrary, the old revolutionary showed great respect to the Pope – the only authority from whom he was able to accept criticism. John Paul II, as usual, did not focus on criticizing the regime, but on encouraging the community he had come to visit. This was his method of achieving "revolution" – the spiritual elevation of the nation. The Catholics there could for the first time leave their churches in order to demonstrate publicly their faith and their hope for freedom. During the mass at the Revolution Square in Havana, where the altar faced a huge portrait of Che Guevara – a symbol of militant Marxism, Castro was forced to listen to millions of his countrymen chanting "Libertad!", "Libertad!" in re-

The Pope sometimes put on national costumes of the countries he visited (Africa, 1988)

Meeting the youth of the world in Manila

action to the words of John Paul II. The seed of freedom, sowed by the pilgrimage of John Paul II, will surely rise in this beautiful island too.

This is what happened in Asia too, where many problems related to poverty, corrupt dictatorships and restrictions of the freedom of religion, were similar to the ones experienced by Latin America. A particularly prominent example of the liberating impact of the Pope's visit, and the force of freedom inherent in the Gospel message, was the most Catholic country in Asia – the Philippines. John Paul II went there already on his first visit to Asia, in February 1981. The island country had been run by Ferdinand Marcos, who from 1972 maintained the martial law there. The leader of the Church in the Philippines, Cardinal Jaime Sin, adopted a similar role to that played by Cardinal Wyszyński in Communist-ruled Poland. There too, the Church was the bastion of spiritual opposition against dictatorship, the principal defender of human rights, and the main spokesman for the dignity of the entire nation. The dictator's wife, the infamous Imelda Marcos, wished to turn the visit of the Holy Father into one more festival of her own person. Every few hours the national television focused on her in a new dress, while the Pope was to appear always in her shadow. And yet he met real people and talked to them directly without restoring to the deceitful media. He talked of the need to organize lay Catholics, of their participation in public life, and of their duty to preach the Gospel by setting a personal example to others. He also reminded the dictators' couple that the state had to serve the people and their rights, and not the welfare of those in power. The beatification of the holy martyrs from the Philippines announced then, for the first time outside of the Holy See, gave the people an example of courage in professing their faith.

The Church in the Philippines did not lack courage after the departure of John Paul II either. Among the growing persecution and treacherous assassinations of opposition activists, the Episcopate intensified the criticism of Marcos' regime in the subsequent pastoral letters. "We have to be obedient to God, not to people," stressed Cardinal Sin. When in February 1986, Marcos fixed the Presidential elections, the Church encouraged the nation to stage a non-violent revolution. The military refused to crack down on defenseless crowds and the regime collapsed. Cardinal Sin had no doubt that without the meeting of the Filipinos with John Paul II, without the example of Solidarity in

John Paul II and Mother Teresa – servants of the Church and humanity at the turn of the millennium

The Pope meets Buddhist monks during the pilgrimage to South Korea

From the very first of his foreign trips, the Pope thus showed respect to the land in which he arrived

Poland, which stemmed from the spiritual inspiration of the same Pope, the Christian liberation of the country could not have been accomplished. The Philippines thanked John Paul II for that in January 1995, when the Pope arrived in Manila to participate in a World Youth Day. The mass which concluded the celebrations on 15 January attracted five to seven million people – the largest gathering in the history of the world. During this joyful gathering, young Filipinos shouted "Lolek, Lolek!" Manila is not the Pope's native Wadowice, however, and so John Paul II suggested that his Asian hosts simply used his first name, instead of the former nickname from his childhood days. The crowds responded by roaring cheerfully "Karol, Karol."

The pilgrimages to Asian countries were not always times of joy. For instance, on that wonderful day in Manila, preparations of Muslim fanatics to organize an attempt on the Pope's life were discovered. Islamic fundamentalists had threatened the Pope before – on his first tour of Asia, during a stopover between flights in the Pakistani capital Karachi in February 1981. In Asia, as opposed to Latin America, Catholicism (except in the Philippines and in Vietnam) is a religion of a small minority – today this is less than 3 per cent of the nearly four billion Asians. Missionary activity, the question of how best to arrange relations with large religions of the continent as well as solidarity with the poor and the persecuted were major issues undertaken during papal pilgrimages to Asia.

Here John Paul II even had to help Christian communities survive in the sea of frequently hostile societies which professed different religions. This is what happened in East Timor, inhabited by Catholics, which had been forcefully incorporated by Muslim Indonesia in 1976. During his pilgrimage in October 1997, John Paul II spoke out about the ruthlessly persecuted inhabitants of Timor, demanding religious freedom for them and respect for human rights, which were abused with regard to everyone, including Muslim subjects of the Suharto regime. A year later the dictatorship collapsed under the weight of its own corruption. East Timor discovered a new road to win independence, although, unfortunately, the bloody fighting inspired by religious differences has not ceased.

At the opposite end of the huge continent, Lebanese Christians suffered a similar fate. Their country, torn apart by the neighboring powers of Syria and Israel, had been practically deprived of a chance to pursue their own independent development since the late 1970s. John Paul II repeatedly issued dramatic appeals to discontinue aggression in Lebanon. He could visit this war-torn country only in May 1997. In Beirut he spoke not only in the name of persecuted Christians, but first of all as a spokesman for peace and the abandoning of violence in the relations between nations and religions. The Middle East and particularly the region where the holy sites of three great monotheistic religions – Judaism, Christianity and Islam – are located, wanted peace very much – and, unfortunately, it still lacks it.

The Pope's call for religious freedom and respect for human rights is still kept out by the rulers of the last Communist powers which have remained in Asia. This problem is particularly acute in China and Vietnam. Catholics constitute a considerable proportion of the population of Vietnam, particularly South Vietnam. However, they are deprived of any rights to manifest and teach their religion in public. Prison and concentration camp sentences are still pronounced there for reading the Bible even in a small group. In spite of the fact that Vietnam has established diplomatic relations with the US, the Communists in power there are still afraid of normalizing relations with the Holy See, knowing (from the example of the nearby Philippines and Indonesia) the threat their despotic

John Paul II celebrates Mass in Benin (pilgrimage to Africa in 1993)

regime could face if they allowed the visit of the Pilgrim of Freedom. John Paul II thus tried to support the Church in Vietnam at least from a distance. The great canonization ceremony of 117 Vietnamese martyrs for faith presided over by the Pope in front of St Peters' Basilica on 19 June 1988 was a gesture of such support. Vietnamese bishops did not lose hope and until the last moment wanted to invite the Pontiff to visit their country.

In China, Catholic bishops faithful to the Pope are subjected to systematic persecution. From among six thousand missionaries which have been active in the country since 1947, only about a dozen have remained. In this most populous country in the world, the Catholic community of a dozen million or so has been completely cut off from the Pope. The totalitarian system, which wishes to retain full control of the religion of its subjects, has forced some of the hierarchs of the Chinese Church to break off their links with the Vatican. Only the clandestine Church did not renounce the allegiance to the Pope. John Paul II tried many times to break through the "Chinese wall" which the Communists raised to separate him from the Catholic community in the Middle Kingdom. In November 1983, he even sent a personal letter to the Chinese leader Deng Xiaoping, addressing these issues. The Chairman of the Chinese Bridge Federation (as this was the one of his titles that Deng appreciated most and kept until the end of his life) never replied to the letter. Therefore, John Paul II used the opportunity of his second visit in South Korea in October 1989, where he took part in the International Eucharist Congress in Seoul, to express publicly his ardent wish to visit the Chinese brothers in Christ. He also stressed

The Pope visits Africa again

*The leader of the Italian Episcopate also travels around Italy:
a visit to Aosta Valey*

John Paul II in India

the heroism of the followers of the clandestine Church and appealed for a reconciliation with the "patriotic Church" maintained by the Communists. Discrete diplomacy and "Vatican intelligence," carried out e.g. with the assistance of the Filipino episcopate (Cardinal Sin, its leader, is Chinese by birth), indicated that in fact the community of the "patriotic Church" did not want to disassociate themselves from the Pope. The hope to pull down the "Chinese wall" did not leave the Pope until the very end, as he saw in it a chance to renew the great tradition of Christian missions started by Jesuit monks as early as the 17th century. This policy found confirmation in the strengthening by the Pope of the legitimate Churches in Hongkong (now incorporated into China) and Taiwan. Such dynamically developing communities are signs of hope for the Church in Asia. Another example is the Catholic Church in South Korea.

For John Paul II the great hope for the entire Church was Africa. Here, as opposed to Asia, Catholics form a more numerous and influential minority – some 16 percent of nearly 800 million inhabitants of the continent. The Pope gave them exceptional attention – he visited Africa 15 times! He was able to discover the distinct character of this Church already during his first visit in May 1980. After the mass in Nairobi he happily appeared in a gift outfit – wearing a plume made of ostrich feathers, and holding a shield and a spear – his throne being a leopard-covered drum. In every country he reached – Zaire, Congo, Ghana, Upper Volta, or Ivory Coast – his visit was accompanied by spontaneous joy expressed by tribal dances, singing and chanting. Catholic rites found new forms here. John Paul II did not criticize them – he enjoyed them, although the limits of this "enculturation" remained a problem. The Holy Father had to remind the Africans, for instance, that monogamy was not an invention of European culture, but resulted from Divine inspiration and was revealed in the Scriptures. Apart from polygamy, the widespread worship of ancestors and belief in the contacts with the spiritual world also constituted both theological and practical problems for the Church in Africa.

The Pope addressed them most fully in a special letter (exhortation) *Ecclesia in Africa*, which he signed during his visit to Cameroon in September 1995. There he emphasized the need to develop the African identity of this Church as well as to maintain its solidarity with the universal Church. He pointed out the errors commit-

*The Pope in Nairobi: wearing a plume of ostrich feathers
and holding a shield of African warriors*

*John Paul II and Chancellor Helmut Kohl in front of the Brandenburg
Gate – symbol of the past division of Europe*

ted by Europeans in their African missions, but did not ignore the immense dedication of the missionaries, who gave testimony to the Christian faith on this continent. Here the Church has been persecuted too – mostly by ruthless military dictatorships, sometimes (as in Sudan) associated with Islamic fundamentalism. Several dozen missionaries still die in Africa every year. Where the Pope could travel, for instance to Sudan in February 1993 or to Nigeria in March 1998, there he demanded respect for human rights, the release of political prisoners and transition to the democratic system of government. At the international forum, John Paul II became one of the most eager defenders of Africa as the continent of the poor who needed help from their former colonizers, and not just the programs of reducing population growth. "Cynical exploitation of poor and ignorant people is a crime against God's work" – these strong words of the Pope in Nigeria were directed both at the local dictators and the countries of the rich North which after centuries of exploitation of African resources turned their back on the problems they had left behind. John Paul II was very strongly involved in African affairs not only due to his natural solidarity with the poor and persecuted, but also because he saw in Africa the hope for the renewal of the Church at large. Until recently Africa has been a mission zone for Europeans, but the number of black priests has been growing steadily and now equals at least the number of priests from Poland. The religious vocations are more and more numerous and the time may come when the African Church evangelizes the secularized Europe.

For the Pope from Cracow, Europe is the native continent. Today its western part, which used to be the mainstay of Catholicism in the Middle Ages and modern times, is now the crisis area

not only for the Church, but for the entire moral order which supports Christianity. Churches are increasingly empty, the number of priestly and monastic vocations is falling and the indifference to advice coming from the Vatican with regards to faith and morality is growing. These were the problems John Paul II had to face in his meetings with contemporary Europeans. Large public and private media companies, run and serviced mainly by those who were either indifferent or hostile to religion, were eager to suggest one solution to these problems: relax the rigors of Christian morality and do not prevent the faithful from choosing those dogmas which suit them and rejecting those which they find inconvenient or outdated. The advocates of this view could be found also within the Church – and they immediately turned into media "stars."

John Paul II consistently rejected this view. He fought for the authority of his office – not for his own sake, but in order to retain the unity of the Church and its unchanging teaching. His faithful supporter in this struggle was the German Cardinal Joseph Ratzinger (maliciously nicknamed Panzerkardinal or Great Inquisitor by his opponents), whom the Pope nominated Head of the Congregation for the Teaching of Faith. Already at the outset of his pontificate, in December 1979, the case of the Swiss Professor of Theology, Hans Küng, broke out. He had developed his own theories for years, which grew increasingly distant from Church teaching and openly questioned its truthfulness. The Congregation finally declared that Küng could no longer teach as Catholic theologian. Küng immediately became a major figure in the media, particularly in Germany, who contributed to creating the image of John Paul II as a "reactionist" who restricted the freedom of opinion in the Church. Critics of the Church were also highly outspoken in the

The Pope meets his theological advisers: Fr. Stanisław Nagy from Cracow (on the left) and Cardinal Ratzinger (in the center)

John Paul II receives Queen Elisabeth II

Meeting with young people in Paris (August 1997)

Netherlands, where from the 1960s a "progressive" trend had developed in the local Church. Its leading theologian, Edward Schillebeeckx, even went as far as doubting the resurrection of Christ and questioning the mysterious presence of his body and blood in the Eucharist – and at the same time he considered himself a Catholic theologian. The "progressive" part of the Dutch Church, however, attacked the Pope primarily for reminding them of Christian morality. They talked of homosexuality as a "special value" which the Vatican was not able to appreciate, they demanded ordination of women, they considered not only abortion, but even euthanasia, to be permissible.

Pilgrimages of John Paul II to Germany and the Netherlands seemed to confirm these difficulties. When the Pope arrived in Cologne in November 1980, his opponents got organized to demonstrate in public. The feminists called him "the enemy of women who wanted to burn them at stake"; the main commentator of the pilgrimage on German television (where only 3 percent of the journalists declared themselves as religious) was – naturally – Hans Küng. But still millions of Germans heard the humble words of John Paul II that it was more worthwhile to "be" rather than "have." The Germans were and have remained one of the most dedicated Christian nations in the entire world with regard to helping the poor. The ratings of the pastoral visit of John Paul II broke records of popularity. It was clear that Küng and "progressive" theologians did not have the mastery of German souls. When John Paul II visited the Netherlands in May 1985, local activists in Utrecht hurled smoke pots and eggs at his car. They even put up posters which promised a reward for the Pope's life: 6 thousand dollars. It was clear, however, that the most ferocious adversaries were the people from the generation of the 1960s. At the threshold of the 21st century these were increasingly the defiant retirees. Paradoxically, their slogan in the struggle with the Pope was the claim that he was an old man and a Pole, therefore he did not understand the demands of modern times.

The response of John Paul II to this criticism and, more broadly, to the critical trends in West European churches was a mirror image of the accusation. First of all, John Paul II addressed his appeal for Christian inspiration in the life of Europe particularly to young people. His unusual skill in breaking the ice between himself – the "old man" – and the youths emerged for the first time at the meeting in Parc des

The Pope hosts Dalai Lama, the exiled ruler of Tibet and spiritual leader of the Buddhist world

World Youth Day in Paris

Princes in Paris, during his pilgrimage to France in June 1980. As was his habit – way back as the academic pastor at St Florian's parish and then bishop and cardinal – he willingly allowed open dialogue in the most important matters which the young people were ready to consider in all sincerity. A question was then asked: "Holy Father, are you not afraid that young people will be turning away from the Church in increasing numbers because of your inflexibility in the issues of sexual morality?" In reply, the Pope addressed the girl who asked the question as well as the whole Western civilization: Yes, the Church does make demands but "only such that are linked to the genuine, that is, responsible love in marriage and parenthood." Its demands coincide with the dignity of the human person. These are demands, "but the crux of the matter is that man can only fulfil himself as long as he is able to make demands from himself... Moral permissivism does not make people happy. Consumer civilization does not make people happy. And it never did." These words and this message were then repeated by John Paul II at consecutive meetings with the youths, for whom he even instituted a special World Youth Day celebrated since 1986. The origin of the idea of these biannual world meetings goes back to 1983. Then the Church solemnly celebrated the Holy Year announced on the jubilee of 1950 years of the death of Christ. John Paul II made a proposal to his Council for the Laity to prepare a separate meeting of the Pope with young people in the same year. Not waiting for the arduous consultations of Vatican officials concerning such an unusual initiative to complete, he invited young people to Rome for Palm Sunday of 1984. On that rainy Sunday over 300 thousand youths from around the world arrived to meet John Paul II. The Pope could find a common language with them. This was not the "buddy" language, but the language of a serious conversation with the father, as contemporary young people increasingly lack a father – someone whom you could ask about the most important matters and receive answers, in full trust that they were dictated by the true authority and real love.

Others, more and more popular world meetings followed: Vienna, Buenos Aires, Santiago de Compostela, Częstochowa, Denver, Manila... – until the youths visited the Pope again in Rome in the Jubilee Year of 2000. John Paul II also invited the youths from all over Europe for a special meeting to Loreto in September 1995. Half a million strong audience were captivated by the words of the Pope: „EurHope: Europe and hope. You have chosen this motto for the vigil tonight. In this motto the words Europe and hope are inextricably linked. This is a beautiful intuition, but also a particular challenge. It demands that you become people who believe in God of life and love and proclaim with unwavering trust that man has a future."

And young people came to him in ever greater numbers and with unfaltering enthusiasm, although he was older and older and less and less "attractive" for modern media culture. And again Paris bore witness to this great feast of young people – they rejoiced in meeting the Holy Father, who only reminded them of the credo of his Teacher. At the World Youth Day in Paris, which took place between 21 and 24 August 1997, 200-300,000 participants were expected at the most – in fact over one million youngsters flocked to meet John Paul II. Holiness, which the Pope recommended to them for their way of life, turned out feasible and attractive to many of them. And this was already another generation from that of the hippie contesters from 1968.

The Pope sought a way to renew Christian Europe not only through youths, but also in another way – again seemingly in response to the contemptuous criticism, which attributed his "backwardness" to the mere fact that he had come from Poland, from the East, from the "worse" Europe. From the beginning of his pontificate, John Paul II demanded that European unity be restored and the division from Yalta be overcome. Eastern Europe used to be no less important part of Christian community of the continent than Western Europe – and it should resume this role. The Pope expressed this truth symbolically when already on 31 December 1980 he proclaimed St Cyril and Methodius, the apostles of Slavic lands, co-patrons of Europe. In June 1985 he devoted a separate encyclical, entitled *Slavorum Apostoli*, to their role. In the heart of unifying Western Europe, when he spoke to the European Parliament in Strasbourg in October 1988, the Pope stated most forcefully that there was another, Eastern Europe. Then he firmly demanded that Europe united in its full shape "within the borders which were marked by geography and, even more strongly, by history." He also demanded the renewal of cultural and moral significance of Europe on the basis of its Christian tradition. He criticized – both from the geographical and moral perspective – the illusive sense of self-sufficiency of today's Europeans who tend to live as if God did not exist and as if to the east of Germany and Italy stretched only wild fields inhabited by strange, backward people.

The Pope talked many times of the two lungs of European Christianity – eastern and western – both of which are necessary for it to be able to breathe. He also did his utmost to revive and strengthen the Eastern "lung" of Europe, quashed by Communism, in the hope that it would help animate entire Europe. The liberation of Eastern Europe from the yoke which restricted its spiritual and material development was treated by the Slavic Pope as his personal mission – and he did succeed in it.

John Paul II listens to the questions posed by young people

The Pope among children (pilgrimage to Poland, 1987)

Victory of Lech Wałęsa and the Solidarity – the moment after the agreement of 31 August 1980 has been signed

John Paul II in Poland following the martial law

CHAPTER X
Return of the king

„Among the 20th-century statesmen, monarchs, leaders, there is not a single figure which would correspond to our image of royal majesty – except Karol Wojtyła. Only he could really play Shakespearean kings. ... At the bottom of its misery, Poland received a king and the one it dreamt about – from the Piast tribe ... not entangled in the "screeching" world of politics ... the King carrying Messianic faith, deeply convinced that the realm of spirits exists which wrestle, struggle, triumph, side by side with the history of the living, and in a close link with it. ... Travels of John Paul II to Poland could be understood as the heavenly struggle to win its soul. As if each gathering of thousands of the faithful in brotherly love moved the heavens, if only briefly, and happened both there and here, on Earth. Could he have known beforehand that he was able to raise the nation from collective humiliation in bloodless insurrection?" These notes from the diary of the poet Czesław Miłosz dated for autumn 1987 faultlessly point to the deep impact of John Paul II on the history of not only Poland, but – through it – on the whole of Eastern Europe too.

With the benefit of hindsight, the majority of the commentators agree that the role of the Polish Pope in setting up the events of 1989 – this "year of miracles" – is unquestionable. Too frequently, however, it is presented in a highly superficial manner – as an element of political struggle carried out as part of the Cold War between two blocs. The Holy Father was to play the role of the best CIA agent. This vision of the involvement of John Paul II in East European affairs was naturally upheld by CIA's opposite number – KBG. The Communists ruling Poland thought in similar terms, both those who imposed the martial law and those who had been removed from power earlier and saw this as a conspiracy of "the western imperialists and the Vatican." For instance, Edward Gierek, in a memorandum drafted in June 1982 (at the time when the former First Secretary had still been interned), wrote emotionally that "the counterrevolution in the country is well in tune with the West and the Vatican; western governments, western radio stations as well as the Pope play their roles with great precision...". For the former KGB resident in Poland, General Pavlov, there was no doubt too that the Vatican and the CIA worked together, in one conspiracy against the Communist system.

Unfortunately, the efforts of John Paul II aimed at liberating Eastern Europe are perceived in similarly primitive terms by esteemed Western journalists, including the authors of one of the most famous biographies of John Paul II Carl Bernstein and Marco Politi. For them the turning point in the history of Europe and the Cold War was 7 June 1982 – the moment when Ronald Reagan arrived at the Vatican. Their conspiracy theory had it that the American President, who publicly referred to the Soviet Union as the "evil empire," was to propose to St Peter's successor a collaboration in intelligence and subversion against the common enemy. The mediator in setting up this "Holy Alliance" was to be the Polish-born Cardinal John Król from Philadelphia, whom the authors of this sensational concept called –

The Pope with President Ronald Reagan and his wife Nancy

John Paul II received by General Jaruzelski and Chairman of the State Council, Henryk Jabłoński, in Warsaw in 1983

with charm typically for journalists – the Pope's "best buddy." Many times, after a game of golf and at the cigars, Król and Reagan were to discuss the plans of involving the Polish Pope in a sweeping scheme against Moscow. Later, the CIA Director William Casey was to act as a courier between the White House and the Vatican, and he met the Pope "half a dozen times." For Bernstein and Politi the fact that Casey was Catholic and – to make it worse – had been brought up by the Jesuits, was tantamount to ideal qualifications for an agent of this great conspiracy. The fact that John Paul II, in turn, never supported the pacifistic offensive of the American Bishops, who in the early 1980s called on their government to declare unilateral nuclear disarmament, was a sufficient proof for them that the conspiracy Reagan-Wojtyła was real and global. Another "proof" of the American-Vatican conspiracy was the critical attitude of John Paul II with regard to the Marxist-inspired Liberation theology in Latin America. The principal subject of the conspiracy, however, was their joint assistance for clandestine Solidarity in Poland.

Both John Paul II and Ronald Reagan had their own reasons to criticize the Communist system. Both the Pope and the American President surely contributed to a considerable extent to the fall of the "evil empire." Nonetheless, the perception of John Paul II as a merchant in intelligence secrets and buyer of the aid for Solidarity in return for silence on American nuclear armaments is shockingly nonsensical. The successor of St Peter did not wage war aiming at the victory of capitalism or strategic triumph of the United States. In fact, he wanted the same he had done prior to 13 December 1981 – for the doors to be opened for the Redeemer both in Poland and in the entire Eastern Europe. He worked to achieve this aim in all his activities on the global scale. Poland, however, was his homeland and this was the simplest motive of the papal anxiety. The Solidarity movement had awakened great hopes in the Holy Father that Poland would actually play the role he had dreamt about in the poems of his youth or in the letters he had exchanged with Mieczysław Kotlarczyk across the border which in the late 1939 separated Wadowice and Cracow. The Pope fought to revive the hope that Poland would turn into the gate to Eastern Europe, to its spiritual revival, liberation of its nations and awakening of Christianity in them. This was truly a great spiritual struggle, the critical moments in which were subsequent pilgrimages to Poland.

John Paul II revealed his intention to visit Poland again on 3 May 1982. He wished to come to celebrate the 600 years of the presence of the image of Our Lady at Jasna Góra, which fell on August that year. The martial law still persisted, however, although the Pope constantly demanded its lifting, expressed his solidarity with the interned Solidarity activists and appealed for their release. He directly addressed the architect of the martial law, General Wojciech Jaruzelski himself, to "respect human rights and the rights of the nation" in two personal letters from 18 December 1981 and 6 April 1982. In contrast, Jaruzelski wished to postpone the visit of the Pope until the moment when he would be able to consider his showdown with Solidarity as completed. On 8 October 1982, the Sejm, controlled by him, voted the law which made the Solidarity trade union illegal. The date when the decision was taken was not accidental, though, because it had been known for a long time that the canonization mass of Father Maximilian Maria Kolbe was planned for 10 October. In the struggle that John Paul II waged to win the soul of Poland, this was to be an important moment. The formal outlawing of Solidarity could be considered a move of the other side. The official broadcast of the mass by the Polish media left out the moment when the Pope took up the challenge and said directly: "depriving the Solidarity trade union of the right to exist legally is a violation of basic human and national rights."

By the end of 1982, Jaruzelski did not feel secure yet. The underground Solidarity declared a national strike for 10 November. Two days earlier the general had decided to announce his decision to allow the visit of the Holy Father in Poland in the following year. He wanted to use this visit not only to defuse the uncertain internal situation, but also to put an end to the international isolation of his regime. John Paul II was ready to take the risk of the game, as he was aware of how much his presence was needed by the Poles, who were tired by the martial law and afflicted by their rapid spiritual and material impoverishment. He knew that both he and they, his countrymen, will come out of this meeting encouraged.

He arrived in Warsaw on 16 June 1983. Already in his very first speech, at the airport, he clearly defined the aim of his trip. He arrived to meet all the Poles and bring

John Paul II in the Capuchins Church in Warsaw looking at the urn with the heart of John III Sobieski

The Pope prays at the tomb of Primate Stefan Wyszyński

peace and comfort particularly to those who suffered and were imprisoned, with whom he kept in touch both by prayer and by letter (indeed, letters from the interned Solidarity activists reached John Paul II at the Vatican, e.g. thanks to the mediation of the editor of the Polish edition of *L'Osservatore Romano*, Fr. Adam Boniecki). During the meeting at Belweder Palace the next day, General Jaruzelski tried to defend his decision to impose the martial law and justify its tragic consequences by referring to the Polish raison d'état. Even the manipulative cameras of the government television could not hide the terrible exasperation of Jaruzelski, whose hands and pant legs trembled uncontrollably. Such trembling must have accompa-

nied all the Communist and military rulers of Poland throughout the following days of the papal trip.

Right after the visit in Belweder, the Pope drove to the Capuchin Church at Miodowa Street where the urn with the heart of King John III Sobieski was stored. The Pope paid tribute to the victorious leader, on the 300th anniversary of the Battle of Vienna. In the church he was welcomed by other, living heroes of contemporary history, which was far from victorious: Solidarity activists linked to the Catholic artistic ministry active in Warsaw. Among them was the poet Barbara Sadowska. Just like

Professor Karol Wojtyła receives an honorary doctorate of "his" Jagiellonian University (June 1983)

To visit the Baltic coast the Pope had to wait till 1987

many other participants of this meeting she worked in the Primate's Committee for Protecting the Imprisoned and their Families. Six weeks before the meeting with the Holy Father the police had stormed the Committee headquarters. The volunteers who brought aid to the imprisoned Solidarity members were beaten up. Barbara Sadowska was among those most brutally treated. Ten days later she lost her son, the 19-year-old Grzegorz Przemyk, who was killed by policemen at one of the Warsaw police stations. The Pope did not say anything, just embraced the suffering mother, as if in her person he wanted to embrace all the victims of the martial law, all the Poles who suffered in this depressing time.

In the sermon at the Dziesięciolecia Stadium in Warsaw, the Pope talked about the defeats of the nation, not only about its victories. And he said that rising after the defeat was possible only through moral revival. "Only the moral victory can put an end to the division of the society and restore its unity. Such harmony may be the victory of both the governed and those who govern." This was the program of John Paul II for Poland, which had very little to do with the wild speculations about Vatican-Reagan conspiracy. The best place to preach about the program was naturally the Jasna Góra Shrine. Here the meeting with young people in the evening of 18 June was the most inspiring. The Pope talked to them about the need to show solidarity, which

was based on the love of their neighbor. He also emphasized the need of responsibility for "that great shared legacy whose name is Poland." Recalling the fact that the Polish freedom always cost a great deal, he emphasized that "only that which costs constitutes a value." Thus, he warned them against escaping from Polish problems, against the temptation to emigrate, to which so many young people yielded at that time of discouragement and lack of perspectives. During the Mass celebrated for nearly two million pilgrims at the Katowice airport and later during the Mass in the church of Mistrzejowice, the Pope tried to support Polish workers in their conviction of the dignity of work and at the same time demanded that they be granted the right to a free trade union.

In Wrocław, which the Pope visited for the first time, the Holy Father raised the question of education in the family and returned to national issues again. In a nation, just like in a family, mutual trust built on the truth is essential. The education, culture, mass media which are based on falsehood inevitably ruin this trust. The future of the nation is dependent on rebuilding this trust, which was still far away in Poland: right after the mass the riot police attacked the participants who had tried to march peacefully towards the center of Wrocław. At the time when the authorities were so untrustworthy and the opposition had to go underground again, John Paul II gave Poland two great patrons, whom he beatified at the Błonia meadow in Cracow. These were the same two saints he had publicly prayed for twenty years earlier on the centenary of the January insurrection: Adam Chmielowski and Rafał Kalinowski. Both the participants of the lost national rising were now presented by the Pope in all their life stories as "signs of victory for the nation ... the victory by the power of the truth, freedom and justice."

After the great ceremonies, like the mass at Błonia, in which nearly two million people took part, the Holy Father had two smaller meetings. The first one, at the Jagiellonian University, was connected with the Pope receiving the honorary doctorate of the university from which he had graduated. The second was a testimony to the ties of the Holy Father with the persecuted Solidarity as well as to his love for the Polish mountains – the Tatras. On 23 June the Pope accompanied by a few friends and former hiking companions, flew on board of a helicopter to the Chochołowska Valley. From here Karol Wojtyła used to set off for the surrounding peaks. In the mountain hotel, the Holy Father met the leader of the banned Solidarity Lech Wałęsa. The whole area was bugged with surveillance microphones so their brief conversation could only be very general. The meeting itself, however, was a very clear symbol for entire Poland. Following the conversation with Wałęsa, the Pope put on his hiking boots and along with his friends went for a walk to Jarząbcza Valley. He walked in front of the group, prayed the Rosary and absorbed the beauty so close to his heart. In a highlander cottage on the way he was offered the goats' cheese. Lacking the security clearance, it was withheld from the Pope by watchful Father Dziwisz. The "cleared" provisions were carried by the Chancellor of Cracow Curia, Bronisław Fidelus, in his backpack. This mountain relief was brief, but important and moving for the Pope.

The relief which that pilgrimage brought for Poland of the martial law was also brief but equally important and precious. It restored hope to many people. "Solidarity" felt that it had not been forgotten by its Father. Those who believed in its revival, however, had to suffer many more sacrifices. Particularly tragic was the sacrifice of the young priest – Jerzy Popiełuszko. This organizer of masses for the homeland, celebrated in the Warsaw Church of St Stanislaus Kostka every month

Evening prayer with young people at Jasna Góra on 18 June 1983

Meeting with workers of Nowa Huta in Mistrzejowice

Hiking trip to Chochołowska Valley (the Holy Father followed by Cardinal Macharski)

John Paul II stops for a while at a highlander cottage in Jarząbcza Valley
The faithful wait for the Pope in front of Jasna Góra ramparts

on the day of the election of Karol Wojtyła as Pope, became one of the best known chaplains of Solidarity and thus most annoying for the regime. Father Popiełuszko did not do anything else than the Pope during his pilgrimages to Poland: he tried to encourage the spiritual, non-violent resistance against evil. He addressed crowds of workers, doctors, intellectuals who gathered around him. John Paul II was greatly interested in the activities of the courageous priest. He asked his friend, Bishop Kraszewski of Warsaw, to protect him. Through his messengers he frequently sent his regards to the defiant priest. He could not save Father Popiełuszko, however, from the assassination by the secret police. The tomb of the priest, kidnapped and murdered on 19 October 1984, turned into a Solidarity shrine. John Paul II himself was to visit his grave too.

The Slavic Pope looked not only on Poland, but on the entire Eastern Europe. The year 1985 brought first harbingers of change in the Soviet bloc as a whole. On 27 February Andrei Gromyko, the "eternal" Soviet minister of foreign affairs appeared at the Vatican again. If removing the Pope turned out impossible, it became necessary to make a deal with him – this seems to have been the message of the visit. Gromyko suggested establishing regular diplomatic relations with the Holy See; this time he was ready to reconsider the situation of Catholics in the USSR. Moscow realized that its empire is crumbling, that it would not win the confrontation with the West, either technological or ideological – the spiritual needs of people being best expressed by John Paul II. The symbol of the change in the Soviet policy was the new general Secretary of the Soviet Party, Mikhail Gorbachev, appointed 12 days following Gromyko's visit to the Vatican. In June 1985 in turn, John Paul II signed his new encyclical on the holy Apostles of the Slavs: Cyril and Methodius. Still before it was announced, in the early April, the aging Cardinal of Prague, František Tomášek had invited the Pope to visit Velehrad in Moravia to mark the 1100th anniversary of St Methodius' death. The Communist authorities of Czechoslovakia did not even consider such a possibility, however. John Paul II was only allowed to send a letter in which he encouraged Czech and Slovak priests to follow in the footsteps of the saint and give courageous testimony to their faith, even if in the current situation it was difficult, burdensome and bitterly. The Velehrad celebrations were attended by nearly

200,000 pilgrims from entire Czechoslovakia. The Catholics in the country cast aside their fears and were regaining their dignity. Just like the Poles earlier, they were now chanting: "We want the Pope!" The doors to Eastern Europe were slowly reopening.

The new political "thaw" in the Soviet Union, started by Gorbachev, enabled the sides to open talks about another pilgrimage of John Paul II to Poland. Jaruzelski, who as the head of the Polish state was received in the Vatican on 13 January 1987, invited the Pope to come to Poland again. He hoped that the visit of the Holy Father would neutralize the radical opposition in the clandestine Solidarity. The Pope, who had requested that his pilgrimage route included Gdynia and Gdańsk, where free trade unions were born, used his visit to obtain full rehabilitation of Solidarity: both in its ordinary, interpersonal sense and as the institution born in August 1980. Just before his third visit to Poland, the Pope emphasized the sense of Solidarity which was not to be limited to the Poles, but was to extend far to the East, where Poland used to reach in the past, and now the Church suffered persecution. On 5 June 1987 he sent his Apostolic letter to Bishops of Lithuania taking the opportunity of the 600th anniversary of the christening of Lithuania to encourage this sister Church, ruthlessly persecuted under the Soviet rule. In order to strengthen the faith and national identity of Lithuanians, the Pope soon beatified the Archbishop from Vilnius, Jurgis Matulaitis. The Lithuanians, just like the Poles before, could now feel noticed behind the Iron Curtain, which had separated them from Europe since the Soviet occupation in 1940. They could now have a sense of belonging not only to the Church, but also to Europe.

The third trip of John Paul II to Poland began on 8 June 1987. The Holy Father did not miss the opportunity to visit Cracow and Jasna Góra Shrine. For the first time as the Pope he arrived in Lublin, where he visited his former university – the Catholic University of Lublin (KUL). On that occasion he not only drew attention to the message of the university: "developing the community of free people in truth," but also referred to the fact that Lublin was the city where the union of the Polish Crown with the nations of the Grand Duchy of Lithuania had been established. He once again encouraged his countrymen to remain faithful to the legacy of their history and open up to the East, once again

During the trips of the Holy Father to Poland, the pilgrims from neighboring countries found their way through the border as they could not wait to see him there

Fr. Jerzy Popiełuszko during one of his masses for the homeland

accepting the role of a mediator in the spiritual exchange between the East and West of Europe. The Pope returned to this idea in his homily delivered at Wawel Cathedral. There he mentioned the Blessed Queen Jadwiga as the patron of Poland's opening to Lithuania and Ruthenia as well as St Casimir – patron of Christian Lithuania. At the Nazi concentration camp of Majdanek, where thousands of East Europeans had perished, John Paul II called for a strong testimony to these tragic chapters of Polish history. He talked about this again in his final homily read out in front of Stalin's Palace of Culture in Warsaw. He then beatified the Bishop of Włocławek Michał Kozal, murdered by Germans in the Dachau

concentration camp. During this trip he also visited Tarnów, Szczecin and Łódź, where he met the female textile workers from Uniontex factory. The Pope blessed them in their work and in their contribution to the struggle of Poles to regain dignity of their work, but he also reminded them of the indispensable role of women in the family and in the education of their children.

The Baltic Coast, however, was the highlight of this pilgrimage. In Gdynia John Paul II met the "people of the sea." Driven to Westerplatte (a Polish bastion of resistance against Germans in 1939) on board a warship, he delivered to the young audience one of the most memorable messages in the history of all papal meetings in Poland. Referring to the symbol of heroic struggle of the Polish unit commanded by Major Sucharski in September 1939, he reminded his "young friends" that in their lives too there must be a Westerplatte – "a range of tasks which they must undertake and fulfill, some just cause for which they cannot fail to struggle." "One cannot desert" – this was his message to young Poles after six years of the martial law. Characteristic was the fact that even here in such a symbolically Polish place, John Paul II wanted his words to be seen in a broader East European perspective. Thus he also delivered a short speech to Hungarian youths who managed to make it to the meeting. All along the pilgrimage, numerous groups of Lithuanians, Czechs and Slovaks made their presence felt. They could not meet the Holy Father in their countries so they followed him elsewhere. And the Pope noticed and greeted them. At the Zaspa housing estate in Gdańsk, in front of the huge altar shaped as a three-mast boat, John Paul II spoke "from the captain's bridge" primarily to the Poles, to the Polish workers, to Solidarity. He contrasted the concept of solidarity and the values implied by its implementation with the Marxist idea of class struggle. In this context he referred to the meaning of Gdańsk agreements of August 1980, and the meaning of the Polish example of peaceful struggle for the dignity of work. He addressed the million-strong congregation saying that the model of Solidarity born there did not belong to the past, but it had its future too: "And not only in our land, but everywhere." The main motive of the Pope's pilgrimage was symbolically framed by the prayer of John Paul II at the tomb of Father Jerzy Popiełuszko.

When several months after the pilgrimage, in October 1987, a group of Pope's friends from the *Tygodnik Powszechny* Catholic weekly arrived at the Vatican, one of them, the popular journalist Stefan Kisielewski, who visited the Pope for the first time, unexpectedly criticized his host. Commenting on the last trip of the Pope to Poland, he said with a cunning smile: "The Holy Father told us that Communism should be overthrown, but did not say how." In fact, John Paul II did not have to say this. The Communist system was visibly collapsing. The political changes in Poland were only a matter of time.

Holy Mass in Gdańsk said before the altar in the shape of St Peter's boat

Holy Mass in Warsaw, in front of the Palace of Culture which symbolized the Communist power over Warsaw and Poland – now collapsing

The demolishing of the wall which separated Eastern Europe from Western Europe and from religious freedom moved ahead in other countries too. John Paul II used 1000 years of Christianity in Russia, celebrated in 1988, as another chance to achieve this goal. He sent a personal letter to Gorbachev, dated 7 June 1988 and delivered through Cardinal Agostino Casaroli. He invited him to undertake a serious dialogue concerning the situation of the Catholic Church in the USSR, praising those initiatives of the addressee which reduced tensions in internal and foreign policy and attempted to liberalize the system. In private, however, in a conversation with an Italian Catholic philosopher, Rocco Buttiglione, John Paul II did not predict any success for Gorbachev's mission: "He is a good man, but he will be defeated as he wants to achieve the impossible. Communism cannot be reformed." The Pope sought contacts with other Russians, who would allow him better to understand the situation in that vast country against which he never intended to raise any "bulwarks." He met e.g. Irina Ilovayskaja-Alberti, editor of the prestige emigration journal *Russkaia Mysl* and close associate of Aleksandr Solzhenitsyn; Yelena Bonner, a prominent dissident activist; and finally (in February 1989) her husband – the unofficial "king" of dissidents, great physicist and defender of human rights – Andrei Sakharov. They kindled in the Slavic Pope the hope for a different, non-totalitarian Russia. They kept dismantling the inhuman system from inside.

To the south of Poland, the road of freedom was symbolically opened by the canonization of St Agnes of Bohemia. The ceremony during which the Polish Blessed, Adam Chmielowski, was also made a saint took place at the Vatican on 12 November 1989. Poland was then almost a free country. Following the elections for the Sejm of 4 June, it now had the first non-Communist government in 50 years headed by the Catholic Prime Minister, Tadeusz Mazowiecki. Czechs, however, were still ruled by the iron hand of the Communist regime. For them, the ceremony in Rome was a blessing for the change, for liberation. It was Czechs who now dominated St Peter's Square. Gathering around their Cardinal František Tomašek, just like the Poles used to gather around Primate Wyszyński, enthusiastic Czech pilgrims chanted slogans demanding freedom. The Pope looked at that with joy.

On the route of his third trip to Poland the Pope was greeted everywhere by Solidarity banners

Meeting with women workers of the Uniontex factory in Łódź

At the tomb of Fr. Jerzy Popiełuszko in the parish of St Stanislaus Kostka in Warsaw

The Pope "conspires" with the American President again – this time it is George Bush Sr. with his wife

John Paul II at the Lithuanian Mount of Crosses

Václav Havel greets the Holy Father in the Czech Republic

First Secretary of the Soviet Communist Party, Mikhail Gorbachev, at the Vatican

The German Democratic Republic then witnessed the collapse of the Berlin Wall. Five days later the "velvet revolution" rolled through Prague. In April 1990, John Paul II could finally stand on Czech soil welcomed by the former prisoner and now President of the country– Václav Havel. The President greeted the Pope with the words, which should perhaps be remembered: "I do not know if I know what a miracle is. Nonetheless I dare say that at this moment I am participating in a miracle: the land devastated by ideology of hatred hosts the messenger of love, the land devastated by barbarians hosts the living symbol of civilization.... For long decades the spirit was banished from our country. Today I have the honor to witness the moment when its soil is kissed by the apostle of spirituality."

Eastern Europe was regaining freedom. Gorbachev, who was received by the Pope on 1 December 1989, did not manage to play a significant role in this process. He even tried to obstruct it in the Soviet Union. This was the case in Lithuania where he tried to prevent the Baltic countries from proclaiming independence by staging a brutal intervention of Soviet troops in January 1991. Nothing, however, could stop these countries now. By the end of 1991 the Soviet Union was gone. And in September 1993, John Paul II could finally arrive in Lithuania too, to bless its reconstruction in the Christian spirit. He could step on

the Ukrainian soil only in 2001, and yet already in June 1997, during a pilgrimage to Poland, John Paul II symbolically summed up an important stage in the liberation of the European East – the restoring of Christian identity to those nations. At the ceremony in Gniezno, where tribute was paid to St Wojciech (Adalbert) – the apostle who had come to Poland from the south – presidents of Czech Republic, Slovakia, Hungary, Lithuania, Ukraine and Germany were present. It was difficult not to see this unique meeting as a tribute paid to the Pope himself, who during a dozen or so years of prayer and service, had gathered the crowds and opened the doors of Christ and freedom in the East. John Paul II asked his audience at this meeting not to forget the Christian foundation of freedom once it had arrived at their threshold.

He wanted Europe to be free and united again and the wall which had divided it into East and West to collapse. He then repeated his prophetic prediction expressed in Gniezno in 1979: "Does Christ not wish, does the Holy Spirit not demand that the Polish Pope, the Slavic Pope, bring to light the Christian unity of Europe right now?" And he added another question: "Can you count on building the joint home for entire Europe if you lack bricks of human conscience fired by the Gospel and linked by the bond of shared love of God?" This question has remained valid until this day.

CHAPTER XI
Lost in Rome?

At the time of John Paul II's election the quotation widely cited in Poland was the piece of Juliusz Słowacki's poetry prophesying the coming of the Slavic Pope. The Pope, whom the prophecy announced, commented on this poem during his pilgrimage in 1987, in Cracow. Before parting with the congregation gathered on Cracow's common, John Paul II reminded them that Juliusz Słowacki wrote other, more ominous words in the poem Beniowski: " Poland, in Rome it is thy loss". Referring to this anti-papal remark, the Pope made a smooth paraphrase giving it a more facetious interpretation: " I thought that he was perfectly right. Loss in Rome, lost in Rome, a man from Cracow, Poland, got lost – and now he is found in Rome!'. However, as he highly esteemed the Polish romantic authors, John Paul II immediately wended his way to the Wawel Cathedral to apologise to the great national poet for such misinterpretation of his words.

Many Poles, immensely proud of having their compatriot at the Papal throne, tended to seriously ask the question whether "our" John Paul II really got lost in Rome? They badly wanted to know the details of everyday life of the Polish successor of St Peter.

Elected to the position of the bishop of Rome, John Paul II was fully committed to take over his new duties. Immediately after his election was announced, he addressed his new diocesans gathered in the St Peter's square in Italian, remarking: "I'm not sure if I can fully express myself in your .... our language, Italian. If I make a mistake, please correct me". At the beginning of his pontificate he was sometimes corrected and instructed by the members of the Curia, particularly in the matters of etiquette. When he sneaked out outside the Vatican walls for the first time, to visit Archbishop Andrzej Deskur in hospital, the prelates trying to catch up with him reminded him to impart his blessing to the whole hospital personnel. John Paul II made a cheerful comment" They want to teach me how to be the pope". Soon after, however, he himself began to teach the Vatican people the new style of his pontificate, associated with his personality and the habits brought over from Poland.

The first symbol of the new times, a novelty soon discovered by sensation-seeking journalists was the swimming pool. The Pope could not bear the thought that he would not go canoeing with his friends in the summer. He needed water and exercise in water to keep in good shape, and opposing some Vatican officials who considered it an unnecessary luxury, had this small swimming pool, eight by eighteen metres, built in his summer residence in Castelgandolfo. In reply to criticism, he said that the costs involved in the construction of that swimming pool would be decidedly lower than the costs of the new conclave. Finally, the swimming pool was not financed by the Vatican Curia, but by the group of the faithful from America, who wanted to help the Pope keep fit. Before he broke the femoral bone and had an artificial hip joint inserted in 1994, John Paul II would go for a swim twice a day, whenever he stayed in Castelgandolfo. After 1994 the swimming pool was used chiefly by the members of the Swiss Guard.

The Pope's secret skiing excursions and mountain hikes marked another departure from the routine life at the Vatican, prompted by Karol Wojtyła's "keeping fit" habits acquired during the "Polish period". The most famous skiing trip took place in the summer

Christmas at the Vatican: the enormous Christmas tree adjoins the traditional nativity crib

On one of his Italian trips, the Pope tries his hand at the popular bowling-like game

Indefatigable hiker – this time not in the Tatras, but in the Dolomites

The relaxed Pope wearing an informal headgear

With harvesters and tourists in Aosta Valley

1984, when the Pope chose to ski on the 3000 m high glacier in the Adamello Massif in the Alps. The Pope would wander or ski in the Dolomites, in the Abruzza Mountains, on the Mont Blanc. In the recent years he frequently stopped in Combes in the Aosta Valley. As he could not get to the beloved Tatra Mountains each year, the Alps had to suffice.

In the face of this sensational news, always being in the centre of attention of the media, John Paul II left the Vatican not only to relax or get medical treatment in Italy. Although his foreign visits (over one hundred) occupied nearly two years of his pontificate, John Paul II most seriously treated his role of the bishop of Rome and the head of the Episcopate in Italy. His duties in the diocese were little different than those he had in Cracow. First of all, he was obliged to pay the pastoral visits in the parishes, and managed to visit nearly 300 out of 328 parishes within the Eternal City, he wanted to miss none. Prior to the pastoral visit, he would receive the parish priest in Vatican to ask about particular problems in the religious community. During his pastoral visits, John Paul II, would celebrate a mass, preach a sermon and meet the congregation, that is exactly what he used to do in Cracow. Furthermore, he visited the sick in hospitals and brought Christian consolation and instruction to the prisoners in the famous Rebbibia prison in Rome.

Unlike his predecessors who had seldom performed the "routine' priest duties, John Paul II would often dispense the sacrament of baptism, marriage, Holy Communion and confirmation. On the Good Friday he would hear confessions of the faithful in St Peter's Basilica. He baptised a girl, Stephanie, a 10 years' old granddaughter of Jerzy Kluger-his Jewish classmate from Wadowice. Then, after many years, the Pope presided over her marriage ceremony in Castelgandolfo. In most cases, however, this great honour was bestowed not on "the select", i.e. the Pope's friends and their families, but the ordinary people from the Roman diocese and from all over the world. Presiding over a marriage ceremony for the first time as a pope, John Paul II administered the sacrament to a daughter of a sewage plant worker in Rome, who had taken part in the Nativity play staged near the Vatican City. The Polish tradition of setting up the Christ-child's manger at Christmas was brought over by the Pope to Vatican. John Paul II revived other traditions, well forgotten in Italy but still alive in Poland – namely the solemn processions along the streets on the Corpus Christi Day. In Rome the main procession now goes from Basilica of Santa Maria Maggiore to the San Giovanni Basilica. In recent years, when the Pope became too feeble to walk that distance, he would lead the procession on the specially designed platform with a praying desk. Nevertheless, he never missed this form of contact with the people. Each year, on Good Friday he would lead the Way of the Cross among the ruins of the Colloseum – the place of martyrdom of many thousand Christians during the first centuries of the Roman Empire. Each year, on Maundy Thursday, he would wash the feet of old men gathered in the St John Lateran Basilica, as a proof of his humility, to show he came to serve others.

Christian celebrations provided the natural link between the Holy Father and his larger "parish" - the whole world. Nevertheless, the Bishop of Rome always attached a great importance to the pastoral service in his second homeland – Italy. According to the pure statistics, the scope of this pastoral work was really breathtaking. The Pope visited nearly three hundred places in Italy. Like in Rome, these visits gave the Catholics in Italy an unique opportunity to get to know the "Polish Pope". They did not need to correct him – it was he who took pains to correct them, which was what each priest concerned about his duties ought to do. Like each priest, he tried to achieve that by his work and his prayers. At the beginning of his pontificate he showed a great commit-

John Paul II administers the sacrament of baptism in the Jubilee Year
The Pope receives gifts from prisoners while visiting the Rebbibia prison

John Paul II challenges the Mafia in Palermo

Palm Sunday at St Peter's Square

The Colloseum in Rome during the Way of the Cross presided over by the Pope

John Paul receives the Brazilian football star Ronaldo

ment in his campaign to protect the life of the unborn Italians, at the time of the referendum concerning the legalisation of abortion. This battle was lost, however, as at that time the Pope was lying, helpless, in the Gemelli Hospital after an attempt on his life. In 1983 he made his way to the very "lion's den" – an Italian town of Palermo, where he waged the war on another plague, born in Italy though spreading all over the world – the Mafia. In 1994 he initiated the nine months' prayers for New Evangelisation in Italy. The Pope tried to attract young Italians, secularised by the contemporary mass culture, and bring them back to the Christian roots using the methods well-tested at the time of his priesthood in Cracow. He chose to seek new ways, appealing to the sensitivity of the young people. During the National Eucharistic Congress in Bologna in September 1997 he invited the rock idol –Bob Dylan to give a performance. Although at the first glance Bob Dylan's songs had little to do with Christianity, the Pope made use of them to encourage young people to follow Christ.

Nowadays, after so many political frauds and moral shocks which rocked Italy in the last twenty five years, nobody had any doubt that this "old man in white", this "pilgrim from Poland" became the greatest, and perhaps the only one, moral authority in this country. Even Massimo D'Alema, a neo-communist and the Italian Prime Minister (1988-2001), trying to gain popularity, would assure his supporters that his favourite book was *Crossing the Threshold of Hope* by John Paul II.

The Holy Father with his priest's duties could not feel lost in Rome and Italy. He was at home there, living in a country which, like Poland, was deeply immersed in Christian traditions. For ages Poland was absorbing the culture and traditions from Italy. It was fully understandable, though, that the Pope as a human being sought ways to maintain contacts with his homeland, his native language, and to keep in touch with his Polish friends. John Paul II did not get lost in Rome, instead he took to Rome as much of Poland as he could...

In the Vatican those in his closest circle were Poles. The key person was Father Stanisław Dziwisz, the son of a railwayman from Raba Niżna, who had accompanied Karol Wołtyła for over thirty five year, first as bishop Wojtyła's chaplain in Cracow. In October 1978 he became the Pope's private secretary. He received his first PhD degree from the Papal Academy of Theology in Cracow, having presented the dissertation on the history of St Stanislaus' cult till the 16th century. He was awarded the title of the honorary doctor from the Catholic University of Lublin in 2001 for taking care of St Stanislaus' successor, and particularly for helping to save his life on 13th May 1981 when Father Dziwisz made a quick decision choosing the Gemelli Hospital to which the wounded Pope was taken. It was in fact the matter of life and death. Fortunately, the exceptionally humble bishop Dziwisz (raised to that dignity in 1998) did not have to make such dramatic decisions as a part of his everyday duties, yet he always seemed indispensable. In a large part he arranged the Pope's plan for the day, made a list of the private guests to be received in the audiences by the Pope, accompanied the Pope during the morning mass and the morning and afternoon audiences, at the meals. When John Paul II was skiing in the mountains, Father Dziwisz would always accompany him. During the last skiing trip in the early 1994 he broke his arm trying to support the Pope when he had a fall. No doubt this man was the Pope's closest collaborator.

The Pope routinely met the Curia officials who rule the Holy See and the whole Church. The first Secretary of State in the Pope's "cabinet" used to be Cardinal Agostino Casarolli – the chief negotiator of the Vatican's policy in the Eastern Europe. On Cardinal Casarroli's retirement in 1990, Cardinal Angelo Sodano, formerly responsible for foreign affairs in the State Secretary's Office, was raised to the position of the person "number two" in Vatican, his previous post being taken over by the Archbishop Jean-Louis Tauran from Bordeaux. Leonardo Sandri from Argentina held the post of the Director in the Pope's cabinet, acting as the Pope's "substitute" in the official matters of lesser importance. These men, beside the directors of the main Congregations of the Curia, were most frequent guests in John Paul II's office.

The Pope carries the cross on Good Friday

John Paul II distributes the First Communion to Roman children

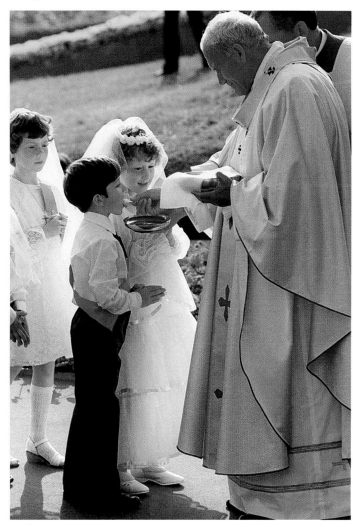

Audience for members of the Papal Pro Vita Academy in the Clementine Hall

The Pope receives the homage of the new cardinals

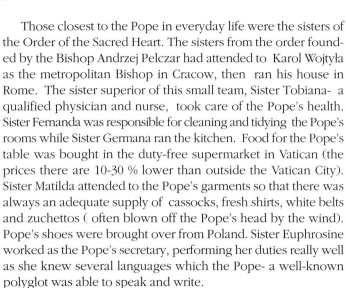

The Holy Father engrossed in prayer during the Mass in his private chapel

Meeting with the pilgrims from all over the world during a general audience

Those closest to the Pope in everyday life were the sisters of the Order of the Sacred Heart. The sisters from the order founded by the Bishop Andrzej Pelczar had attended to Karol Wojtyła as the metropolitan Bishop in Cracow, then ran his house in Rome. The sister superior of this small team, Sister Tobiana- a qualified physician and nurse, took care of the Pope's health. Sister Fernanda was responsible for cleaning and tidying the Pope's rooms while Sister Germana ran the kitchen. Food for the Pope's table was bought in the duty-free supermarket in Vatican (the prices there are 10-30 % lower than outside the Vatican City). Sister Matilda attended to the Pope's garments so that there was always an adequate supply of cassocks, fresh shirts, white belts and zuchettos (often blown off the Pope's head by the wind). Pope's shoes were brought over from Poland. Sister Euphrosine worked as the Pope's secretary, performing her duties really well as she knew several languages which the Pope- a well-known polyglot was able to speak and write.

Amidst this close circle, including Father Mieczysław Mokrzycki- the Pope's second personal secretary, the Pope led his "ordinary' life in Vatican. John Paul II woke up at five thirty- half an hour later than in Cracow. The light was switched on in his third floor apartment in the Vatican Palace, meaning that the Successor of Peter was up and praying at the start of the new day. After the morning toilet, he wended his way to the private chapel to pray in solitude. On the praying desk awaited slips of papers with the names of people who asked him to pray in their intentions. At seven o'clock the Pope celebrated the Mass, together with Bishop Dziwisz who would climb downstairs from his apartment on the fourth floor. As a rule, about ten special guests would be invited to participate in this Mass: Pope's friends from Poland or Catholics from all over the world. The invitation was a token of distinction and a great privilege. After the Mass the Pope found time to speak to them for a while. Some of the guests had another honour bestowed on them- they were invited to have breakfast with the Holy Father at eight and got an opportunity to have a longer conversation with Him. The breakfast menu was not very elaborate: scrambled eggs, ham, cheese, rolls, tea or coffee. The guests were encouraged to eat by the Pope's valet- Angelo Gugel, indispensable on such occasions. At eight o'clock people began to flock to the Pope's office, here came Cardinal Sodano, Archbishop Tauran and Father Dziwisz. From nine to eleven the Pope was always busy in his library. He would peruse the major Italian newspapers, and also *Die Welt*", *Le Figaro, The International Herald Tribune.* In the library he prepared the major documents of the papal teaching: encyclicals, pastoral letters, sermons. Written in this library were his most personal books published after 1978: *Crossing the Threshold of Hope* and *Gift and Mystery,* containing his reflections on his priesthood. At eleven the Pope would begin the official audiences, as in his bishop's days in Cracow. The audiences were held on the floor below. The Pope would receive in the audience politicians, bishops arriving in Rome, Vatican officials, people from the world of culture and science and sometimes even sportsmen. Presents offered on these occasions would land in the Pope's private museum whilst food products would go to one of the children hospitals or the poorhouses in Rome. At two John Paul II had dinner, sitting at the table with some of the guests received during the audience. Sister Germana carefully chose the menu, adapting it to the specificity of the cuisine in the guests' home countries. Dinners provided an excellent opportunity for conversation – an unforgettable experience for the guests and a rich source of information and comments from all over the world for the host.

After dinner the Pope would rest on his own. Afterwards he would read and recite the breviary. His walks on the terrace with a magnificent view of Rome had to substitute for hikes in the Wolski Forest in Cracow or the weekend trips to Kalwaria Zebrzydowska where he would walk the Way of the Cross. At half past six the Pope met the major Curia officials in his private apartment to discuss the current issues in Vatican and the Church. Before supper the Holy Father often went down again to the official apartments on the floor below to receive a select group of guests whom he wished to distinguish particularly. John Paul II had supper accompanied only by Bishop Dziwisz, during the meal they would arrange the plans for the next day. After supper he went to the chapel to pray, then returned to his study. Unlike in Cracow, it had a TV set, so the Pope watched the news in the Italian state-owned TV station, sometimes also the Polish News (TV1) transmitted via the Polonia Channel. On rare occasions the Pope had a film show at home. That happened, for example, when the movie *Pan Tadeusz* was shown in Vatican, the performance attended by the film director Andrzej Wajda and actors starring in the movie. At eleven the Pope still would be busy, working or praying. The light in the third floor apartment would go out before midnight.

During the general audiences on Wednesdays the Pope met large groups of Catholics – and there were always Poles among them. The audiences were held on St Peter's square or in the Paul VI's Hall – under an expressive huge bronze Cross, made to the order of the Patron of the room. On Sundays the Pope would recite the Angelus Domini and communicate his reflections leaning from the window of his apartment. Similarly, the Wednesday meetings provided the Pope with an excellent opportunity to present his teachings and to address the current social or political issues. In the summer the Pope moved to Castelgandolfo for a couple of weeks, accompanied by Bishop Dziwisz, the Sisters of the Order of the Sacred Heart, the valet and the members of the Swiss Guard; from there he travelled to Rome to take part in the general audiences by helicopter. John Paul II usually spent these summer weeks in Castelgandolfo in the company of his Polish friends. The most personal and intimate meetings with friends were always at Christmas time. Pope's friends from Wadowice, Cracow, Lublin were just like his family. They met at the supper table on Christmas Eve, observing the traditional customs of breaking the wafers and exchanging good wishes, together sang the Christmas carols and talked – about Poland, of course.

John Paul II accompanied by his friend, Cardinal Deskur, at the screening of the Pan Tadeusz *epic poem at the Vatican*

Christmas Eve in Rome: the Pope sings his favorite carols in the company of his KUL friends

Service in the Castelgandolfo chapel (the wall painting, commissioned by Pius XI, represents the 17th-century defense of Częstochowa against the Swedes)

The Holy Father receives a group of pilgrims from Cracow

CHAPTER XII
Quench not the Spirit!

The situation in Poland in the 1990s was a major challenge for John Paul II. At the first glance it seemed that as soon as the new Parliament was elected in June 1989 and the Solidarity-led opposition came into power, the great hopes for the Pope's homeland freed from the Communist oppression would come true. He himself expressed those hopes in the great encyclical *Centesimmus annus*, published on the 100th anniversary of the first encyclical on social issues: *Rerum novarum*, by Leo XIII. Proclaimed on 1 May 1991, the new encyclical had a separate chapter praising the way Poland gained its freedom – through solidarity, with no recourse to violence, "using only the weapons of truth and justice". It summarised the failure of the Communist ideology as 'spiritual void" and the braking force, stifling the man's economic initiative. For the first time the papal teachings admitted that the capitalist system could be approved on the grounds of the Catholic social doctrine as long as it was incorporated in the legal framework recognising and protecting the ethical and religious foundations of man's freedom. Though sometimes presented in a simplified way as the affirmation of capitalism, the encyclical *Centissimus annus* gave a direct warning in a closing chapter. Freedom gained after the fall of the Communist totalitarian system "cannot refuse to be bonded to truth". Formal democracy and market economy are not sufficient to develop a just and good system. The Pope warned people, as he had warned the western societies many years before, not to succumb to consumer attitudes, the striking example of which is the use of drugs. On the other hand, he clearly admonished certain liberal ideologists for their desire to create a "secular religion', to oppose the values defended by the Church: "As history demonstrates, a democracy without values easily turns into open or thinly disguised totalitarianism".

These strong words were prompted by the first experiences of political transformations in Poland, which seriously worried the Pope. After 1989 the media and newly formed political parties began to question the till-then obvious goals and objectives of the Solidarity movement, aiming to build the new national and spiritual iden-

A Mass for the Polish army: Koszalin, June 1991

Meeting with President Lech Wałęsa and his wife Danuta

John Paul II blesses Poland

tity of Poles in the free country. One of the goals was the re-introduction of religious instruction in schools, withdrawn from curricula by communists in the 1960s. Suddenly it appeared that this postulate was being questioned by members of the influential political elite. Though emphasising their Solidarity backgrounds, they began to threaten people with the gloomy perspectives of 'intolerance at schools", "ideology in education", "domination of the clergy" in the public life, "dictatorship of the black (i.e. priests)". The debates on those issues in the Polish papers in 1990 were a painful shock to the Church and John Paul II following them from Rome. The Pope was further pained by the growing resistance to the postulate that legal protection be given to the unborn from the moment of conception. This legal protection was withdrawn by the Communists in 1956. This postulate appeared to be the logical consequence of the Catholic majority regaining their right to express their views. The Pope - Successor of Peter responsible for the Church and her teachings and a Pole feeling responsible for the

community of his compatriots, could not close his eyes to several hundred thousands abortions each year in Poland. Left-wing politicians and intellectuals promoted by the media propagated the slogans of "neutral" state and the postulate of maintaining the abortions legal was on the banner of their ideological campaign. The Pope was greatly disappointed by the fact that those participating in this campaign or at least not trying to oppose it were his former friends from the Catholic weekly *Tygodnik Powszechny* in Cracow. The Pope gave vent to his disappointment in the letter written to the editors of *Tygodnik Powszechny* on the 50th anniversary of its foundation by Archbishop Adam Sapieha. The Pope expressed his acute sorrow: " Regaining of freedom seemed to coincide [paradoxically] with intensified attacks of the left-wing groups and liberal forces on Church, the Episcopate and the Pope. I became distinctly aware of it during my visit in Poland in 1991. I could not but feel it keenly, especially as attempts were made to make people forget what the Church meant for the nation in the recent years".

Actually the pilgrimage to his homeland in 1991 turned into a clash between the Holy Father and the forces mentioned in the letter to *Tygodnik Powszechny*, whch started an open war with the Church aiming at the "control of the souls" in the Polish society. On 16 May, two weeks before the Pope's fourth visit in Poland, the non-communist parliament passed the draft law supported by the Union of Freedom whereby abortion was permitted with few restrictions only. Shortly before the arrival of the Holy Father, a prominent newspaper *Gazeta Wyborcza* took great pains to promote a counter-culture event, the song festival in Jarocin as the reaction of the "free" Poland to the threat of theocracy, embodied by the pilgrim from Vatican. In this situation John Paul II decided to assume the role of Moses, reminding people God's commandments. The Decalogue became the moot point in his teachings during that pilgrimage.

Instead of communist officials, this time he was welcomed by the first leader of Solidarity and newly-elected president Lech

Paulite monks gather at Jasna Góra Shrine before the Holy Father visits their monastery one more time

The Pope in Wawel Cathedral

Wałęsa. Symbolic was the fact that in Koszalin- the starting point of the tour, John Paul II met the soldiers of the Polish Army at a field mass. Those who were recently sent to fight against the members of their own society, were reminded of the noble traditions of knighthood by the Pope- a son of a military man from Wadowice. He called back the momentous events from the Polish history: from the battles of Legnica and Grunwald, the victory at Vienna, the war in 1920, right through to September 1939, the battle of Narvik, Monte Cassino and the Warsaw Uprising. He was telling Poles they should be proud and cherish those traditions, they must not be ashamed of them as they are prompted to do by contemporary critics. In Rzeszów the Pope emphasised the major role played by the Church in the resistance against the communism. There he paid tribute to the mainstay of this resistance movement, Ignacy Tokarczuk, Bishop of Przemyśl. His commitment and heroism in this struggle for the human rights, the rights of the nation and the citizens' rights to confess their religion became the symbols of what the Church had done to give Poles their freedom, which the people were being made to forget.

In Przemyśl, near the Ukrainian border (formally at that time Ukraine was not an internationally -recognised independent state but still a part of the Soviet Union) John Paul II emphasised the role of Poland as a gate open to the east. He made a tremendous effort to reconcile the parties in the Polish-Ukrainian conflict, alas at that time the conflict was fuelled by the question whether to let the Uniate community (of the Byzantine-Ukrainian rite) use one of the Roman Catholic churches in Przemyśl. The Pope put in marked endeavor to establish peaceful relations with the Ukrainians who at that time were regaining their independence and national identity. Towards the end of the meeting he spoke Ukrainian, expressing his hope to say more in that language 'if the Lord allowed him to come to Lvov some day". After ten years this hope came true.

During the Mass celebrated in Łomża, attended by over ten thousand Catholics from Lithuania, the Pope expressed his intention to visit this Baltic republic. The visit took place two years later. The Pope tried to breach the gap between Catholics and the Orthodox Church and Russia when he visited St Nicholas Orthodox Cathedral in Białystok. Two months later, when John Paul II came back to Poland to meet the young people from all over the world in

Częstochowa on the Assumption Day, there came nearly seventy thousand pilgrims from the Soviet Union, including two hundred Red Army soldiers.

In June, however, the Pope made a direct appeal to Poles. During the Mass celebrated at the Masłowo Airport near Kielce, John Paul II spoke strongly and even raised his voice. Referring to the fourth commandment "Honour your father and mother", he reminded people that in order that children should honour their parents, they must be first accepted as the God's gift. The Pope directly addressed the problem of abortion, speaking vehemently and with feeling: "That is why I say so, this is my mother, this land. This is my Mother, my homeland! These are my brothers and sisters! You have to understand, you who take those matters lightly, that I cannot remain indifferent. These things hurt me and ought to hurt you as well. It is easy to destroy things and more difficult to build them up again. The destruction process has been too long! Now we have to rebuild things! The destruction must stop!". John Paul II was speaking amidst the raging thunderstorm, like a prophet appealing to human conscience. He continued to do so at the places he visited next: in Radom ("You shall not murder"), in Białystok ("You shall not steal") and in Olsztyn ("You shall not bear false witness"). Here the Pope pointed out that in contemporary world the mass media serve the cause of falsehood, thus becoming the means of spiritual oppression, in Włocławek and Płock the Pope referred to the commandments "You shall not covet your neighbor's wife" and "You shall not covet neighbor's goods". During Father Rafał Chyliński' beatification mass in Warsaw the Pope reminded people the Commandment of Love. On that occasion the Pope commented on the Polish inferiority complex towards the western Europe, cultivated by some media and liberal intellectuals. He told the Poles that "too often do we hear this humiliating argument that we have to join Europe some day". He encouraged people to think first what Europe they would like to join: Christian or anti-Christian. The affirmation of our own cultural and historic identity rooted in Christianity and in Christian Europe, accompanied by a warning to avoid the dangers of the "sleeping spirit" and fascination by the material goods – these were the key messages left by the Pope in 1991. He put them in a nutshell at the end of his visit, quoting St Paul: " Give thanks to God... quench not the spirit".

John Paul II looks at Poland with concern

Skoczów, 1995: appeal for a life ruled by conscience

land joining Europe, yet I do not accept that this desire become a sort of fetish, a false fetish'.

These sentiments voiced during the pastoral visit in 1991 were professed again during the Pope's next visit in Poland. The Pope would visit his homeland every four years. Following this regularity, he arrived there again in 1995. As if willing to show his criticism of the political, and first of all, of moral and cultural tendencies prevailing in Poland at that time, he spent there a couple of hours only. As a part of the pastoral visit in the Czech Republic to canonize Father John Sarcander, a priest tortured to death during the 30 years' war in the 17th century, the Pope celebrated the Mass in Skoczów- Jan Sarcander's birthplace. He also visited the nearby town of Żywiec and Bielsko-Biała. He addressed the members of the new post-communist government, including the Prime Minister Józef Oleksy", pointing out that those believing in God must not be marginalized in the name of tolerance. The Pope clearly distanced himself from the main intellectual centers in big town where his teachings were contested: "this time I arrived neither in Warsaw nor Cracow, but in Skoczów. Perhaps that is where I should go. Not to the very centre of things, but nearer the mountains and the sea".

Nevertheless, the Pope returned two years later to pay his longest visit to Poland. This time he did not go to Warsaw, though the atmosphere of that visit was entirely different than previously. It would appear that new political events in Poland should further strengthen the Pope's critical attitudes. In the autumn 1995 Aleksander Kwaśniewski from the Polish Left Alliance was elected president. The parliament passed the new law whereby abortion was permitted on a larger scale. These facts did not leave much room for optimism, yet the Pope gladly accepted the invitation extended to him by the new president in Vatican on 7th April 1997. The next pastoral visit was a part of the project of New Evangelization for Europe, its main purpose being to revive the Christian foundations of this continent. Unlike most western societies, Poland, still striving to be incorporated in the European political and economic structures, did adhere to the Church and the Christian traditions despite the shortcomings branded by John Paul II. Hence the Pope's desire to strengthen what was good, so that Poland, together with other Catholic countries in the Eastern and Central Europe, should play a positive role in reviving the

Has the Pope remained in the hearts of Poles only for show?

The next months and years seemed to confirm the view that John Paul II" expectations did not coincide with those shared by a large portion of the Polish society. The failure of political parties stemming from the Solidarity movement in the parliamentary elections in the autumn 1993, when post-communist parties came into power, blocking the ratification of the Concordat –a diplomatic agreement between Warsaw and the Vatican – and the most aggressive and offensive propaganda in the media demanding that abortion be widely permitted –all these seemed to suggest that Pope's words spoken in 1991 fell into an exceptionally arid soil. Meditating on the possible causes of this state of affairs, John Paul II did not lose hope that this was just a passing thing, marking a transition period which would end as soon as people's fascination with "the ultra-liberal, consumerism system deprived of any values and imposed by the aggressive propaganda - the system identified with Europe" was over. He expressed that view on the 15th anniversary of his pontificate, when interviewed by Jaś Gawroński, a journalist from the Turin paper *La Stampa*: Actually the media representing a certain ideological orientation in Poland take much trouble to show the pope in the negative light. On the other hand, it appears that the strategy of the Polish media did not represent the feelings and opinions of the whole Catholic nation. One has to understand where these critical attitudes have their roots. In my opinion, the root of all evil is the misunderstanding over the desire of "joining Europe. [...] I am not against Po-

moral values in the united Europe. The sixth pilgrimage could be regarded as the crowning touch in the series of Pope's pastoral visits: in Lithuania (September 1993), Croatia (September 1994), Czech Republic (May 1995), Slovenia (May 1996), Germany (June 1996), Hungary (September 1996).

John Paul II did not show anger any more, this time he was given a better reception by his countrymen than in 1991. His incessant warnings against consumerism, indifference to poverty and unemployment of others and manipulation by the media were then better understood by Poles eight years after the first breadth of freedom. The Pope began his pastoral visit on 31 May 1997, where he presided over the ceremony of closing the International Eucharistic Congress in Wrocław. Despite pouring rain and cold which awaited the Holy Father in Wrocław, the atmosphere during that visit was more cheerful. The Pope made facetious remarks, as he used to do in the circle of his friends. In the tone of a joke he told everybody about his loud "ecumenical" sneezing, which interrupted his speech at the Congress, and which was witnessed by representatives of various Christian religions as well as Jews and Muslims. During the Mass celebrated in Gorzów, he appealed to the congregation to pray for the fulfilment of Cardinal Wyszyński's hope, so that the Polish Pope should lead the Church into the third millennium. In reply he heard a loud assurance "we will help". The Pope immediately responded, alluding to the assurance given to the Party leader Edward Gierek by Polish workers in 1971 and replied: "Perhaps it will turn out better this time"..... And indeed, this time it turned out better.

The Pope visited Legnica and Gorzów and finally arrived in Gniezno, to celebrate the jubilee of the martyrdom of St Adalbert, an apostolic and missionary man, who one thousand years ago brought the Gospel to the peoples in the Central Europe. For John Paul II he became the "symbol of Europe's spiritual unity in the name of Christ." In 1979 on the Victory Square in Warsaw the Pope warned the powers that be that the attempts to depreciate the role of Christianity in the Polish history, culture and modern life should bring no good. In the similar spirit he appealed to the whole Europe, and to the heads of States gathered in Gniezno: the presidents of Germany, of the Czech Republic, Hungary, Slovakia, Ukraine, Lithuania, and Poland. Beside St Adalbert, the other patroness of this pilgrimage was the Polish Queen Jadwiga

The Mass celebrated to end the Eucharistic Congress in Wrocław

John Paul II meets rectors of Polish universities and colleges during his visit in St Anne's Collegiate Church in Cracow

The Pope receives homage of Polish highlanders

Canonization Mass of St Jadwiga the Queen in the Cracow Common

Holy Mass in Sopot in 1999

John Paul II visiting Poland

Following the footsteps of St Adalbert: Gniezno, 1997

– the Lady of Wawel, always venerated by the Pope. On Cracow's common on 8th June, the Pope raised Queen Jadwiga to the honours of the altars during the ceremony attended by one and a half million people. Referring to Queen Jadwiga, the Pope set her as an example for modern politicians, thus paying tribute to her discernment and dedication to the reasons of State. Cracow witnessed another important meeting: in the University Collegiate Church of St Anne the Pope met the representatives of the academic world. He spoke about the duty to serve the Truth, emphasising that science and education need to firmly oppose the moral and utilitarian relativism whereby a man is regarded as "raw material" while education is likened to the production processes. Each meeting was important: that with the young people in Poznań, the meeting with farmers in Krosno, the canonisation mass of St John of Dukla in his hometown. The most moving, however, was the Pope's meeting with the group of highlanders from Zakopane. That time the Pope took a rest for one day in the Tatra mountains where – as in the days of yore – he

In front of the Basilica of Our Lady of Licheń (under construction)

The Mass in Ełk – here the Holy Father is also greeted by Lithuanians

The Mass in Drohiczyn where the ecumenical meeting took place

In Stary Sącz – the Pope looking at the familiar mountains

went to Kasprowy Wierch by cable railway, visited the Morskie Oko Lake and met his schoolmates from Wadowice. On 6 June he celebrated a mass in Zakopane and the Association of Podhale Region presented him with a white shepherds' belt, calling him the "shepherd-in-chief in the world". Dressed in regional folk clothes , Mr Adam Bachleda-Curuś -the Mayor of Zakopane knelt down in front of the Pope as he said these memorable words: "Thank you Holy Father for delivering us from the red bondage. Teach and show us how to remove from our homeland all that brings us shame, devastation, misery and ruin". Towards the end of his homily in Zakopane the Pope pointed to the Cross on top of the Giewont Mountain, adding the key message of his whole pilgrimage: "This Cross speaks to the whole Poland: - *Sursum corda.* Lift up your hearts!'

In purely political context these hopes were realised very soon. In the autumn 1997 the parliamentary elections were won by a political party whose name and programme were derived from the Solidarity tradition. Finally, the Concordat was ratified. President Kwaśniewski wanted to establish good relations with the Holy Father and so John Paul II was able to return to Poland once again, after two years, in June 1999. This pastoral visit proceeded in an exceptionally friendly atmosphere. The first patron of this pilgrimage was again St Adalbert. Following the paths of St Adalbert's martyrdom the Pope finally arrived in the seaside town of Gdańsk. Once again he took an opportunity to remind the Poles of their heroic past and over one thousand years' old links

with the Church. During the Mass celebrated in Sopot, he passed from the testimony of St Adalbert, to the defendants of Westerplatte and the Post Office in Gdańsk to that given by Polish workers in 1970 and 1980- the Solidarity movement. This was not a call to struggle, but an encouragement to show magnanimity, to forgive without forgetting and, first of all, to serve others. "Without solidarity there is no love" – became the motto of this pilgrimage. The Pope alluded to the past history during the mass celebrated in Pelplin, where he brought back the memory of priests murdered during the World War II, one hundred and eight of whom were beatified by him on the Victory Square in Warsaw. In Radzymin and in the Warsaw district of Prague he recalled the momentous battle of Warsaw of 1920, of grave importance for his generation, when Poland and Europe escaped the threat of bolshevism. The painful reminiscences of the persecutions of the Uniate Church by the Tsarist authorities were awakened during the Pope's meeting with a large group of pilgrims from Ukraine, headed by Archbishop Myrosław Huzar. As usual, John Paul II made efforts to come to terms with the modern Russia and the Orthodox Church – these aspirations were professed during the mass celebrated in Drohiczyn. On the papal route were also Elbląg, Ełk, short relax by the Wigry Lake, a boat trip to the Marian Sanctuary in Studzienniczna, the towns of Toruń and Bydgoszcz and Licheń- the construction site for the largest church in the modern Europe, erected to commemorate the Mother of God's appeals for the sobriety of the Polish nation. On 11 June John

The Pope wonders about the new Poland...

During the mass at the Błonia meadow in Cracow common, Cardinal Macharski reads the homily of John Paul II and Cardinal Sodano takes the place of the ill Pope on his throne

Meetings at the Sejm: official with some MPs, cordial with others

Taking the opportunity of the Pope passing by, nuns from enclosed orders could have a glance at the world

Paul II paid a visit in the Polish Parliament in Warsaw, where he assumed the role of the king of Poland, though without a crown. Then he visited Łowicz and Sandomierz, appealing to the young and encouraging them to "to live in opposition to the common opinions and proposals contradictory to the God's laws". In Sosnowiec the Pope condemned the violation of human rights in the conditions of new economy "when the economy justifies depriving a person of work, this person now loses all perspectives to maintain himself and the family". In the end the Pope succumbed to tiredness and sudden fever. Over one and a half million people who gathered on Cracow's common in the rain to hear the mass, could only have a brief glimpse of John Paul II in the window of the Archbishop's Palace. Millions of Poles at that moment went to pray for the Pope's health. Having resumed his pilgrim-

age, the Pope visited Gliwice, Stary Sącz, finally arriving in his hometown: Wadowice. This meeting was an unforgettable experience for those taking part and for those watching it on the Polish TV. This journey back to the land of his childhood, so well portrayed in his friendly conversations with the inhabitants of Wadowice, showed us the smiling face of nearly eighty years' old Pope. Through his gentle smile Karol Wojtyła communicated to his countrymen a clear message "We are at home now!" and was better understood than when preaching sermons. The people knew that the Pope wanted to come home again. He wanted to stand on the Polish soil and see his beloved mountains. Before the departure from the Balice Airport near Cracow, he told his countrymen what they already knew, ensuring them that "In my thoughts and prayers Poland and Poles occupy the unique position".

CHAPTER XIII
On the Threshold of the Third Millennium

John Paul II was the Pope on the turn of the third millennium of Christianity. On 24 December 1999 the world saw the stooping figure of Pope who, with the utmost difficulty, was opening the Holy Door of St Peter's Basilica, marking the beginning of the Jubilee of the Year 2000, two thousand years after the birth of Christ. John Paul II wanted this Jubilee year to be the sign of 'the new spring in Christian life'. This hopeful message appeared in the letter written in 1994, announcing the preparations of the Jubilee: *Tertio millenio adventiente*.

Responding to this message, the Pope in the first place had to find a way out of the crisis aggravating the Church – not the inner crisis of Christianity, but the overpowering crisis of religion in the secularised world. The first step involved maintaining the unity of the Catholic Church, with the strict adherence to the Church teachings. The threats posed by the leftist "liberation theology" were discussed in the previous sections and so were the teachings of some trendy "progressive" theologians at the time of the onset of John Paul II's pontificate. To a large extent these threats were marginalised thanks to the fall of 'progressive' communist centres and finally dispelled by patient testimony of the Pope himself acting towards the truth. In that lay the major difference between him and thousands of "moral authorities" launched by the media and lasting just one season: the Pope not only taught but acted in accordance with those teachings. He acted not only as a guide, but gave people a living testimony, which might convince them.

Alas, not all of them were convinced. A French traditionalist, Archbishop Marcel Lefebvre, openly resisted the Pope, as he could not accept the reforms of liturgy and the teachings of Vatican Council II. In Switzerland Mons. Lefebvre founded a Fraternity of priests opposing the reforms in the Church and in 1988 he decided to create new bishops from among his brethren – without the Pope's consent and without renouncing his errors. That meant the establishment of the new church, not united with Rome. John

John Paul II opens the Holy Doors, thus announcing the Jubilee year

The Holy Father prepares the Poles for a new millennium

John Paul II embraces children – the hope for a new age of the Church

Shepherds of the Church gathered at the Holy Mass in St Peter's Basilica

Paul II, for many years trying to convince the opposing Archbishop, could not hesitate any further: Lefebrve and his followers were excommunicated. This contradiction of the unity of the Church and her teachings, on the "right hand side", though extremely painful to the Pope, was still a narrow margin in the life of the ecclesiastic community of nearly one billion Catholics all over the world.

To provide guidance in moral dilemmas presented by the contemporary world and to give the faithful a better understanding of the problems of faith, John Paul II decided to present the Catholics with the new Catechism. A joint effort of the group of distinguished theologians and priests headed by Cardinal Ratzinger, the first Catechism of the Catholic Church for four hundred years, was shown to the public in December 1992. It would appear at the first glance that the lecture on the articles of faith written in the form of 2856 paragraphs might be regarded as "dry" and hard to follow, yet it proved to be a clear presentation of the truth, providing a guidance in recognising good and evil in one's conscience. Modern in its methods and examples, yet strictly adhering to the unchanged teachings of Christ, the Catechism became one of the best-selling books in the late 20th century, the number of copies sold amounting to over ten million. It is, without doubt, a symbol of the unity of Catholic faith.

Throughout the whole pontificate of John Paul II his efforts to build bridges between people reflect the pledge and appeal for unity not only of Catholics, but of all Christians. This aspect was duly emphasised in the programme of preparations for the "spring" of the III Millennium. The fact the Christian world was allowed to get divided was regarded as one of the major sins, which the Pope publicly confessed in the name of all Catholics on the Day of Forgiveness – 12 May 2001. Standing in front of the Crucifix in St Peter's Basilica, the Successor of the First Apostle repeated the words directed to God: "we forgive and beg forgiveness". He decided to make this unprecedented act of penance being fully convinced that "forgiveness gives rise to reconciliation'. His continued efforts towards reconciliation with other Christian communities were emphasised in numerous documents, including the encyclical *Ut unum sint* of 1995 and during ever so many ecumenical meetings. The major achievement of John Paul II in this field was the reconciliation with one of the oldest Christian churches – the Armenian Church. He established close relations with other ecclesiastical communities in the East: Syrian, Chaldean, Syrio- Malabar communities and with the Coptic church whose head, also titled as ' the pope' met John Paul II during his pastoral visit in Egypt in 2000.

Unfortunately, there appeared hindrances in the dialogue with the largest ecclesiastical communities divided from Rome by lesser differences in doctrine: the Anglicans and the Orthodox Church. In the first case, the apparently near agreement (announced in the joint declaration by the Pope and Archbishop of Canterbury, Robert Runt in October 1989) was annulled due to the doctrinal changes introduced by the Anglican Church under the pretence of "progress". The decision of the Anglican Church allowing women priests and overruling by voting of an article of faith thus negating the existence of hell, openly contradicted the deposit of faith guarded by the Catholic Church. In the consequence, many members of the Anglican Church, including the Church ministers, chose to leave their ecclesiastic community to join the Catholic Church. Other protestant communities were also going through the period of identity crisis, which did not render the ecumenical dialogue an easy task.

In 1979, when John Paul II visited the patriarch of Constantinople- Successor of St Andrew, he made clear his intentions to improve the relations with the Orthodox Church. After ten years it seemed that these relations would be given a strong stimulus as the Orthodox Church in Russia was freed from the oppression imposed by the communist rule. However, the Orthodox Church and her hierarchy were not able to reject the image of Catholicism as the major rival of the Orthodox Church and the tool in the western offensive against Russia and its civilisation. The main bone of contention in the early 1990s was the revival of the Byzantine-Ukrainian Church which, after long years of clandestine activity, demanded the right to operate and requested the return of church buildings mostly taken over by the Orthodox Church during the communist rule. Even in the context of the ecumenical dialogue with the Orthodox Church, John Paul II could not sacrifice the five million community of Uniate Church

The Pope prays with a commission of theologians in his private chapel (next to the Pope sits Cardinal Christoph Schönborn – co-author of Catholic Catechism)

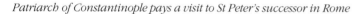

Patriarch of Constantinople pays a visit to St Peter's successor in Rome

Archbishop Marcel Lefebvre

John Paul II and Archbishop Christodoulos, leader of Greek Orthodox Church, sit at the Areopag rock in Athens

Fanatic Orthodox clergymen staged loud protests against the visit of the Pope to Greece

John Paul II in Syria – following the footsteps of St Paul

Meeting with Ukrainian young people at the Sikhov housing estate in Lviv

members – recognising the authority of Rome, even at the price of martyrdom. Neither could he relinquish the idea to organise the system of pastoral care of the Catholics in Russia. The Pope's efforts to meet the Patriarch of Moscow Alexei II in person came to naught, and so did his plans to visit Russia. Though John Paul II was invited to visit the country by the political leaders: Michail Gorbatchev, Borys Yeltsin and Wladimir Putin, the patriarchs of Moscow would always say "no'.

The Slavic Pope, for whom the reconciliation with the eastern Churches and with Russia remained a major issue, never gave in. Using his own devices he tried to bring down the walls of mistrust built by history and fresh prejudices (associated with political conflicts dividing the Catholics and the members of the Orthodox Church over the question of the Balkan war). In May 1999 for the first time the Pope visited Romania, a country where members of the Orthodox Church formed the majority. The Patriarch of Bucharest, who in the early 1990s perceived the Catholicism as "deceptive heresy', decided to recite the prayers together with the Pope. This visit, proceeding in a friendly atmosphere without any discords, prompted the further endeavours. Later John Paul II went to Greece- the country strongly identified with the Orthodox tradition and with deep rooted feeling of being wronged by the Catholics over the centuries (starting from Middle Ages). An opportunity to overcome this hostility presented itself on the occasion of Pope's planned journey following the footsteps of St Paul- the Apostle of Nations. His visit in Athens, where St Paul had been teaching the pagan world about the real God, was to become the key event of this pilgrimage. The leader of the Greek Orthodox Church, Christodoulos, the metropolitan bishop of Athens, ranked among the most vehement opponents of the dialogue with the Catholics in the previous decade. In May 2001, however, he and the whole Greek Orthodox Church faced an old, stooping man dressed in white, who most humbly begged their forgiveness for the wrongs inflicted by his Catholic brethren. At that moment Christopoulos and the members of his Church realised that this Pope did not embody the spirit of conquest or hostility, but of love and reconciliation. The protests on the part of the most radical Orthodox clergy against the Pope's visit in Greece died down shortly. The meeting in Athens did more good for the establishment of better relations between the Churches than numerous declarations and documents worked by the committees of theologians.

Long-desired visit in Ukraine, for which the Pope prayed devoutly, took place in 2001 and marked the next step on this path. However, the situation was more complicated because of the Uniate Church issue (in the first place the Pope was coming to visit this ecclesiastic community) and because of the divisions of the Orthodox Church in Ukraine into three religious groups. Open hostility was demonstrated only by the hierarchy recognising the authority of the Patriarch of Moscow. The patriarch Alexei II was ostensibly visiting Belarus ruled by president Lukashenko and the Russian – Ukrainian- Belarus border regions, as if to emphasise that political unity of Slavic republics of the former Soviet Union was his ultimate goal and achievement, threatened by the "Polish" and "western" Pope. Whilst John Paul II repeated his plea for forgiveness for the wrongs inflicted by Catholics on the members of the Orthodox Church in Ukraine and did not request that the party reciprocate these sentiments, the patriarch of Moscow was repeating the gestures characteristic not of the defender of the real faith, but of the Russian empire. Millions of Orthodox Church members in the Ukraine saw with their own eyes that the Pope did not pose any threat, just the opposite – he brought new opportunities to overcome the bad influence of communism and historic prejudices. The visit in Kiev, and first of

Beatification Mass of Archbishop Bilczewski and Father Gorazdowski in Lvov

Holy Mass on the Chaika airfield in Kiev

all, the joyful meeting in Lvov where the Mass was celebrated in the Uniate rite gathering nearly one and a half million of people, showed to the whole world the new face of Ukraine: not a poor country torn apart by political struggle but a country in which serenity and spirituality would reign and in this way the newly established state of Ukraine was strengthened.

The dialogue with the Orthodox Church awaited further steps – in the direction of Russia, and the Pope never lost hope.

Throughout his pontificate John Paul II never confined to promoting reconciliation among Christian communities only. He did more than any of his predecessors to breach the gap dividing the 'children of one God" – three billions of confessors of the three great monotheistic religions: Christianity, Judaism, Islam. Karol Wojtyła, a schoolmate of many Jewish brethren, a witness of Holocaust, was the first bishop of Cracow who entered the synagogue in this town. Likewise he was the first pope who paid a visit to the synagogue in Rome on 13 April 1986. During each visit in Poland he would meet the representatives of the Jewish communities. On several occasions he openly condemned the sin of anti-Semitism. He recognised the state of Israel and in September 1994 the diplomatic relations were established between the Israel and the Holy See. The major breakthrough in the relations between Catholics and Jews came in March 2000, when the Pope visited the Holy Land as the part of the celebrations of the Jubilee Year 2000. "The old friend"- that was the cryptonym of the security operation to protect the Pope during the pilgrimage, reflecting the cheerful atmosphere of that visit. Jews, who for ages suffered the persecutions from Christians and responded with deep distrust and, sometimes, with open hostility, now received the successor of Christ on this earth as a friend. Along his way, Jewish children cheered and greeted him, shouting "el baba", a Hebrew word for "father'. When John Paul II met a group of former prisoners of concentrations camps who escaped Holocaust, he was approached by an old woman from Poland, his contemporary. She recalled that after leaving the concentration camp she had met a young cleric who gave her some food and drink and, as she was too feeble to walk, he carried her in his arms to the railway station whence she was to travel further. It appeared that this cleric was "the old friend", standing before her. Jews would never forget that. Neither would they

New Russian President, Vladimir Putin, visiting the Holy Father

Canonization Mass of St Teresa Benedicta – the great Jewish convert Edith Stein

Historic visit of the Pope to the synagogue in Rome

forget the moment when the Pope, in perfect silence, stood before the Wailing Wall. In the wall –the remnant from the destroyed Jewish temple in Jerusalem, religious Jews insert slips of paper with their prayers. John Paul II also put in the slip of paper with his intention: he wanted to pray for forgiveness to those responsible for sufferings of the Jewish nation.

The Pope visited the Holy Land not only to meet the community of the children of Israel. Like forty years ago, he arrived there to pray in those places where the Catholic faith and Church were born. He was able to stand in the place where Christ had been born, where he had preached his Sermon on the Mountain, had been crucified and buried. Again the Pope would kiss the ground in the Grotto of Annunciation and the stone in the Church of Holy Sepulcher, on which the Christ's body had lain. He prayed for peace in this land, peace among those believing in one God.

During this pilgrimage the Pope visited the Yad Vashem Institute commemorating the victims of Holocaust and also the camp of Palestinian refugees. He never meant to get involved in the conflict tearing apart the Middle East region and the Holy Land – the conflict between Jews and Arabs. He aimed to establish friendly relations with these two communities, supporting all peace initiatives. It is worthwhile to mention that apart from being the first pope who visited a synagogue, he was also the first one who entered a mosque – during his pilgrimage to Syria in spring 2001. This was preceded by another unprecedented event: the meeting with eighty thousand young Muslims in Casablanca. This meeting was held towards the end of the Pope's third visit to Africa, in August 1985. Invited by King of Morocco, Hussein, the Pope had an opportunity to address those young Muslims, professing their faith in Allah. Discreetly alluding to the prosecution of Christians in many Muslim countries, the Pope spoke to them about the need to respect the religious freedom. He stood before them as a believer in one God, emphasising the aspects common to all great religions: 'the importance of praying, fasting, alms-giving, humility and forgiveness".

This fundamental aspects, shared by Christians, Jews and Muslims, distinguish them from a large and still growing part of the modern world which rejects God and lives their life as if God did not exist. The Pope was apparently trying to promote an alliance between the faithful of the three monotheistic religions, so that together they

John Paul II and Chairman of the Palestinian Authority Yasir Arafat during the pilgrimage of the Pope to the Holy Land

The Pope born in Wadowice slides a card with his prayer to the God of Jews and Christians into the Wailing Wall in Jerusalem

should more effectively defend the man from the dangers and threats posed by the modern neo-poganism. That such an alliance existed was confirmed by the media in connection with the International Conference on Population and Development held in Cairo in September 1994 under the auspices of the UN. The US president Bill Clinton, who never hid his pro-abortion attitudes, was reaching for the world leadership and never had any difficulty finding allies in western European leaders. Threatening to cut down the international financial assistance, he managed to gain the votes of some Third World leaders, too. The draft of the final document of the Cairo Conference, as prepared by the Clinton administration, was in fact revolutionary. Marriage was regarded as the means of oppression and discrimination; sexual activity of teenagers was called "an undeniable right." Furthermore, all countries were prompted to put in place the policy of population control. A new program was planned to organise the world-wide propaganda campaign promoting abortions, sterilisation, contraception and destruction of the traditional family model. John Paul II found the right term for this vision of the new world, referring to it as: "civilisation of death", described in more detail in his new encyclical proclaimed in March 1995 *Evangelium vitae: On the value and inviolability of human life.* Before the conference in Cairo at all public meetings he steadfastly spoke in defence of married life, family and, in the first place, of human life. The Papal Academy pro Vita, founded by the Pope to group distinguished lay academics, it its statement brought back to our minds the truth that" the care we owe every human being does not depend on their age or disability which might afflict them." Vatican diplomats continued to seek alliance with pro-life movements not only in Catholic countries, but in Muslim states and in Jewish communities which, like the Catholic Church, discerned the threat posed by the attempt to "impose adultery, sexual education and abortion in all countries'. And the Pope did get support. During the Cairo Conference the administration of the world superpower clashed with the smallest state- the Holy See wielding spiritual power only and finally lost the battle. In the end the final document of the Cairo Conference, which was to settle the global population policy for the next decade, recognised the parents' rights and responsibility for their children and rejected abortion as a "method of family planning".

Catholics from Syria receive Communion from John Paul II during his visit to Damascus in 2001

During his visit to the Holy Land, the Holy Father had an opportunity to visit the Grotto of Annunciation in Nazareth

The Pope signs an encyclical – a contemporary interpretation of unchanging faith

CHAPTER XIV
Love conquers all

"In many areas the world resembles a powder-keg ready to explode and shower immense suffering upon the human family" – the words found in one of John Paul II's last papal writings, his apostolic exhortation *Pastores Gregis,* signed at the end of 2003, unfortunately reflected the sad reality of the beginning of the new millennium. The Pope made every effort to avoid this explosion.

Just at the turn of the century he had to take on one of the biggest challenges in the whole course of his pontificate: the prospect of the "war of civilizations" begun by the terrorist attacks of Islamic fundamentalists in New York and Washington on 11 September 2001. Already the next day, John Paul II condemned the terrorists and sent a telegram to the newly-elected American President George Bush, in which he expressed his solidarity with the American nation. He also reminded the people: "Even if the forces of darkness appear to prevail, those who believe in God know that evil and death do not have the final say. Christian hope is based on this truth; at this time our prayerful trust draws strength from it". Having experienced war himself, the Pope in his reaction to the tragic events of 11 September wished to prevent the spiral of hatred from developing, inevitability of which was claimed in view of the envisaged confrontation of the two civilizations, the post-Christian West and Islam.

In his message, which he delivered after the al-Qaeda's terrorist attacks, for the World Day of Peace on 1 January 2002, he again encouraged the dialogue between cultures and national traditions, the dialogue between the "civilizations". He warned against the consequences of "the slavish conformity of cultures, or at least of key aspects of them, to cultural models deriving from the Western world, which, detached from their Christians origins, are often inspired by an approach to life marked by secularism and practical atheism and by patterns of radical individualism". He pointed out that such a globalization might lead to a defense of the cultural and national identity with the use of violence and terror. In his message and ecumenical prayer for peace offered in Assisi on 24 January 2002, John Paul II called for finding ways to make inter-cultural communication pos-

The Pope listens to his guest, George W. Bush, at the Vatican

Ecumenical prayer for peace in Assisi

sible and to build up an inter-cultural harmony, which he considered the only "path towards the civilization of love and peace."

Pontifex, or a bridge builder, as the title of the Bishop of Rome proved particularly relevant at that time. During his pilgrimages which now required ever greater physical and spiritual effort, John Paul II built bridges between civilizations so that war could never divide them again. His pilgrimage to Kazakhstan and Armenia at the end of September 2001 had already taken on such overtones. In Kazakhstan, where Muslims constitute the majority of the population, though they are far from the fundamentalist models, John Paul II referred to the tragic events of 11 September in New York during his meetings with young people and with representatives of the world of art and culture. He emphasized that hatred, fanaticism and terror profane the name of God, the one God of Christians and Muslims. The Pope encouraged the Kazakh people to oppose the spurious logic behind the idea of the confrontation of the civilizations and to turn their country into a bridge joining Europe and Asia.

The Pope's pilgrimage to Azerbaijan and Bulgaria at the end of May 2002 became another occasion to appeal for peace between religions, between cultures and nations. "As long as I have breath within me I shall cry out: 'Peace, in the name of God!'," said the Pope at the meeting with political and cultural representatives of the Caucasus country inhabited mainly by Muslims. In Bulgaria, where the Catholics also form a minority of the population, John Paul II wished to make an appeal with his ecumenical message to the Orthodox Church prevailing in this country. He pointed to St Cyril and St Methodius, Apostles to the Slavs, as the finest patrons of the communication between Christian churches. Regrettably, the majority of the Bulgarian Orthodox bishops boycotted the meeting with John Paul II. Still, he was very well received by the inhabitants of the city of Sofia, who showed great enthusiasm when he talked about the significant role of their country in building the bridge between West and East and when he denied that he had ever associated the attempt on his life in 1981 with Bulgaria, where some traces had allegedly led according to press reports.

At the turn of 2002 and 2003, marked with the particularly dramatic papal message for the 25th World Day of Peace, John Paul II focused all his spiritual efforts on averting the military intervention being

Visit to Azerbaijan

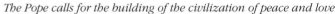

The Pope calls for the building of the civilization of peace and love

prepared by the US and their allies against Saddam Hussein's regime in Iraq. With his prayers and the use of diplomacy, the Pope searched for a peaceful way of resolving the crisis, which he perceived as a threat of a more serious, long-lasting conflict between the Islamic and Western worlds. The consistency with which he opposed this war effectively deterred it from being turned into a religious "crusade". Although its outbreak could not be prevented, the repeated papal appeals to both Muslim and Western societies largely contributed to the moral disapproval of military intervention policies by public opinion.

"Peace remains possible. And if peace is possible, it is also a duty" – with this message written for the next World Day of Peace on 1 January 2004, the Pope continued his trip around the world. He reminded people that there was no peace without forgiveness. Justice, which frequently cannot free itself from resentment and hatred, must be complemented by the 'logic of forgiveness', a form of love. John Paul II kept repeating this truth as the only solution to the conflicts in Palestine and the Middle East. He also recalled it in his special letter published in July 2003 for the 60th anniversary of the tragic events in Volhynia, which had deeply divided Poles and Ukrainians: "Just as God forgave us in Christ, so believers must be able to forgive one another the offences received and ask pardon for their own failings".

In June 2003, John Paul II repeated the same truth, often so hard to accept for victims of injustice or crime, as a warning on his pilgrimage to the countries of the former Yugoslavia: Croatia and Bosnia and Herzegovina, which not so long ago had suffered dreadful hardships of the war and ethnic cleansing. In Croatian Dubrovnik, severely affected by the recent war and in Banja Luka, mainly inhabited by Bosnian Serbs, the Pope talked about the necessity to overcome the feeling of hatred, a legacy of national and religious conflicts. In Banja Luka, from which Croatian Catholics had been banished, John Paul II himself showed how the logic of forgiveness and love transcended the logic of resentment. He expressed remorse to God for the sins committed on this land also by "children of the Catholic Church" and called on its inhabitants to clear their hearts and memory and to pursue a moral rebirth.

As a response to the threats revealed at the beginning of the 21st century, the Pope consistently pointed to mercy, for-

"Three Magi" at the Vatican

Young people listen to the Pope: World Youth Day in Santiago de Compostela (1989)

giving love, and just like previously, he still found grateful and fervent listeners among young people. The World Youth Day in Toronto in July 2002 became another manifestation of that specific relation the Old Man in White was able to establish with young people anywhere in the world. Before its beginning, John Paul II decided to have a few-day rest on Strawberry Island in Canada – it was the only such vacation during his pontificate which he did not spend in Italy. During his first meeting (27 July) in Toronto with the young people

who flocked there from all continents to participate in a veritable festival of joyful Christianity, John Paul II called on his attentive listeners not to postpone the time of their "stepping onto the path of holiness" until they became older. He convinced them that only through the relation with God could they find the meaning of life. The next day, during the main ceremony, in the streams of rain, the Holy Father gave hundreds of those gathered a simple answer to the question about the sense of their meeting, the sense of their witnessing: "Why have you come together from all parts of the world? To say all together to Christ: 'Lord, to whom shall we go? You have the words of eternal life' (Jn 6:68). Jesus – the intimate friend of every young person – has the words of life".

With these words – words of life he continued his pastoral trips. The next year, during his visit to Spain (3 – 4 May 2003), over 600,000 young people attended a special meeting with the Pope held at a former air base near Madrid. John Paul II himself made a joke, saying: "I am a young person aged 83". Indeed, his message appealed to the young: he talked to them about the necessity to overcome the evil of the modern world with the "fascinating power of love" and about the necessity to make peace together. He made this appeal in the context of his determined attempts to prevent the war in Iraq, which was also opposed by the majority of the Spanish, as well as in the context of the Basque terror, with which the Spanish people had to contend themselves.

The teaching that John Paul II so persistently passed on to the modern world – "the powder-keg ready to explode" – was summarized in his message for the World Day of Peace on 1 January 2004: "Love is the loftiest and most noble form of relationship possible between human beings. Love must thus enliven every sector of human life and extend to the international order. [...] *Omnia vincit amor* (love conquers all)! Yes, dear Brothers and Sisters throughout the world, in the end love will be victorious! Let everyone be committed to hastening this victory".

John Paul II reminded the world that the victory of love was not possible without God and His mercy. This thought also became a major theme of his next pilgrimage to Poland in August 2002. Three years after the previous one, John Paul II intended to make up for his absence at the Cracow Błonia meadow back in June 1999, where over a million of the faithful had awaited him and he had not been able to arrive due to his illness. According to some observers, the route of the rather brief pilgrimage was to follow the places he came to love in his youth: the town of Kalwaria Zebrzydowska, Cracow and its surroundings, thus giving a somewhat sentimental dimension to it. However, the Holy Father would never have come to Poland for his own pleasure. The main purpose of his visit was passing on the message of Divine Mercy, for which the best place was the world centre of its cult established by the

At the Basilica of Divine Mercy at Łagiewniki

Spanish Queen Sophia greets the Holy Father during a canonization Mass in Madrid

Holy Sister Faustina in Łagiewniki, a district of Cracow. There, where Sister Faustina had devoted her last years to prayer, John Paul II dedicated a new basilica. He blessed the water with which the church walls were sprinkled afterwards, anointed the altar with holy chrism and burned incense at it just like he had done so many times before as the Archbishop of Cracow. During the Nazi occupation, he frequently had stopped at the old convent church, now standing in the shadow of the new basilica, to pray on his way from work at the nearby Solvay factory. At present, hundreds of thousands of pilgrims from all continents arrive at the Shrine of Divine Mercy. There, John Paul II talked about the magnetic power of merciful and forgiving love of God, which all people – sinful but ready to convert – need so greatly. In Łagiewniki, the Pope, using remarkably powerful and probably the most significant words during that pilgrimage, entrusted the world to Divine Mercy and called on all Poles, the Church in Cracow in particular, to undertake a special mission in the new millennium: "May the binding promise of the Lord Jesus be fulfilled: from here there must go forth 'the spark which will prepare the world for his final coming'. This spark needs to be lighted by the grace of God. This fire of mercy needs to be passed on to the world. In the mercy of God the world will find peace and mankind will find happiness! I entrust this task to you, dear Brothers and Sisters, to the Church in Cracow and Poland, and to all the votaries of Divine Mercy who will come here from Poland and from throughout the world. May you be witnesses to mercy!". Only 14,000 people participated in the Holy Mass in Łagiewniki as there was no more room inside the Basilica.

The following day at the Cracow Błonia, two and a half million people turned out to listen to the Pope, which proved to have been the largest gathering of the faithful in the history of Poland and Europe. John Paul II arrived here not only to make up for his absence at Błonia three years earlier, but also to beatify four servants of God of the Polish Church: Archbishop of Warsaw Zygmunt Szczęsny Feliński (died in 1895), exiled by the tsarist authorities into the interior of Russia after the insurrection of 1863 for his open defense of the persecuted; Father Jan Beyzym (died in 1912), who devoted his life to caring for lepers in Madagascar; Father Jan Balicki (died in 1948), the Rector of the Seminary of Przemyśl, who offered help to the sick and poor

and above all to sinners in the confessional; Sister Sancja Szymkowiak (died in 1942), who gave herself to the poor and war prisoners in the Second World War. Their example was to give rise to "a new 'creativity' in charity" among the contemporary Poles. The Pope wished to "arm" his compatriots spiritually so that they could overcome – as he put it –"the mystery of iniquity", which continued to prevail in the world. To clarify this term, the Pope described our reality as one in which man

"frequently lives as if God did not exist", through genetic manipulation he tries to interfere in the mystery of human life and he wishes to establish the limit of death. The Pope also emphasized that "when the noisy propaganda of liberalism, of freedom without truth or responsibility, grows stronger in our country too, the Shepherds of the Church cannot fail to proclaim the one fail-proof philosophy of freedom, which is the truth of the Cross of Christ. This philosophy of freedom finds full motivation in

John Paul II meets young Cracovians

*New Blesseds of the Church: Archbishop Feliński, Fr. Balicki, Fr. Beyzym, Sister Szymkowiak,
beatified at the Błonia meadow in Cracow*

the history of our nation". Thus, the Pope once more undertook a spiritual battle for the moral face of his nation. He truly relished the fact that he could still encounter young people who wished to follow him and the words of Christ which he kept proclaiming. At the end of the solemn Mass in Błonia, deeply moved, he listened to *Barka*, his favorite song of the "Oasis" movement, performed by the choir consisting of several hundred people. He called it "a hidden breath of his homeland", which had accompanied him at the time of the conclave and on the variety of paths during his pontificate. Also filled with emotion, he thanked Cracow's Błonia for the hospitality shown so many times: "May God reward you! I would like to add: See you again. But this is completely in God's hands".

Still on that day, John Paul II prayed alone by the relics of St Stanislaus in Wawel Cathedral. He visited the crypt with the tombs of Adam Mickiewicz and Juliusz Słowacki and the urn with earth from the grave of his favorite poet Cyprian Norwid. He paused at the foot of the Crucifix of St Jadwiga the Queen, under which he had served at Mass on 1 September 1939, and later had so frequently come to pray as a priest, then as a bishop and finally as an archbishop – the host of the cathedral. As usual, he visited his parents' grave at the Rakowicki Cemetery in Cracow and met with his school friends from Wadowice in the Archbishops' Palace. Out of 42 classmates in his final year only eight were still alive. As always on his papal visits to Cracow, John Paul II engaged himself in a witty conversation with a crowd of young people assembled under the windows of the Archbishops' Palace. "We say to someone who is leaving: 'Come again' and I say that to myself too", he said. The next day, before his departure, the Pope unexpectedly visited the Benedictine Abbey of Tyniec near Cracow and the Camaldolese Priory of Bielany in Cracow, where he used to meditate before making major decisions in his life and before embarking on new missions. Earlier, he had presided over the celebrations of the 400th anniversary of the Sanctuary of Our Lady in Kalwaria Zebrzydowska. In this place, to which he had made his frequent pilgrimages as a young boy, then as a student, as a priest and finally as a bishop, he delivered perhaps the most beautiful prayer of his pontificate – a prayer to God's Mother, worshipped in the Shrine of Kalwaria. He asked Her to:

Future Christianity in Europe does not look bad from the perspective of the Błonia meadow

Jubilee of the Kalwaria Shrine

Look upon this nation,
which has always placed its hope in your
maternal love.
Turn your eyes of mercy towards us,
obtain what your children most need.
Open the hearts of the prosperous to the
needs of the poor and the suffering.
Enable the unemployed to find an
employer.
Help those who are poverty-stricken to
find a home.
Grant families the love which makes it
possible to surmount all difficulties.
Show young people a way and a horizon
for the future.
Cover children with the mantle of your
protection,
lest they be scandalized. [...]
Most Holy Mother, Our Lady of Calvary,
obtain also for me strength in body and
spirit,
that I may carry out to the end the
mission given me by the Risen Lord...

John Paul II met Poles not only in Rome – here he converses with the crowd from the famous window of the Archbishops' Palace in Cracow during his last trip to Poland

John Paul II tried to compensate the fact that his health continued to deteriorate (which was so frequently commented on by the world media) with the strikingly ever more powerful spirit. Indeed, it had given him strength to continue his mission as a successor of St Peter for 26 years. In the history of papacy, only Blessed Pius IX (1846 – 1878) held office longer than John Paul II did so far. By the year 2003, John Paul II had gone on 102 apostolic journeys world-wide and altogether visited 129 countries in which he had spent nearly 580 days (about 400 days the Pope devoted to pastoral trips around Italy). Difficulty with walking, only to a small extent overcome with the help of technology (a mobile podium used by John Paul II for various ceremonies in the Vatican), undoubtedly seriously limited the activity of the Pilgrim Pope. At meetings with his close associates he would sometimes quip: "It's good I have begun to break from my legs and not from my head". That the mental activity of the Head of Church was not at all in decline could have been proved by his pastoral writings he still issued at that time. Among them was the encyclical *Ecclesia de Eucaristia* proclaimed (five years after the previous one) on 17 April 2003. It was a theological analysis of the Eucharist as an actual sacrifice of Christ and of its role in building Church community. The encyclical also provided the Pope's answer to the threat of the "reductive understanding" of the Eucharist. He reminded people that under normal circumstances the Catholics may receive Communion only from Catholic priests. He also called atten-

John Paul II engrossed in prayer (Wawel Cathedral, 2002)

The Pope still " behind the wheel"...

tion to the fact that ecumenical unity cannot be built by the Eucharist being celebrated jointly by the Catholics, who perceive the actual presence of Christ in it, and others (such as most Protestant communities) for whom it has only a symbolic meaning. "The path towards full unity can only be undertaken in truth."

The apostolic letter *Rosarium Virginis Mariae*, published half a year earlier, on 16 October 2002, also had a considerable significance to millions of believers, providing them with religious guidance in their spiritual life. It was dedicated to the prayer of the Rosary and in it the Pope also suggested that the fourth part should be added to the traditional pattern of the Rosary, namely the mysteries of light. In the course of these mysteries the public life of the Savior from his Baptism in the Jordan to the beginning of his Passion should be contemplated. As John Paul II wrote, "this suggestion has the goal of expanding the horizon of the Rosary so that it may be possible for those who recite it with devotion and not mechanically, to go more deeply into the content of the Good News and to conform their lives more to that of Christ".

Another important document which might be regarded as a summary of the Pope's spiritual program, realized throughout his pontificate, was the apostolic exhortation *Ecclesia in Europa* (28 June 2003). It urged Europe's return to its Christian background and heritage. Alluding to the attempts made in our times to build a united Europe with no reference to this heritage, without which it would be impossible to embrace the European history, culture and identity of the previous generations of its inhabitants, John Paul II rhetorically asked whether a tree that had no roots could grow and develop. He voiced his hope that the Church would succeed in reviving the faith in Jesus Christ, the highest good, among the inhabitants of the uniting Europe.

It remained evident that the Holy Father had a deep conviction that Poland and the Polish Church had a mission to complete in pursuing this goal after joining the European structures. John Paul II frequently confirmed this belief during his apostolic visits to Poland. Once more he did so at a meeting with the Polish pilgrims, who had arrived in Rome for the canonization (18-19 May 2003) of four blesseds among whom were two Poles: Bishop of Przemyśl Józef Sebastian Pelczar and Mother Urszula Ledóchowska. In Mother Urszula John Paul II saw someone who had tirelessly proclaimed the Good News, which she had

The Pope, standing on a special mobile podium, meets the faithful in St Peter's Basilica

Canonization of Bishop Józef Pelczar and Mother Urszula Ledóchowska

Mother Teresa – the new Blessed of the Catholic Church

"brought first of all to children and young people, but also to all who were in need: the poor, the abandoned, the lonely." The Pope regarded her as an apostle of the new evangelization, who "with the message of God's love crossed Russia, the Scandinavian countries, France and Italy." St Józef Sebastian, the founder of the Congregation of the Handmaidens of the Most Sacred Heart of Jesus, was presented as a great worshipper of the mystery of the Eucharist, to which John Paul II devoted his last encyclical. Addressing his fellow countrymen, the Pope pointed to these two saints as spiritual patrons of the Poles, who, faithful to their Catholic identity, should undertake their mission in the service of evangelization of the Old Continent in the era of its uniting.

The May canonizations were the culminating point of the celebrations held to mark 25 years of John Paul II's pontificate, together with the beatification of Mother Teresa of Calcutta, held on 19 October 2003, almost on the anniversary of the day when Karol Wojtyła had been elected Shepherd of the Roman Church. The Holy Father, who had met Mother Teresa (she was the 1315th blessed proclaimed in his pontificate) many times and spiritually supported her in her work of bringing help to the poorest, wished to bear testimony to Christianity through the example of her life: being Christian means being a witness of charity. Whoever wants to be great must become a servant of their neighbors.

The attempts made to assess John Paul II's pontificate on the occasion of the 25th anniversary proved premature. The pontificate continued. Soon after the conclusion of the anniversary celebrations, the Pope convoked another consistory of the College of Cardinals, and, for the ninth time, increased their number by appointing new members (among them was one of the closest friends and theological advisers of the Holy Father, Fr. Professor Stanisław Nagy from Cracow, a member of the Congregation of the Priests of the Sacred Heart of Jesus). Relying on his associates, among whom 194 cardinals were his closest advisers, and supported by 4,649 bishops, 405,000 priests (140,000 religious priests among them), 55,000 friars and nearly 850,000 nuns, 140,000 secular missionaries and almost 3 million catechists, John Paul II continued his service to the Church in the 21st century. His huge effort left ever more visible marks on its shape, though it was still hard for people to perceive them clearly.

The Pope – sign of hope for those who seek the good

John Paul II at St Peter's confession surrounded by cardinals and bishops of the Catholic Church

CHAPTER XV
Way of the Cross

The more and more evident physical suffering, which was the price the Holy Father had to pay for carrying on his apostolic ministry, did not diminish his spiritual authority but, in fact, it displayed a greater power of faith, courage of faithfulness and intensified the radiance of Love and Truth, to which John Paul II continued to bear testimony. Although his body grew fragile, his spirit became a more powerful sign of protest against evil and blindness existing in the modern world. He was still a sign of hope for those who sought the good.

The Holy Father brought this hope to people on his subsequent pilgrimages. In the mid-September 2003 he visited Slovakia. On his trip from Bratislava, via Trnava, Banská Bystrica, Rožňava and back to Bratislava, the Pope reminded Slovaks about the long Christian tradition existing in their country, dating back to the ninth century and the mission of SS Cyril and Methodius. He called on them to sustain it in the new era – in the school of "a mature freedom". During the most important ceremony of this pilgrimage, the Beatification Mass in Bratislava, he proclaimed two martyrs of the Communism blessed: Bishop Vasil' Hopko, imprisoned and poisoned by the Communist repressive apparatus and Sister Zdenka Schelingová, tortured to death for helping a group of priests in their escape from prison. "Both shine before us as radiant examples of faithfulness in times of harsh and ruthless religious persecution", John Paul II said about the new blesseds. He left Slovakia with the message in which he urged it to remain faithful to the Cross.

When the next year at the beginning of June the Holy Father arrived in Switzerland, his primary aim was to meet the young Catholics taking part in a national rally in Bern. Conversing with them on the first day of his visit, the Pope warned against the illusions of the consumerist society. He reminded them that Christianity, which was the true answer to man's existential questions, was neither an ideology nor a system of values or set of principles. "Christianity is a person, a presence, a face: Jesus, who gives meaning and fullness to human life." The figure of the old Pope, following in the Christ's footsteps through his suffering, enlivened the reactions of the Swiss, usually remaining rather aloof. Nearly 80,000 people turned up for the Mass on 6 June, which commentators, skeptical before the pilgrimage, now defined as "the spiritual miracle of Bern". Before the end

John Paul II and Cardinal Joseph Ratzinger celebrating Mass
"We are all pilgrims" (Santiago de Compostela)

of his visit, John Paul II also found time to meet with a group of 300 members of the Association of Former Swiss Guards and their families. Before the approaching 500th anniversary (in 2006) of the founding of the Papal Swiss Guard, he thanked for their faithful service to the successors of Peter.

On his next foreign journey John Paul II went to Lourdes on 14 and 15 August 2004, on the occasion of the approaching 150th anniversary of the promulgation of the dogma of the Immaculate Conception. Greeted by President Jacques Chirac, John Paul II paid homage to the Christian heritage of France and asserted the right of the Church to participate in public life, which right was persistently denied to the Church in France by the French authorities (who even at the end of the pilgrimage caused affront to the Head of Church, and, contrary to the expectations, none of the highest authority officials came to the farewell ceremony at the airport). The Pope's primary goal of the pilgrimage was a visit to the Grotto of Massabielle, where in 1858 Our Lady revealed herself to St Bernadette. From there John Paul II led the rosary procession to the Basilica of Lourdes. "Kneeling here, before the Grotto of Massabielle, I feel deeply that I have reached the goal of my pilgrimage", said the Pope in the moving introduction to the prayer. His emotion spread to over 2,000 sick and disabled people with whom the Holy Father said the prayer. Jean Vanier, the founder of "Faith and Light" and "L'Arche", the great movements of communities which gather people with disabilities and their friends, could not hold back his tears: "Poor though my words are, I pray to the Lord for our Pope and thank Him for giving us this Pope". The Holy Father, ill among the ill, spent the night in Lourdes among them on one of 904 beds at the Accueil Notre-Dame, a residence for sick pilgrims. The next day at the Prairie of Lourdes, the Pope celebrated Mass attended by over 300,000 believers. As usual, he had the good message for them: "But evil and death will not have the last word! Mary confirms this by her whole life, for she is a living witness of the victory of Christ". This message, so characteristic of all his pilgrimages, was to be the last one. As he had sensed it in the Grotto of Massabielle, the 104th apostolic journey was to mark the end of his extensive travels.

The Marian sanctuaries – again how symbolically – were the last places to which John Paul II traveled on his pastoral trips across the land of Italy. In October 2003 he visited the ancient Pompei, where he solemnly concluded the celebrations of the

Concert at the Vatican to mark 25 years of the pontificate of John Paul II

John Paul II during his pilgrimage to Lourdes

Year of the Rosary he himself had announced. Together with 30,000 believers he prayed for peace in the world reciting the mysteries of light which he himself had introduced into the meditation on the Rosary. Reviewing the 143rd apostolic journey made in Italy, John Paul II referred to its destination, the ancient Roman city flooded by the lava of Vesuvius in the year 79. "Today", he said, "as in the times of ancient Pompei, it is vital to proclaim Christ to a society that is drifting away from Christian values and even forgetting about them." Eleven months later, on 5 September 2004, the Holy Father went on his last journey outside Rome to the Marian Sanctuary of Loreto. There he met with the community of the Italian Catholic Action, whose three activists he proclaimed blessed during the Beatification Mass attended by over 300,000 believers. The people gathered for the ceremony prayed for the victims of terror in Beslan in North Ossetia: "For those who suffer violence, look down upon your people in Russia, for the dead, the wounded, for children, for families who suffer, may they find strength for a new unity and justice through carrying the cross of Christ", the Pope prayed in Loreto.

His desire to reach Russia with the mission of Christian reconciliation remained unfulfilled. When in November 2003 the Holy Father again received Russian President Vladimir Putin in a private audience, he hoped that, at least symbolically, he would be able to make his ecumenical pilgrimage to Russia. He wished to return the icon of Our Lady of Kazan to the authorities of the Russian Orthodox Church in person. This religious painting, the object of profound veneration in the Russian Orthodox and national tradition, had been lost at the beginning of the 20th century and finally landed in the Vatican. The Orthodox hierarchs, however, remained steadfast in their hostility towards the Polish Pope. On 25 August 2004, in a solemn manner the Holy Father bid farewell to the icon, famous for its divine graces. It was to be returned to Russia but the Pope was not to go there. "The Bishop of Rome asks you, Holy Mother, to intercede so as to hasten the time of full unity between the East and West, of full communion among all Christians", John Paul II prayed before the icon of Our Lady of Kazan for the last time.

The Pope was no longer able to make his trips around the world. Yet, he never ceased to continue his service as a "prophet of justice". In his exhortation *Pastores Gregis* (Shepherds of the Lord's Flock) of 16 October 2003, he called on all bishops to do their service of justice, too. As he

John Paul II giving the "Urbi et Orbi" blessing

Meeting the Russian President, Vladimir Putin (the icon of Our Lady of Kazan in the background)

Ash Wednesday celebrations at the Vatican

emphasized in his document, in today's world in which "the war of the powerful against the weak" continued, the bishop had to play the role of "the defender of human rights, the rights of human beings made in the image and likeness of God". In a feeble physical condition but still with a prophetic power, John Paul II referred to the violence, injustice and poverty of the modern world also during the Holy Week ceremonies in 2004, over which he was able to preside himself. On the Palm Sunday he appealed to young people worldwide: "Do not be afraid to swim against the tide". A week later in his "Urbi et Orbi" message on Easter Sunday, alluding to the recurrent acts of terror in the Sudan, Iraq, Spain, Chechnya and the Holy Land, the Pope prayed: "May the temptation to seek revenge give way to the courage to forgive; may the culture of life and love render vain the logic of death; may trust once more give breath to the lives of peoples".

John Paul II also left a special message for Poland, which he had no more opportunity to visit during his earthly ministry. One of the occasions for passing it on became his meeting with the pilgrims of the Polish Solidarity Union, whom he received on 11 November 2003, celebrated in Poland as the Day of Independence. He called their attention to the fact that Poles need to remember all the victims of the struggle for independence, without whom regaining freedom would not have been possible. The Pope said that the younger generation, who could not remember the successive uprisings in the fight for sovereignty and who failed to remember the "Solidarity" of 1980 and the attempts to quell it under the martial law, should really appreciate the freedom they now possessed as well as they should learn about the price that had been paid for it. " 'Solidarity' cannot neglect to pay attention to this history, both so near and yet so distant. [...] We must constantly refer to this heritage so that freedom will not degenerate into anarchy, but take the form of joint responsibility for Poland's future and that of every one of its citizens."

He also expressed his concern for the necessity to preserve the national heritage in the memory of all Poles in a special letter to the President of Warsaw Lech Kaczyński, which he sent at the end of July 2004 for the 60th anniversary of the Warsaw Uprising. In the letter, he voiced his solidarity with this important anniversary: "When I think back to those events and to the people involved in them, I am under the impression that Warsaw, the Indomitable City, rebuilt from its ruins and just as splendid today as other European capitals, is an eloquent monument to their moral victory. As such it will stand for ever", wrote the Holy Father.

Memory and Identity, the book by the Pope published in March 2005, turned out to be his most eloquent spiritual testament, principally addressed to the Poles, describing Poland's place in Europe, its 20th-century experience and goals to be attained in the new age. In the book, the Holy Father presents a moving account of his understanding of such notions as homeland, patriotism, nation, history and relations between a nation and its history. He reminds the Poles of the contribution they had made throughout the centuries to the formation of Europe, admonishes them against turning their back on the national heritage while building Europe today and asks them "not to exchange the nation for a democratic society". This great lesson on memory, based on the Author's own experience, has been framed in a broader, Christian message of the presence of Divine grace, which helps man transcend the boundaries of the history, nations and continents to reach the order of love. Divine grace sets limits to evil, its totalitarian ide-

John Paul II praying for peace in Iraq

ologies and the violence they cause. This is presented in a deeply emotional way especially in the last chapter of the book, which recalls the assassination attempt on the Pope's life from 13 May 1981. "Ali Agca – as I believe – understood that above his power, the power of shooting and killing, there is a greater power. He began looking for it. I wish for him that he finds it", wrote the Pope.

Memory and Identity was not the only book written by John Paul II as his personal testimony in the last years of his pontificate. Ten months earlier, exactly on the day of the Holy Father's 84th birthday, his biographical book came out entitled *Rise, Let Us Be on Our Way.* In the book, the Pope elaborated on the themes discussed in *Gift and Mystery,* though he mainly concentrated on the experience he gained conducting his bishop ministry in Cracow. He amusingly recalls how he was summoned by Primate Wyszyński to come to Warsaw, where he found out about his bishop nomination. He hesitated before finally accepting it: "Your Eminence, I am too young, I am only 38". The Primate replied without hesitation: "This is a weakness that we quickly recover from ...". Describing the subsequent years of his bishop life: the day he took holy orders in Wawel Cathedral, his pastoral visits, administration of the sacraments, defense of the church in the District of Nowa Huta in Cracow, his close relations with the world of culture and science, with the youth and their "Oasis" movement and with various religious orders, John Paul II once more emphasized the importance of prayer. He pointed to Cracow saints such as Sister Faustina or Brother Albert, who played a particularly significant role in his prayer. He confessed that every day he still said, even as a Pope, "the litany of the Po-lish nation" addressing all Polish Saints.

In his prayer, John Paul II returned to poetry. For the first time since 1978 he turned to it during his vacation in Castel Gandolfo in September 2002, where he wrote his *Roman Triptych,* published the following year in spring. In the main, it contains his meditations on the passing of life, the indestructible aspects of human existence and on the essence of the papal mission. In the central part of the *Triptych – Meditations on the Book of Genesis on the Threshold of the Sistine Chapel –* the Pope, in a deeply moving manner, described the election of a new successor of Peter:

Those to whom the care of the legacy of the keys has been entrusted
gather here, allowing themselves to be

The Pope blessing the faithful on Palm Sunday

John Paul II present in spirit at the Way of the Cross service in the Colloseum

enfolded by the Sistine's colors,
by the vision left to us by Michelangelo —
so it was in August, and then in October
of the memorable year of the two
Conclaves,
and so it will be again, when the need
arises
after my death.
They will find themselves between the
Beginning and the End,
between the Day of Creation and the
Day of Judgment.
It is given to man once to die and after
that the judgment!
A final clarity and light.
The clarity of the events —
The clarity of consciences —

(Trans. by Jerzy Peterkiewicz)

The 27th year of John Paul II's pontificate, the third-longest in the history of the Papacy (after those of Saint Peter and Pius IX), marked the time during which he proceeded along the path of ever more intense suffering, faithfully following in the footsteps of his Master in the direction of "a final clarity and light". In this light the magnitude of his pontificate was brought to prominence. It was not established by his "countable" records, that is 104 pilgrimages, 14 encyclicals and thousands of blesseds and saints proclaimed, but above all, it was determined by the spiritual power of the old and suffering Pope, carrying his cross to the end.

The documents he wrote at the end of his life as well as beatifications, celebrations and liturgical ceremonies in which he participated all acquired a wider dimension in view of his suffering and inevitable end of his earthly pilgrimage. This was already the case when on 7 October 2004, the Holy Father proclaimed his apostolic letter *Mane Nobiscum Domine* (Stay with us, Lord), written for the Year of the Eucharist (October 2004 – October 2005). In his letter the Pope designated the Eucharist – the breaking of the bread – as a solidarity program for all humanity. "Stay with us, Lord, for it is almost evening" (Lk 24:29) – this was the invitation that the two disciples traveling to Emmaus addressed to the Wayfarer who had joined them on their journey. The old, suffering Pope was now on the same journey. His day was drawing to a close. With his letter, however, he tried to remind the faithful weighed down with sadness that their Master has risen from the dead, that he had to leave them so that he could come back in the Eucharist.

John Paul II wished to provide more examples of holiness, also by new beatifications. In October 2004, he included new God's servants in the circle of blesseds,

The ill Pope attempting to speak from the window of his suite to the faithful gathered in St Peter's Square

The Papal Rock at the Błonia of Cracow in the wake of the Pope's death

A young girl laying flowers at the building of the Cracow Curia

among whom were Katharina Emmerick, a German mystic (*The Passion of the Christ,* a deeply emotional movie by Mel Gibson, watched also by the Pope, was based on her revelations) and Charles of Austria, the last emperor of the Austro-Hungarian Empire (who was the only one among political leaders to support peace efforts of the Holy See in the First World War). Another beatification ceremony, during which the Pope would beatify Fr. Władysław Findysz, a Polish martyr of the Communism (a parish priest in the city of Przemyśl, imprisoned and tortured by the Polish Secret Police (UB)), was planned to be held in the Vatican on 23 April...

On the eve of the Lent in 2005 the last stage of the Pope's earthly journey began, dominated by suffering and prayer. On 1 February John Paul II was taken to the Gemelli hospital with flu complications. The acute inflammation of the trachea and larynx made it difficult for the Holy Father not only to speak but also to breathe. Long suffering caused by progressing Parkinson's disease now grew so intense that it was life-threatening. Joaquin Navarro-Valls, the papal spokesman, issued reassuring announcements, the faithful kept praying, the less faithful wanted to see the Holy Father, the media waited for a miracle or death.

On the Ash Wednesday of 10 February 2005, late in the evening, the Holy Father returned to the Vatican following the hospital treatment, which, as it turned out later, had not been sufficient. Before noon Archbishop Stanisław Dziwisz sprinkled ashes on the Pope's head in the room of the Gemelli hospital. The Lenten Season began. John Paul II had already prepared his Message for Lent (signed on 8 September the previous year), in which he called on the faithful to reflect on the role of the elderly in the Church and in society. "Knowledge of the nearness of the final goal leads the elderly person to focus on that which is essential, giving importance to those things that the passing of years do not destroy" – reminding others of this should become the most important role of the elderly people in the modern world. No one played this role in a way that would affect people's imagination more than the way the Pope did it himself.

On 24 February due to a sudden increased difficulty in breathing, the Pope was again taken to the hospital, where he underwent a tracheotomy operation, during which a tube was inserted into his trachea to ease his breathing. As a result, however, his ability to speak became severely limited, which must have caused a real suffering to John Paul II, for whom the contact with the faithful through the spoken

Body of John Paul II lying in state in St Peter's Basilica

National Mass celebrated at Piłsudskiego Square in Warsaw

word had always been extremely important. On 13 March he was released from the hospital and returned to the Vatican to prepare himself for the ceremonies of the coming Holy Week. When seven days later, on the Palm Sunday, at the end of the Holy Mass celebrated in front of St Peter's Basilica, he appeared in the window of the Apostolic Palace to greet the faithful with a palm held in his hand, an almost deadly suffering showed on his face. It became clear that he had commenced his own Holy Week, too.

As the Pope's condition remained serious, he could not participate in the liturgy of Holy Thursday. On Good Friday, in his silent prayer he joined the traditional Way of the Cross procession at the Colosseum via television. The Pope's figure, shown with his back to the camera, sitting in a chair in his private chapel and holding a Cross in his hands with traces of intravenous therapy, became poignant part of the meditations and prayers prepared by Cardinal Ratzinger: "Lord, help us resolutely to set out on the Way of the Cross and to persevere on your path".

When on Easter Sunday at the end of the Mass celebrated on St Peter's Square, Cardinal Angelo Sodano read out the Pope's *Urbi et Orbi* message, John Paul II appeared in the window of his suite. He turned the successive pages of the message as if he was reading it out himself. How many prayers must have been offered for the "departing" Pope when Cardinal Sodano presented the Pope's meditations based on St Luke's Gospel – "Stay with us, Lord!", and when tens of thousands of the faithful gathered on St Peter's Square and millions of others observing the ceremony on television saw the Pope struggling with his own pain and inability to say his "Urbi et Orbi" blessing. "Stay with us, Lord!" These fifteen minutes of Easter Sunday, during which John Paul II wanted so much to speak to the faithful for the last time – and could not – remained one of the most deeply affecting moments of his pontificate.

Two days later on 29 March, Joaquin Navarro-Valls released a statement in which he informed the world about a grave condition of the Pope, who was now fed through a nasal tube. The next day John Paul II appeared in the window of his apartment for the last time and blessed the faithful. On 31 March he developed a high fever as a result of an urinary tract infection and suffered circulatory and respiratory insufficiencies. He asked not to be taken to hospital. Millions of people everywhere in the world prayed for his recovery, tens of thousands arrived at St Peter's Square to keep vigil for the ill Pope.

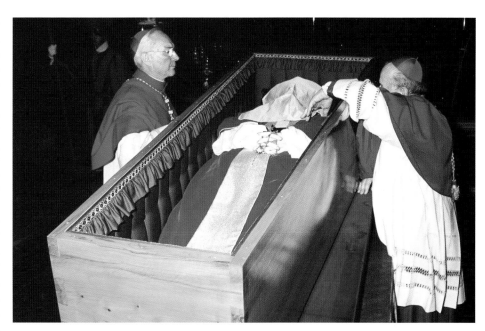

Archbishop Stanisław Dziwisz covering the face of his closest friend with a veil

Funeral of John Paul II in St Peter's Square

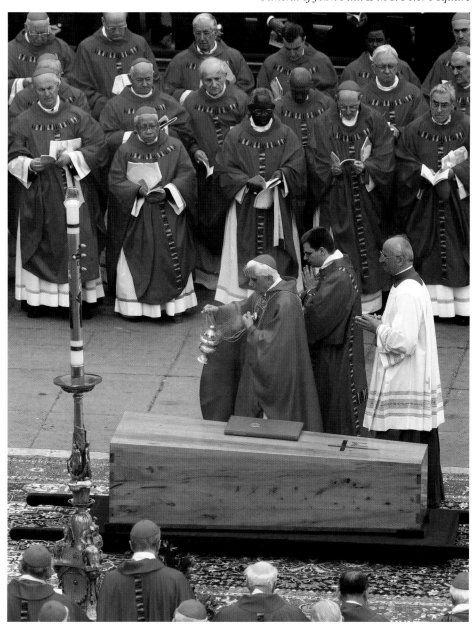

The Holy Father remained conscious; on 1 April he concelebrated a Mass from his bed, read his breviary and participated in the service of the Way of the Cross presided over by Archbishop Stanisław Dziwisz. At a press conference Joaquin Navarro-Valls, holding back tears, said: "Certainly, it was an image I have never seen in these 26 years. He was lucid and extraordinarily serene, but obviously having trouble breathing". In the evening, John Paul II was told about the thousands of the young people who had gathered on St Peter's Square to offer their prayers and songs for him. He said with broken words: "I have been looking for you and now you have come to me. I thank you for this".

The following day was the last one in Karol Wojtyła's earthly life. He passed into eternity on 2 April 2005 at 9:37 p.m. "On the vigil of Divine Mercy Sunday the Angel of the Lord passed by the Vatican Apostolic Palace and said to his good and faithful servant: 'Enter into the joy of your Lord'." With these words Cardinal Angelo Sodano referred to the death of the Holy Father during the Mass celebrated at St Peter's Square the day after. In medical terms, as stated by his private doctor Renato Buzzonetti, "John Paul II (citizen of the Vatican) died [...] because of septic shock and irreversible cardiocirculatory collapse".

John Paul II died surrounded by fellow Poles: Archbishop Stanisław Dziwisz and Msgr. Mieczysław Mokrzycki, his two personal secretaries; Archbishop Stanisław Ryłko; Cardinal Marian Jaworski, the Archbishop of Lviv (the Pope's friend for nearly sixty years); Fr. Tadeusz Styczeń, his friend, who succeeded him at the Chair of Ethics at the Catholic University of Lublin and Polish nuns of the Order of the Handmaidens of the Most Sacred Heart of Jesus. At 8 p.m., a Mass to Divine Mercy was celebrated in the presence of the Pope, in the course of which the Communion for the dying and the Sacrament of Anointing of the Sick were administered to the Holy Father. A short moment before he died, the Pope tried to raise his hand moving it in a gesture as if he wanted to bless the faithful gathered at St Peter's Square. Lastly, he whispered "Amen" (Let it be so).

"Vere papa mortuus est" (the Pope has truly died) – when Camerlengo of the Roman Catholic Church Cardinal Eduardo Martinez Somalo pronounced this formula to verify the death of the Pope, for 100,000 faithful gathered on St Peter's Square and billion worldwide began the time of prayer for the soul of Karol Wojtyła, the great John Paul II. Poland turned into a place of spiritual insurrection, brought about once again by the Pope. That was his last pilgrimage to the homeland. Once more he united millions of people, who in all Polish towns and villages attended masses, prayers and marches, and lit candles to express their deepest gratitude to the deceased Pope.

About 5 million pilgrims arrived in Rome for the Pope's funeral on 8 April. When the wind that was blowing the pages of the book of the Gospel, lying on the plain wooden coffin, suddenly shut it, people could see a symbol of the departure of the faithful follower of Christ. But it was only the end of his earthly life. "We can be sure that our beloved Pope is standing today at the window of the Father's house, that he sees us and blesses us. Yes, bless us, Holy Father." These words from Cardinal Ratzinger's homily best rendered the feelings and hopes of all believers. John Paul II, one of the greatest popes in the Church history, was already in heaven. The Pope's body was buried in the crypt under St Peter's Basilica, in which until the year 2000 (the year of his beatification) the tomb of John XXIII had been located – in the immediate vicinity of St Peter's grave.

Cardinals gathered at the tomb of John Paul II